THE YEARLONG PANTRY

FOR MACK: THE
REASON I LOOK
FORWARD AND
RARELY BACK.

ERIN ALDERSON

THE YEARLONG PANTRY

*Bright, Bold
Vegetarian Recipes
to Transform
Everyday Staples*

Hardie Grant

NORTH AMERICA

CONTENTS

GRAINS

RECIPES

LEGUMES

NUTS AND SEEDS

BOONVILLE
BARN COLLECTIVE

CALABRIAN
CHILE FLAKES

SINGLE ORIGIN
GUNTUR
SANNAM
CHILLI

NET WT. 2.29 oz (65g)

A LOVE ACROSS WITH SOUL
Natierra
nature + earth

ORGANIC SHIITAKE
Mushroom Powder –

No Salt Added

NET WT. 1.8 OZ (51g)

프리미엄콩   JayOne
된장   Fermented
Soybean Paste

Doenjang

NO 첨가물

Net Wt. 1.1 lbs(500g)

Em

AR FREE

an.

WED

gan

MOTHER
IN LAW'S
GOCHUJANG

FERMENTED
CHILE PASTE
CONCENTRATE

ORIGINAL

VEGAN   NET WT. 10 oz

NO MSG · VEGAN · NO CORN SYRUP

PREFACE

While it took me a while to realize it, loving food has been a constant in my life.

My grandfather had a garden that I would always help with. My great aunt made sure I knew how good butter could be. And I owe my adoration of spices to my mom, who occasionally would make meals full of spices and richness that felt out of place in our Midwest lives, but laid the groundwork for my cooking journey.

My relationship with food was affected by two events during my college years: my father had a heart attack at the age of forty-five and my grandmother bluntly confronted me about my path toward diabetes. Up until that point, I aspired to be healthier (code for thinner in the diet culture of the '90s), yet never seemed to be motivated (a fact I can now trace to having ADHD). So I started to cook for myself, often on a hot plate in my dorm room. I became obsessed with food but less in a "it's so delicious" way and more in a calorie-counting way. I ended up building my relationship with food on a weak foundation.

Eventually I started to grow out of that mindset and channeled my energy into a food blog in the mid-aughts, Naturally Ella, as a way to document my exploration of food, and it lasted until 2020. By that time, I'd constructed a whole career in food through recipe development and photography. Naturally Ella became a destination for vegetarian recipes. I'd written two books and hosted countless dinners and classes. Then, when the pandemic hit, I had time to reassess where I'd been and where I wanted to go, and I realized just how disconnected I felt from my personal journey in food. It had become a business and not the creative outlet I needed. I had two options: walk away, or rebuild it with a stronger foundation.

I walked away from everything. Stopped the blog and let go of all my clients. I was terrified, but I knew it was the correct decision. I spent my free time poring through cookbooks and making food that genuinely sounded delicious. I ripped out my entire front yard to start a garden and took up more food-based projects than one probably should (luckily my family is patient). I had (and still have) an unquenchable thirst for understanding.

Out of this time came a deep respect for plants and all the things they can provide for us. I became stauncher in my belief that vegetarianism is not a sacrifice but rather a joy and a way of cooking that keeps me learning.

And so, while I hope this book encourages everyone to rethink their relationship with their pantry and explore vegetarian cooking, it's also a bit of a thank-you to those who helped me rebuild my love of food.

WHY THE YEARLONG PANTRY?

Time and again I find beautiful vegetarian cookbooks that are, not surprisingly, heavily vegetable focused. What does surprise me is how often those cookbooks don't feature a large number of grains, legumes, nuts, and seeds. Occasionally you'll see a vegetarian book heavy on beans, or one that devotes a chapter to grain-based meals. But these dynamic ingredients add so much flavor and texture. They are beautiful seasonal ingredients in their own right that just happen to last a bit longer than ripe tomatoes or fresh greens. My intention with this book is to showcase them as such.

Look at cultures that have grains, legumes, nuts, and seeds embedded in their cuisines. Think of rice and soy in many Asian cultures, lentils and chickpeas in Middle Eastern and Indian cuisines, and legumes and drought-tolerant grains like teff and millet in numerous African cultures. Many of these ingredients have been around for as long as humans have been foraging food, which means inspiration and knowledge abounds.

In the United States, our reliance on processed food has drawn us away from these ingredients, and instead we grow grains for oils, sugars, and flours stripped of their nutrients, not to mention for fuel and animal feed! Add to that certain diets pushing narratives that many of these ingredients are bad for our bodies.

My love of grains and legumes blossomed with the unexpected gift of a flour mill. When the flour I traditionally used for rye bread had been discontinued, I searched for new flour to use. A company contacted me and offered to send me a mill to see if home-milled flour would be the answer.

The same day I received the mill, I had fresh rye flour, and that freshly milled flour had more flavor. Over time, I realized that the same rye berries could be milled into flour, turned into sprouts, pickled, fried, cracked, or rolled. I was hooked.

Soybeans are another ingredient that can be transformed into something delicious (something Asian cultures have known for centuries)! Growing up in rural Illinois, we watched the soybean harvests year and after year without realizing what we were really missing. Tofu! Tempeh! Soy milk! Miso! Shoyu! Those tiny beans, with a little time and salt, can truly make magic.

I've spent the better part of the past fifteen years exploring and learning how these ingredients can be used to create an endless number of meals. I strive to make food that inspires everyone to fall in love with vegetarian meals as I have—a feat that started in my own home with my husband and son, neither of whom are vegetarian. The ingredients explored in this book make that possible and bring every meal together.

INTRODUCTION

I happen to live in a household of neurodivergent humans, and this has an individual and deep impact on my relationship with food and the cooking I do. I have been forced to explore many different options and flavors because I try hard to respect everyone's preferences. There is no "You'll eat what I made and you'll like it" here.

Often this means I'm making a couple variations on the dishes because of flavor or texture preferences. I've accepted this because I cook for myself and then adapt to suit my husband and son. This way, we can all enjoy the meal.

Seasoning to Taste

Often, you'll see "to taste" in my recipes. By that, I don't mean just salt. "To taste" is at the core of who you are as a cook and your preferences for what something should taste like.

For example, I am a bright and salty person (a bit of a match for my personality). I'm heavy on acid, and fermented products like miso, and often use salt to honor my great aunt, who would sneak into the kitchen, give a wink, and wantonly add more to every dish.

However, this might not be you, and I often develop recipes with the seasoning at a base level and allow you to adjust for what you like. Add salt, whether that's kosher salt, soy sauce, or miso. For acid, a teaspoon of vinegar or lemon juice can make all the difference! Drizzle a bit of olive oil or butter into a dish if it feels like it's lacking richness. Or a sprinkle of sugar if it feels too tart. Or, if you're feeling like something is missing but you can't quite put your finger on it, a little pinch of MSG can do wonders.

Recipes are a guide for you to start your journey. Keep a few small bowls on hand so you can take out a bit of what you're making and try adjusting it to taste. This keeps you from accidentally over-salting the entire dish! Also, don't be afraid to push it. Embrace your inner child and push boundaries, you'll know when you've pushed too far, but you'll have learned what tastes good to you.

Now you might have stopped in your tracks at the mention of MSG if you were raised like I was in a predominantly white American area. "MSG is bad! It causes headaches! Makes you sick!"

Fear not, MSG, monosodium glutamate, is a naturally occurring amino acid that a Japanese biochemist discovered in an attempt to isolate the savory taste of kombu (seaweed). Modern MSG is produced through fermentation (a process we all know and love).

In My Pantry

Beyond the grains, legumes, nuts, and seeds high-lighted in this book, I stock my pantry with various items that make these recipes come to life.

VINEGARS

I have a small vinegar obsession and am learning to make my own vinegar, which means I keep quite a few varieties on hand, but I do have a core set.

Rice vinegar has become my all-purpose vinegar. It's on the mild side, making it great for balancing while not overpowering. I use it as a base for pickles, for boosting sauces, and, generally, for replacing distilled vinegar any time it's mentioned in a recipe. **Sherry**, **red wine**, **Champagne**, **balsamic**, **apple cider**, **malt**, and **black vinegar** are great when I'm looking for more pronounced flavors.

Vinegars will never really go bad, just decrease a bit in punchiness.

FATS

Diet culture gave fats a bad rap, but embracing them has become an essential part of how I make my meals feel whole. I use **olive oil** (often Séka Hills) with wild abandon for nearly everything. **Avocado**, **rice bran**, **sunflower**, and **safflower oils** come in handy for frying or applications that require a neutral oil. **Butter** provides a distinctly rich flavor and is perfect for adding interest in the form of compound butter, while **ghee** is the right choice for lending buttery flavor when you need to use high heat. **Toasted sesame oil** and **peanut oil** are great for adding their unique flavors to various dishes.

CHILES

I'm a chile fan and like to have a wide variety at the ready. What you stock will depend on your taste and heat preferences.

I stock whole dried **ancho**, **chiles de árbol**, **guajillo**, **New Mexican**, and **pasilla chiles**. Some dried chiles can also be found in ground/powdered form. Substitute 2 to 3 teaspoons ground chile for 1 large dried chile and ½ to 1 teaspoon ground chile for each smaller, hotter dried chile. Always start with a small amount and add to reach your desired heat level. The ground chile powders and chile flakes I stock include **hot**, **smoked**, and **sweet paprikas**; **urfa biber**; **gochugaru**; **Aleppo**; and **Kashmiri**.

Beyond the dried versions, chile pastes are a must (and can either be homemade or store-bought). My favorites and the ones typically on hand are **sambal oelek**, **chipotles in adobo**, **gochujang**, **harissa**, and **aji amarillo**.

HERBS AND SPICES

I can't live without **cinnamon**, **turmeric**, **ginger**, **cumin**, **coriander**, **allspice**, and **fennel seeds**. More on these can be found in the spice seed section on page 212. I keep the majority of spices whole and grind as needed with the exception of ground turmeric and ginger, which are easier to source in their ground forms. I also rely heavily on dried herbs such as **oregano** (Mexican and Greek), **bay leaves**, **sage**, and **thyme**.

SWEETENERS

I don't shy away from using sweeteners, even in savory dishes. While I acknowledge that copious sugar consumption is bad for our health, I firmly stand for everything in moderation, even sugar. Beyond desserts and sweet breakfast items, a little hint of sweetness can go a long way to balance flavor, just like salt and acid.

I keep **brown** and **cane sugar**, **molasses**, and **brown rice syrup** (see page 75) on hand for broad, neutral sweetening, while **maple syrup**, **honey**, and **sorghum syrup** (see page 104) not only enhance but bring their own flavor to dishes. Also, **barley malt syrup** (see page 54) gets an honorable mention because we're a bagel household and I make them near weekly.

FERMENTED FLAVORING INGREDIENTS

I keep a small extra refrigerator for the fermented items that play a crucial role in adding texture and flavor to many meals. Fermentation adds layer upon layer of flavor.

I have on hand a variety of traditional Asian pastes and sauces. I stock few varieties of **soy sauce**, including **double-fermented, mushroom**, and **light**.

I use homemade and store-bought **miso pastes** in large quantities (**chickpea, shiro [white] miso**, and **awaze [red] miso**). I also keep *doenjang*, a Korean fermented bean paste made with salt and water, on hand because it has a different flavor and salt level from miso. All of this is highlighted more under soybeans on page 172.

Also of note, I use **vegetarian oyster sauce** and **vegan Worcestershire**, both made from a soy sauce base, to replace their seafood-based counterparts. I also use **hoisin sauce**, a thick, flavorful sauce often found in Chinese cuisine, made from a base of fermented bean paste.

Beyond the sauces and pastes, having different kinds of **preserved citrus** on hand allows me to extend California's citrus season throughout the year, and I ferment seasonal vegetables to enjoy year around. This includes fermented cabbage in all forms (think **kimchi, sauerkraut**, and *curtido*), **pickles of all kinds**, and **brined olives**.

ODDS AND ENDS

The shelf that sits to the right of my stove houses a collection of jars that, while not terribly exciting, act as my glue. This includes salt, for which I use Jacobsen Salt Co. **kosher salt** and **Maldon** finishing salt. I keep jars of **MSG** and **nutritional yeast** on hand to add their essential umami flavor to many dishes. **Cornstarch** and **potato starch** are key for making crispy tofu.

In another part of my pantry, an assortment of **noodles** (Italian pasta and a variety of Asian noodles), **nori**, and **rice papers** are kept along with some items that don't really fit a category, such as **vegetable bouillon cubes, tamarind paste, fried shallots, mushroom powder, Japanese-style panko**, and extras of **mustard, mayo, barbecue sauce, ketchup, jams**, and **vinegar-based pickles**.

Finally, I'm never without a host of jarred tomato products, including **tomato sauce, crushed tomatoes**, and **tomato paste**.

SEED SCIENCE

Before we dive into the grains, beans, nuts, and seeds, I want to interject a small bit of science. While this knowledge is not necessary for enjoying the food and recipes in the following pages, it can be extremely helpful to understand terms used in the marketing and cooking of these ingredients so you may combat all the misinformation and fear mongering that often surrounds them.

Every ingredient highlighted in this book is a seed. If you were able to procure a whole walnut, you could plant it in the ground and in around seven years have a tree that produced new nuts. Toss amaranth into a patch of soil in the spring, and by fall you'll be surrounded by beautiful flowers and more seeds. Many of the seeds in this book go through processing to get to our pantries, and as such, would not be able to produce a plant; however, at one time in their life, they could have.

When cooking with seeds, it's helpful to have a basic understanding of parts of the seeds, both seen and unseen. These impact how we process, cook, and eat the ingredients highlighted in this book.

Seed Layers

On the outside, a seed has a protective layer called the **pericarp**. For some of the nuts and seeds, such as almonds and pistachios, the pericarp is soft and fleshy. For all other edible seeds, the pericarp is dry and hard: the shell of a sunflower seed and peanuts that we crack to eat what's inside, the start of the bran layer for grains, the pod that encloses mature beans.

Past the pericarp is the **seed coat (testa)**, which is a protective layer that keeps the seed safe. The seed coat is what we contend with when we're cooking grains (see page 28), what we're removing when nixtamalizing corn (see page 84), what we remove when making creamy hummus (see page 157), and what we're removing when we blanch nuts such as hazelnuts and almonds (see page 185).

As we move farther in, we hit the living **aleurone layer** that is the bridge between the pericarp and the endosperm. This is the final layer of bran in grains and also where pigments reside that give us black rice, blue barley, and many of the colors we find in beans.

The bran layer, which is the pericarp, seed coat, and aleurone layer, contains mostly fiber. In grains these three layers are fused together. Bran is removed to make pearled grains (see page 24), white rice (see page 73), and all-purpose flour (see page 30).

Once we're past the bran layer, we hit where all the energy resides that a plant needs to grow. In grains and spice seeds, this is the **endosperm** and it's primarily made of starch cells which is what we love for flour; in legumes, nuts, and seeds mostly there is a **cotyledon**, stocked with proteins.

Finally, tucked deep inside is the **germ/embryo**. This is where the seed begins to grow. It's vital for the malting process in grains (see page 26) and the start of sprouting. It is also removed when making all-purpose flour.

Husks and Hulls

One other important part of the plant is the husk, also called the hull. In nuts, like almonds, pistachios, walnuts, and pecans, the husk surrounds the seed coat. Chances are, unless you find yourself with some green almonds, you won't run into this.

For grains, the hull is a protective layer. These hulls are not toxic to humans but are extremely fibrous, tough, and rather unpleasant to eat (think corn husk). So the first process grains go through upon harvest is to lose the hull. Grains are on a spectrum when it comes to hulls and how tightly they adhere to the grain. On one end, modern wheats, some barley, and oats have been genetically altered so that the hull is brittle and falls away without effort. These grains are referred to as being **hulless** or **naked**.

On the opposite end, rice, emmer (also known as farro), spelt, rye, and the unmodified oats and barley have hulls that take a bit more work to remove. These grains are referred to as **hulled**.

The remaining grass grains, such as millet and sorghum, fall somewhere in between, depending on the varieties. As for the three pseudograins, amaranth, quinoa, and buckwheat, they are simply shaken from their flowers.

Legumes have no husk or hull as the pod is the pericarp.

Seed Makeup

Foods are primarily made up of water, lipids (fats/oils), carbohydrates, and proteins. Minor components include vitamins, minerals, and flavoring elements—all of which play a role in the texture, flavor, color, and how they react during storage, processing, and cooking.

WATER

The simplest but also one of the most important compounds in food. Water likes to bond with other, non-water molecules and it does this by surrounding these molecules, and separating them from each other, effectively dissolving the non-water compound. If a compound is able to dissolve in water it is water soluble.

Many grains contain low levels of water-soluble compounds. This leads to the chewiness we often associate with whole grains, as the proteins react to the water and clump together.

LIPIDS

Natural fats, in solid and liquid form, are composed of a variety of fatty acids that fall into three broad categories—saturated, monounsaturated, and polyunsaturated—which have to do with their molecular structure.

Fats play a vital role in energy needs for our body. Also, we can take advantage of compounds that are fat-soluble, such as those in spices and chiles. By combining these ingredients with fats, the fat-soluble compounds dissolve, which in return releases and intensifies flavors.

Saturated fats are found in greater amounts in animal products, coconut products, and palm products. When turned into a usable fat, like ghee or coconut oil, they tend to be solid at room temperature and more heat stable. **Monounsaturated fats** are found in greater amounts in olives, avocados, almonds, hazelnuts, pecans, and pistachios. When turned into oil, they are liquid at room temperature and have a moderate heat stability. **Polyunsaturated fats**, such as fats from walnuts, pine nuts, sunflower seeds, corn, soybeans, fish, and flax, are liquid at room temperature but have a lower heat stability. Polyunsaturated fats tend to be labeled the healthiest of the fats but can also be the most susceptible to degradation (becoming rancid).

CARBOHYDRATES

Carbohydrates are quite important for our body and the way we cook, especially in relation to grains and legumes.

The simplest form of carbohydrates is **sugar**. **Glucose**, a simple sugar, forms the foundation for starches, and that's why we're able to get sweetener from grains, such as corn syrup, which is starch broken down into individual glucose molecules or in the case of malted barley syrup, two glucose units. **Sucrose** comes from the photosynthesis of plants, which is how we get sugar from sugar cane and sugar beets along with sorghum syrup from the cane of certain varieties of sorghum. Sucrose also accounts for the majority of sugar compounds in maple syrup.

Beyond the simple sugars, we move into the carbohydrates that contain "few" sugar molecules, the **oligosaccharides**, and "many" sugar molecules, the **polysaccharides**.

Oligosaccharides, made up of several sugar units, are part of the energy supply of plants but are compounds that only our colon has the enzymes to process. They can be responsible for the discomfort some people experience when eating beans. For more information on how to manage oligosaccharides when you cook legumes, see page 118.

Polysaccharides, made up of potentially thousands of sugar units, are where we find **starch** and **fiber**. The majority of a seed's bulk, the endosperm, is starch. In whole grains, starches plump an otherwise hard and chewy seed. Different types of starches are also the reason certain grains appear sticky while others are distinct. And starch's ability to have structure and hold water is what creates pockets of air in baked goods.

Beyond sugar and starch, **fiber** plays a large role in our diet and in our use of these seeds. The cells that make up the seeds are composed of large amounts of soluble and insoluble fibers, creating the cell structures and more storage. These include cellulose, which is a bit like the bricks forming the cell walls, and pectin, which is the cement holding these bricks together. These types of fibers are important in understanding how grains and legumes cook (see page 27 and page 118).

PROTEINS

Proteins consist of molecular units or chain(s) of amino acids, made up primarily of carbon, hydrogen, oxygen, and occasionally sulfur atoms. Plants and humans alike need amino acids to function, but unlike plants, humans need nine essential amino acids that our bodies are not able to produce. Pseudograins, pumpkin seeds, and soybeans are "complete" proteins, which means they provide all nine essential amino acids, while the other grains and beans in this book don't have all nine essential amino acids. However, if you're eating a variety of nuts, seeds, legumes, grains, and vegetables on the regular, you should be more than covered.

Different legumes, nuts, seeds, and grains consist of varying amounts of albumins (water soluble), globulins (water-salt soluble), glutelins (acid soluble), and prolamins (alcohol soluble). These storage proteins are what tell us we should soak beans with salt and that grains do better with a splash of acid. These are also the proteins that help us understand gluten.

GLUTEN

A subset of proteins form the gluten structure found in grains of wheat. These proteins interact with water and each other to form the network that gives us elasticity and plasticity in doughs. The more a dough is worked, the more these proteins interact with each other, creating a stronger network. This is why bread is kneaded to create a strong gluten network and cakes should barely be stirred. Some people have a drastic autoimmune reaction to the presence of gluten. This is why people with Celiac disease cannot eat any grain from the wheat, barley, and rye family.

ANTINUTRIENTS

Both grains and beans contain compounds that are labeled as antinutrients, which tend to block the absorption of nutrients in our bodies. However, the effect of antinutrients can be mitigated, and research even suggests that antinutrients are not all bad and some can actually provide our bodies with antioxidants, compounds that can fight disease and promote general health. There are two primary antinutrients of importance, lectins and phytic acid.

Lectins are proteins that react and bond with carbohydrates. The lectin phytohaemagglutinin **(PHA)** is made up of two different proteins and is found in smaller amounts in grains and larger amounts in legumes, with the highest amounts in kidney beans. In its raw state, PHA can cause food poisoning. Lectins are water soluble. When dealing with beans, a sustained 10 to 15-minute boil will destroy PHA, after which you can return to a simmer.

Phytic acid is a compound found in plants that is used to store phosphorus, which is essential for their growth. Without phosphorus, plants won't grow and produce the food we eat. Phytates bind to minerals, rendering them unavailable to our bodies. While I don't go out of my way to reduce phytates in my day-to-day cooking, I am naturally reducing some phytates. Soaking, sprouting, lacto-fermentation, acidulated pickling, and cooking all reduce phytates in legumes and grains. And, as you'll see throughout this book, these are all techniques I use to enhance flavor, texture, and presentation.

Final Advice

Make your meals diverse and fill your plates with fruits and vegetables. Research continues to show that diets high in whole grains, legumes, and nuts/seeds are good for our health. Now it's time to start cooking.

GRAINS

Grains make up a rather large part of everyone's diet as breads, pasta, porridges, flatbreads, beer, whiskey, ferments such as soy sauce, seed oils, and a range of sweeteners. These powerhouse ingredients have stood the test of time, climate change, and disease to continue to fuel our bodies.

WHAT IS A GRAIN?

Grains are, for the most part, seeds of the grass family, which includes grass that grows in our yards, bamboo, sugarcane, and native grasslands. However, for this section, we're focusing on the grass plants that produce the edible seeds we eat on a daily basis, including wheat, barley, rye, rice, corn, millet, and more.

Pseudograins

There are a few seeds we use like grains that are not actually part of the grass family. These include amaranth, quinoa, and buckwheat. These pseudograins are often small but can be cooked and used in similar ways to grains. More information and recipes for these three ingredients can be found on page 94.

GRAIN PROCESSING

Once a grain is harvested and the hull removed (see page 19), the grain can stay in its whole-grain form and either be sold as is or made into true whole-grain products. The grain can also go through a secondary process where some or all of the bran and germ is removed, at which point it is no longer considered a whole grain, but it still has nutritional value.

Whole-Grain Products

A whole grain is a seed that remains intact, directly out of the husk. In the food world, this is occasionally labeled as a "berry," such as a wheat berry.

There are a few products made directly from whole grains, and while the grains are processed, all the layers of the grain are kept, locking in the nutrition from the bran layer. These products are often marketed as flaked or rolled, steel-cut or cracked, parboiled, and whole-grain flour.

I prefer to keep whole grains on hand and crack or grind into flour at home, primarily because whole grains are more shelf-stable than their processed versions, and I'm able to pick and choose which nutrients I leave out at any given time and how far to process the grains for individual recipes. I use a food processor, high-speed blender, and mill for processing whole grains.

Non-Whole-Grain Products

Grains that do not stay whole are typically stripped of the fibrous outer bran layer. This allows for faster cooking with a potentially creamier and softer result. These products are marketed as pearled, white (as in rice), semi-pearled, quick-cooking (often code for pearled). Some flours are also made from grains that have had some or all of their bran and germ removed, such as all-purpose flour or pastry flour.

Flaked Grains

Many co-ops and online stores that stock whole grains will also stock flaked grains, such as oats, spelt, rye, and barley. Grains can go through a flaker with little preparation and come out in variable levels of thickness. Oats work best because they are a softer grain, while the harder grains, like rye and spelt, will be thick and crack as they are processed. Smaller and pearled grains, like pearled barley, quinoa, and millet, can also be found in flake form. They can be a nice addition to baked goods and porridges. Flaked grains can be stored at room temperature for weeks.

Cracking Grains

In my recipes, I occasionally call for cracked grains, not to be confused with specific commercial products such as steel-cut oats, bulgur, and freekeh. Cracked grains can easily be made at home with either a food processor, blender, or grain mill. I often use cracked grains in place of pearled grains. By cracking the grains, the tough seed coat is broken, which allows the grain to cook more readily. Cracked grains can be cooked with a range of liquid amounts, resulting in a range of textures and uses, including risotto, polenta, and porridge.

For my cooking purposes, I grind whole grains into three textures of cracked grains.

Finely cracked grains: Finely cracked grains can be ground with a finer setting on a mill or run a bit longer in the blender, and are marked by nearly equal amounts of coarse flour and small pieces of cracked grains.

I'll use this size for quite creamy porridges or I've occasionally sifted out the flour and used the small pieces of grain for a quick-cooking pilaf (and then used the reserved flour for cream-of-wheat-type porridge the next morning).

Medium-cracked grains: These grains are run through a grain mill on a coarser setting than for the finely cracked grains, or they are run in a blender or food processor for a bit less time. These grains have nearly all been cracked, but they're still more cracked grain than flour.

I use medium-cracked grains for textured porridges, often savory, like the Parmesan Cracked Barley with Braised Leeks on page 58. This size lends a creamier consistency but still has texture.

Coarsely cracked grains: These are grains that have been run through a grain mill on a nearly open setting or pulsed in a food processor or blender a few times. Coarse cracked grains have many grains that are still whole but a few have been cracked, creating pieces and a small bit of flour.

I prefer coarsely cracked whole grains for risottos. The longer cooking time allows the whole grains to fully cook while the small amount of flour/starch created by cracking the grains makes for a creamy texture without the dish turning into a porridge.

Flour

If you continue to grind cracked grains in a high-speed blender or a home mill, eventually your grains will reach flour consistency. I have a KoMo FidiFloc mill that takes up a solid amount of counter real estate but is a machine I use nearly every day.

Milling flour with a machine is as simple as selecting the coarseness, turning the machine on, and adding the grains to the hopper. Machines such as the KoMo use self-sharpening stone burrs to grind the flour, keeping it cool enough to not lose nutrients in the process.

No grinder? No problem! Visit page 230 and get yourself some flour from a miller.

SIFTING FLOUR

I'll often sift freshly milled flour to remove some or almost all of the sharp-edged, fibrous bran that can hinder gluten development (if that is what I am after). Flour sieves look like cake pans with mesh at the bottom and are labeled by size—not to be confused with the sieves used for straining. Passing freshly milled flour through a no. 60 sieve will extract the sharp bran pieces and allow all the pillowy starch-heavy flour to pass through. Any finer mesh sieve and the flour doesn't quite pass through as well.

From here, you can keep all the bran out (and make the porridge on page 33 or add it to some pancakes on page 61) or add some percentage of bran back in.

Freshly milled flour has a higher probability of going rancid and, as such, should be stored in a well-sealed container and used within a few weeks. The flour will store in the freezer for longer time, but age can impact the flavor.

TOASTING FLOUR

Heat a large skillet over medium heat and add the flour. Cook, stirring often, until the flour has deepened in color and developed a nutty aroma, 4 to 5 minutes. This technique is great for all types of flours, and I especially love it for the Buckwheat Crepes with Burnt Honey Butter (page 102), Buttermilk Barley Pancakes with Roasted Black Raspberries (page 61), and Spoon Pudding with Greens (page 87).

Note: I only toast a small portion of flour destined for bread. When heated, proteins needed for gluten development break down. Heating a small amount of flour lends flavor while leaving the majority of flour able to produce the gluten network.

Malted Grains

Often the first step for making beer, malted grains are whole grains that go through an initial sprouting process and are then dried. By allowing the seeds to germinate, enzymes begin to turn the starch into sugars, as though the seed was about to become a plant. From there, the dried grains are used as a fermentation starter, made into a syrup, or ground into powder.

BUYING AND STORING GRAINS

Grains are one of the most shelf-stable pantry items, given their low fat content, so the likelihood you will encounter bad grains is fairly low. The biggest issue I've run into over the years are moths that like to feast on the grains.

Storing whole versions of the grains can be done at room temperature in well-sealed jars or bags for years, but I like to cycle through them yearly. Grains that are processed such as pearled, cracked, and flours, have a shorter shelf life and can become a bit rancid, with a slight, playdough-like odor.

You can store these items in the freezer, but I find occasionally the taste is not the same once it's been frozen for a month or longer. So instead, I like to come up with a plan to work through whatever items might need to be consumed first.

A list of purveyors and farmers I recommend can be found on page 230.

HOW TO COOK GRAINS

Chances are you've eaten undercooked grains, grains that were gummy, or grains that were so overcooked they turned into mush. On the spectrum of grain cookery, there are a lot of ways to go wrong, but once you get a handle on it, you'll never have to eat a poorly cooked grain again.

What follows is a bit of a general practice on how I cook a wide variety of grains with detailed instructions highlighted in each grain section.

Rinsing Grains

Commercial whole grains are fairly clean and free of debris and excess starch and therefore, I don't rinse the majority of whole grains. If I'm buying grains from a local, less commercial source, I do check for debris and sometimes rinse. This is especially true for quinoa, which has a layer of saponin, an outer coating that can cause a bitter taste, which isn't always removed by smaller growers. I also rinse pearled and white grains to remove extra starch when I'm going for a fluffy pilaf-like texture.

Toasting Grains

Toasting grains before cooking them adds layered depth of flavor. If you plan to toast your whole grains, do so before any soaking.

Dry toasting: Over medium heat in a dry skillet, add your grains and toast until you begin to smell them and you notice a slight color change, 3 to 4 minutes. This provides just an undertone of nuttiness, but any more than that and the risk of burnt and bitter grains rises. I prefer dry toasting grains for soups, stews, casseroles, and dishes where fats are added later in the process.

Oil/butter toasting: Over medium heat in a skillet with 1 to 2 tablespoons of butter or oil, add your grains along with optional aromatics, such as onion and herbs, and toast until fragrant and you notice a slight color change, 4 to 5 minutes. I use this method for infusing flavor early—it's great for pilafs and porridges.

Soaking Grains

While all grains can be cooked without a soaking step, some grains really benefit from soaking. However, each grain and processed version of the grain will react differently to soaking. As such, I vary my soaking methods. Detailed instructions can be found on the specific grain pages.

Long soak: Some grains benefit from an 8-hour soak in a bit of acid to start the breakdown process, particularly of the acid-soluble proteins. Soaking grains with a bit of acid, such as vinegar, lemon juice, or even better, a fermented liquid like whey, kombucha, or brine from something previously fermented, such as sauerkraut, is a great way to start the process. Soaking in this manner enables the grain to become more tender during cooking, creating a more palatable bite.

Short soak: I often use an optional 4-hour soak for smaller grains. While they don't need it to shorten cook time or make them more tender, the soak still helps to get a more even cook for older grains, reduce phytates, and create a more creamy consistency.

Water-only soak: I soak in water only for grains that may become overly mushy with the addition of acid, such as small and pearled grains, or when a pilaf-like, fluffy texture is desired.

What if you don't want to soak or just forget? You can start the process at any time and still have some benefit. Or, to cook without soaking, add 2 tablespoons of mild-flavored vinegar and ½ teaspoon of kosher salt to the cooking liquid. The fermented liquid doesn't work as well in this application, which is why I recommend vinegar. Grains will take upward of an hour but will still be more tender than if you didn't soak at all. Use this only if grains are compatible with an acidulated soak.

Will everything taste like vinegar? The vinegar flavor is subtle and rarely out of place in the savory meals I make. However, you can soak in whey or use vinegar in the soak and replace with fresh water upon cooking for a more neutral grain.

Should I cook with my soaking liquid? Yes, unless you want to minimize vinegar flavor, then use fresh.

COOKING WHOLE GRAINS

When it comes to cooking grains, I rely on two different methods, depending on my end goal for the grains.

Pasta method: With this method, grains are cooked, after any soaking or toasting, in enough water to cover by about an inch (2.5 cm) at a rapid simmer, covered, until the grains are plump. If the grains are still chewy and you're low on water, add a bit of hot water to keep the grains covered. Once the grains begin to burst and are tender, I like to take it one step further by draining the grains, returning them to the pot (off heat), covering, and leaving the grains to absorb any small amount of moisture left for 10 minutes.

This results in grains that are pleasantly chewy. The grains will begin to harden upon cooling as the starches begin to bond again. If the grains are undercooked, this will make the grains nearly inedible within minutes.

Absorption method: This method cooks grains, after any soaking or toasting, in just enough water so that the grains are cooked once all the water is absorbed. The grains are brought to a rapid simmer, covered, and cooked over medium-low heat until the water is absorbed, then removed from the heat and allowed to sit with the lid still on, for 10 to 15 minutes, before using.

My hope is that you take the ratios in the chart as a bit of guidance instead of the rule, because texture can vary greatly with just a bit of change. Find your grains are too soft? Decrease the amount of liquid slightly the next time you cook them. Want a softer, more porridge-like consistency? Increase the ratio of water to grain by a factor of 1 (for example, 2 parts water to 1 part grain becomes 3 parts water to 1 part grain) and increase the cooking time as needed.

SPECIAL METHODS FOR PREPARING AND COOKING GRAINS

Beyond simply cooking grains, I have a few techniques I like to use to enhance flavor or alter the texture of grains.

Smoking Grains

Smoking grains is a fun way to infuse a smoked flavor into raw grains before cooking and can be done without a large outdoor smoker.

To smoke grains, place a piece of parchment paper in the bottom of a dutch oven and layer with ½ cup (50 g) small smoker wood chips of any type of wood. Place a metal steaming basket over the wood chips and put 1 to 2 cups (240 to 480 ml) of your chosen raw grain in either a cheesecloth or a bowl that fits in the steamer basket. Cover and smoke over medium heat for 10 minutes, then let the pot rest for another 30 minutes.

I recommend taking the pot outside before removing the lid as the smoke smell will linger in your house. Your dutch oven and steaming basket will also have a lingering smell of smokiness, but I find it dissipates quickly after washing and letting air dry.

Smoked grains can be stored for a few days in a sealed jar before they find they begin to lose some of the smokiness.

Popping Grains

Popped grains are lovely as a soup topping, tossed with roasted vegetables, or added to granola.

While corn is our beloved popping grain, every whole grain and pseudograin can technically pop, but the question becomes, is it worth it?

I stick to sorghum, corn, amaranth, and quinoa because the tough seed coat on other grains creates an uneven pop. The seed coat on most grains doesn't allow the starch to really expand as it does with corn. As such, the end result is just a bit of puffed-up starch peeking out from the seed coat.

To pop, heat a dry skillet over medium heat until it reaches around 250°F (120°C)—an infrared thermometer is helpful for this. Add the grain and immediately start swirling the pan. Don't stop until most of the grain has popped. All grains but sorghum and corn can be popped without a lid.

Popcorn is often popped with oil to reduce the risk of burning. You can pop corn dry, just continuously shake the pan as stated above.

Air poppers are great for corn, but smaller grains clog the machine and can cause it to burn out (from personal experience).

Frying Grains

There are two ways I like to fry grains, and both start with cooked grains. Non-sticky grains like quinoa or spelt berries fry up into crispy bits perfect for sprinkling anywhere you might want a crunchy topping. Millet, teff, amaranth, polenta, grits, and short-grain rice will stick together in a solid mass upon cooling thanks to their starch makeup, and they can then be sliced and fried. These fried grain slices are fantastic under a salad, beans, sauces, and more.

Non-sticky grains: Add about 1 inch (2.5 cm) of oil to a small saucepan and heat until it reaches 325°F (160°C). Add cooked whole grains, being careful not to crowd the pan, and fry for 4 to 6 minutes, until grains have substantially darkened in color. Use a spider strainer or slotted spoon to remove from the oil and place in a medium bowl. From here I like to toss with a pinch of salt and spices such as cumin, coriander, and ground chile.

Sticky grains: When storing grains to fry later, place in an oiled food container before cooling and refrigerating. Cut the saved grains into any shape you desire (I like triangles), about ½-inch (1.3 cm) thick, and heat a bit of neutral oil on a well-seasoned cast-iron skillet over medium heat. Place your grains on the skillet and fry until one side is nice and golden, 2 to 3 minutes. Repeat with the second side and remaining grains.

LEFTOVER GRAINS

It is inevitable that you will begin to accrue a stash of grains in your refrigerator. Smaller amounts are great for frying (see page 43) or pickling (see page 41) to use as a garnish for soups, salads, and grain bowls. Larger amounts can be reheated and used as bases for bowls, tossed in eggs, or added to soup.

To store cooked grains, cool them quickly to avoid bacteria growth. For larger batches, it helps to spread them on a sheet tray. Putting food directly in the refrigerator can disrupt the overall refrigerator temperature, which is why we cool before putting away.

To reheat larger grains, place in a saucepan and add enough water to cover. Bring to a rapid simmer and cook until hot and somewhat soft. Drain and use. To reheat small cracked and pearled grains, place in a saucepan and add a generous splash of water. Cover and cook on low, stirring occasionally, until the grains are hot. Upon reheating, the grains might seem just a touch chewier.

WHEAT

Unlike most ingredients in this book, we tend to encounter wheat in its processed forms, as breads, pastries, cereals, and more. While this leads us to think of wheat as a generic ingredient, the diversity of wheat is quite grand.

Today we have access to the varieties grown thousands of years ago, known as the ancient wheats, as well as the many common wheats (heritage and modern) and durum wheat varieties.

Ancient wheats include einkorn, emmer (also known as farro), and spelt. The grains of einkorn are the smallest and have a slightly nuttier and more subtle flavor. Emmer is middle-of-the-road in size and wheatiness, and spelt is the largest grain, with slightly grassy notes. These wheats have high levels of protein, but the ratio of gluten proteins does not lend itself to developing gluten networks when milled into flour.

Common and durum wheats are classified by hardness, color, and growing season.

WHEAT CHARACTERISTICS

Hardness: A wheat berry is categorized as either hard or soft, depending on certain proteins contained in the endosperm. **Hard wheats** are high in overall protein (11% to 15%) and best for using when a strong gluten network is desired, as for bread. **Soft wheats** are lower in overall protein (5% to 9%) and provide less gluten development. These wheats are best suited for pastries, biscuits, and cookies, which do not require strong gluten development.

Color: The color of the outer bran layer is either red or white. **Red wheat** contains tannins that lend it a slightly bitter, more robust flavor and a reddish color. **White wheat**, on the other hand, has no tannins, giving it a milder flavor and a light color.

Season: The season refers to when a grain is grown and harvested. **Winter wheats** (sown in autumn) need a period of growing when the temperature rests below 40°F (4°C). **Spring wheats** do not require a period of rest and are sown in spring and grown through summer. Spring wheats can have slightly elevated protein levels, impacting gluten development; however, this is highly dependent on the variety of wheat.

MILLED WHEAT

Hardness, color, and season are all considered as flours are milled and blended.

Many of the common wheat varieties grown and milled locally will be sold with information about protein content to allow you to create your own types of these flours, often with more flavor.

All-purpose flour: This flour is typically made from a mixture of hard red wheat and soft wheat to reach a protein level of 10% to 11%. The grains are milled and bran removed. This creates a great "all-purpose" flour because there is enough protein for gluten development, but the flour can also work in pastry applications.

Bread flour: Milled from hard wheats, bread flour is also milled with the bran removed. It is higher in protein, usually around 12%, to help develop the gluten network needed for a good rise in bread.

Pastry flour: Made from the soft wheat varieties, the grain is milled and the bran removed. It has a protein level around 9%. This lower protein level means a weaker gluten development, which keeps the dough flaky and light.

Semolina flour: This is the flour that results from milling durum wheat. Durum wheat, often characterized as being one of the hardest wheats with the highest gluten protein content, produces a flour that has good plasticity but not as good elasticity, making it a choice flour for pastas, but not breads.

COOKING WHEAT

GRAIN	UNCOOKED QUANTITY	WATER	SOAK	SOAKING ADDITIONS (OPTIONAL)	COOKING METHOD	COOKING TIME (SOAKED)	COOKING TIME (UNSOAKED)	COOKED GRAIN YIELD
Cracked grains	1 cup (140 g)	3½–4 cups (840 to 960 ml)	4 hours (optional)	½ tsp salt 1 Tbsp acid	Absorption	30–35 minutes	50–60 minutes	3½ cups (740 g)
Pearled grains	1 cup (180 g)	2½ cups (600 ml)	4 hours (optional)	½ tsp salt 1 Tbsp acid	Absorption	15–20 minutes	30–35 minutes	3 cups (600 g)
Whole grains/ berries	1 cup (190 g)	Cover with 1 inch (2.5 cm)	8 hours	½ tsp salt 1 Tbsp acid	Pasta	30–35 minutes	50–60 minutes	3 cups (420 g)

Pasta method: Place the grains and soaking liquid, if using, in a pot and add enough water so that the grains are roughly covered by about an inch (2.5 cm). Cover, bring to a rapid simmer, and cook until the grains are quite plump with a few that have burst open, using the chart times as a guide. Once the grains are done to your liking, drain, return to the pot off heat, cover, and let rest for 10 minutes.

Absorption method: Place the wheat grains and cool water or their soaking liquid, if using, in a pot over medium heat. Once the cooking water comes to a rapid simmer, cover the pot, reduce the heat to medium-low and cook for the specified time, checking 5 to 10 minutes before the grain might be done. The grains are done when they are tender and the water has been absorbed. For pearled grains, remove the saucepan from the heat and let it sit, covered, for 10 to 15 minutes. For cracked grains, serve immediately.

Notes: You can replace the mild vinegar in a soak with liquid from a ferment, just double the amount (see page 27).

You can omit the acid or start with fresh water for cooking if desired.

Toasting your grains is a great way to add layers of flavor before cooking (see page 27).

Cracked grains refer to home-cracked grains (see page 25).

WHEAT RECIPES

Cream of Wheat with Caramelized Pears

Serves 4

One of my firm beliefs is that you don't have to eat whole grains to reap the benefits of cooking with whole-grain ingredients. Most of the time I don't make 100% whole-grain doughs for bread and pizza (page 38) because I prefer a bit of lightness to the doughs that can be hard to achieve with 100% bran inclusion. Because I don't want to waste the bran as I sift some of it out, I find ways to include it in recipes. My favorite, by far, is this porridge.

Cream of wheat was a staple in my house when I was growing up, and this porridge is a nod to that. However, using bran and freshly cracked grains creates flavor that the boxed stuff just can't match. It's warm, filling, and one of the best ways to start the day. Instructions for cracking the wheat berries are on page 25. Of course, wheat bran can be store-bought as well if you're not grinding flour at home.

BRAN PORRIDGE

2 tablespoons unsalted butter

⅔ cup (80 g) finely cracked wheat berries

⅔ cup (40 g) wheat bran

2 cups (480 ml) whole milk, nondairy milk, or keffir

2 cups (480 ml) water

½ teaspoon kosher salt

Heavy cream, whole milk, or nondairy milk for serving (optional)

PAN-FRIED PEARS

¼ cup (56 g) unsalted butter

8 to 10 green cardamom pods

2 tablespoons maple syrup

½ teaspoon kosher salt

2 bosc or other firm pears, peeled, cored, and quartered

MAKE THE PORRIDGE: Melt the butter in a medium saucepan over medium-low heat and add the cracked wheat berries and wheat bran. Stir, coating both with the butter, and let toast until the color deepens slightly, 3 to 4 minutes.

Stir in your choice of milk, water, and salt. Bring to a boil, reduce to a simmer, cover, and cook until the porridge is creamy and the cracked wheat berries are tender, 30 to 40 minutes depending on the size of your cracked grains.

MAKE THE PEARS: Melt the butter in a medium skillet over medium heat. Place the cardamom pods on a cutting board and crack them open using the butt end of your knife. Add them to the skillet and toast for a minute or so. Stir in the maple syrup and salt. Place the pear slices in a single layer in the pan. Cook, flipping the pears occasionally, until the maple-butter mixture has deepened in color, and the pears are tender. Remove the cardamom pods.

TO SERVE: Divide the cream of wheat between four bowls and top with pears, maple-butter mix, and a bit of cream, if desired.

Notes

The cardamom pods add a very subtle amount of flavor. For a more pronounced flavor, use ground cardamom or a mix of warming spices, including cinnamon, clove, and ginger.

Seasonal Variations: During the spring, cook halved strawberries in the butter mixture. In the summer, I turn to peaches and nectarines.

Make Ahead: Porridge can be made ahead of time and stored in the refrigerator for a few days. Reheat with enough water or milk to loosen into a good porridge consistency.

Yeasted Einkorn Waffles with Honey Butter and Nectarines

Serves 4

I believe my son would disown me if I didn't at least include a few breakfast recipes in this book, because we are breakfast people. Waffles rank high on our list, and this yeasted version, with its light texture and crisp outsides, is my favorite.

Einkorn flour is great for baked goods. This ancient wheat provides a delicate, sweet, earthy flavor without the heaviness of whole wheat. This recipe uses 100% whole-grain einkorn flour. Jovial, the most common einkorn brand, also sells a bran-removed, all-purpose einkorn flour, which is less absorbent. If you use all-purpose einkorn flour, I recommend starting with 1 cup (240 ml) of milk and adding more, if needed, after the batter has rested.

NECTARINES

2 to 3 ripe nectarines, halved, pitted, and cut in wedges

1 to 2 tablespoons cane sugar

WAFFLES

1½ cups (360 ml) whole milk

¼ cup (56 g) unsalted butter

1¼ cups (150 g) raw or toasted whole wheat einkorn flour (see page 26)

1 tablespoon cane sugar

1 teaspoon instant yeast

½ teaspoon kosher salt

1 large egg

¼ teaspoon baking soda

PREPARE THE NECTARINES: Combine the nectarines and sugar in a small bowl. Cover and refrigerate until you are ready to serve. The nectarines should have released a bit of juice and softened considerably.

MAKE THE WAFFLE BATTER: Warm the milk either on the stovetop or in the microwave until hot. Cut the butter into small pieces and add to the hot milk, stirring until the butter has melted and combined with the milk. Let the mixture sit until the temperature reaches around 100°F (38°C).

Combine the einkorn flour, sugar, yeast, and salt in a medium bowl. Whisk in the cooled milk mixture until the batter is mostly smooth. Cover and let rest at room temperature for an hour or so, until the mixture is bubbly. Alternatively, the batter can rest in the refrigerator for up to 2 days, creating a more developed flavor.

CONTINUES

Yeasted Einkorn Waffles with Honey Butter and Nectarines

CONTINUED

HONEY BUTTER

¼ cup (55 g) unsalted butter at room temperature

2 tablespoons honey

½ teaspoon smoked finishing salt

FOR SERVING

¼ cup (30 g) crushed roasted hazelnuts (see page 140)

MAKE THE HONEY BUTTER: Combine the butter, honey, and salt in a small bowl and vigorously stir together until lightened in texture. Taste and adjust flavors as desired. Set aside.

MAKE THE WAFFLES: Preheat the waffle iron. Stir the egg and baking soda into the batter until just combined. If using the 2 by 2 square waffle iron, add half the batter. If using a Belgian waffle iron, add about one-quarter of the batter. Cook according to the manufacturer's directions. Repeat until all the batter is used.

TO SERVE: Divvy the waffles among four plates. Top each with a tablespoon of honey butter, a spoonful of the nectarines, and a sprinkle of hazelnuts.

Notes

Waffle batter should be thicker than pancake batter, but not quite as thick as muffin batter. If you find your waffle doesn't have an airy texture, I recommend adding a splash of milk. Add a little at a time so you don't thin the batter too much.

Seasonal Variations: In spring, swap the nectarines for strawberries and apricots. In the cooler months, my waffle toppings of choice are roasted pears, citrus curd, or jam.

Make Ahead: The yeast in the dough keeps the batter active, allowing the dough to be made up to 2 days ahead of time. Or make a double or triple batch of waffles, cook until just golden, then freeze for the future. To heat, pop a waffle into the toaster, toaster oven, or waffle iron and heat until hot and crisp—a lovely way to have waffles on a weekday.

Emmer e Ceci

Serves 4

Finding Deb Perelman's Smitten Kitchen recipe for *pasta e ceci*, a classic Italian comfort meal of tomato-based soup with pasta, filled a SpaghettiOs shaped hole in my cravings for childhood staples. Deb finishes the dish with a hearty herb oil, a must in my opinion, and as I went back to the recipe over and over, I soon began to incorporate whole grains. Here, the emmer takes the place of the pasta for a hearty whole-grain meal that's as delicious as the pasta version (which I also still make).

SOUP

2 tablespoons olive oil

1 large yellow onion, minced

1 rib celery, minced

½ teaspoon kosher salt

4 garlic cloves, minced

6 tablespoons (90 g) tomato paste

1 (15-ounce / 425 g) can tomato sauce

2 cups (320 g) cooked and drained chickpeas

4 to 5 cups (960 ml to 1.2 L) vegetable broth

2 cups (200 g) cooked whole-grain emmer (see page 31)

1 cup (80 g) grated Parmesan, plus extra for finishing

CHILE-DILL OIL

2 teaspoons crushed red pepper flakes

½ cup (120 ml) olive or neutral oil

¼ cup (12 g) minced fresh dill

MAKE THE SOUP: Heat a medium saucepan over medium heat. Add the olive oil, followed by the onion, celery, and salt. Cook until the mix has softened and begun to turn golden, 14 to 16 minutes. Add the garlic, cooking for a minute more. Next, stir in the tomato paste and cook for another minute or so. Add the tomato sauce, chickpeas, and 4 cups (960 ml) of broth. Bring to a boil, decrease the heat to a simmer, stir in the cooked emmer, and continue to cook until the soup has thickened, 10 to 15 minutes. If the mixture is looking too thick, add more broth, ½ cup (120 ml) at a time.

MAKE THE CHILE-DILL OIL: Place the red pepper flakes in a heat-safe bowl that's large enough to hold the hot oil too. Heat the oil in a pan over medium heat until the oil is hot (it should appear to shimmer). Carefully pour the oil over the crushed red pepper and let cool, then stir in the dill.

TO SERVE: Once the soup has thickened, stir in the Parmesan. Taste and add more Parmesan and/or salt as desired. Divide into four bowls and top with a small drizzle of the chile-dill oil before serving.

Notes

I traditionally make this with whole-grain emmer, which lends a nice, pronounced texture to the dish. However, if you'd like to make this meal day-of, without soaking the whole-grain emmer, I recommend switching to pearled emmer, cooked with a small splash of vinegar (see page 31).

Also, when working with grains in soups and stews, I prefer to cook them separately, then add them at the end. Grains, depending on age and storage, can be a bit unpredictable and not all cook evenly or react to ingredients in the same way.

Seasonal Variations: In summer, fresh tomatoes can be used in place of canned, and you can swap the dill for basil. In the cooler months, I often find myself looking for ways to use greens. Kale, chard, or spinach work well wilted into this soup.

Make Ahead: The base chile oil can be made ahead and stored at room temperature for a few days. Stir in the dill right before serving.

Pizza with Asparagus and Charred Scallion Sauce

Makes 1 (12-inch / 30 cm) pizza plus dough for 2 more pizzas

I am a person with many hobbies that revolve around food, primarily because I realized that with a little research and practice, I could make the meals I loved most. And so it seems only natural that I would fall in love with making pizza at home. I'm able to combine my love of vegetables, cooking with fire, and playing with grains all into one meal.

This same-day pizza dough is a riff on a recipe from *Flour Water Salt Yeast* by Ken Forkish that I've been making for years. I've tested it time and again with varying levels of wheat flour, sifted and unsifted. While I've been known to make 100% whole wheat versions, this dough is a good introduction for those who might not be as comfortable working with whole wheat flour. The dough recipe will leave you with enough for two more pizzas to top as you please or save for later (see Notes). You can also triple the sauce and toppings if everyone in your house wants to eat the same pizza (not common in my house).

PIZZA DOUGH

2½ cups (350 g) white whole wheat flour

1 cup plus 1 tablespoon (150 g) all-purpose flour

1½ cups plus 2 teaspoons (370 ml) warm (115°F / 46°C) water

1 tablespoon plus ¼ teaspoon kosher salt

1 teaspoon instant dry yeast

MAKE THE DOUGH: Combine the flours with the water in a medium bowl and mix until the most of the flour is incorporated into a shaggy ball. Cover and let rest for 30 minutes, or until the dough reaches a temperature of around 100°F (38°C).

With a damp hand, dimple the dough and sprinkle the salt and yeast over the top. Alternate bringing the sides of the dough over the top and pinching the dough, like a claw coming together, until the yeast is well incorporated. Continue to dampen your hand if the dough begins to stick.

Let the dough rest for 10 minutes, then complete a set of stretches and folds by taking part of the outside dough, stretching it up without tearing, and laying that part over the top of the dough. Repeat this action around the ball.

Cover, let the dough rest again for 30 more minutes, then repeat another set of folds and stretches. Cover and let rest until the dough has doubled in size, 1 to 2 hours depending on the ambient house temperature.

Once the dough has risen, turn it out onto a clean, dry surface. Divide the dough into three balls. Take one ball. Fold the edges again to the center, then flip the ball so the folded ends are on the bottom. Begin to roll the dough in a small circular motion so that it drags and begins to create a tighter ball. Once you have a dough that feels quite a bit tighter, transfer it to a floured sheet pan. Repeat with the remaining two balls if you plan to use them right away, or freeze the rest of the dough for a rainy day. Cover and refrigerate for at least 4 hours or for up to 2 days.

Preheat the oven to 500°F (260°C) with a baking stone and cast-iron pan in place. Let the dough rest, covered, at room temperature while you make the sauce.

CONTINUES

Pizza with Asparagus and Charred Scallion Sauce

CONTINUED

CHARRED SCALLION SAUCE

5 to 6 scallions, trimmed

2 tablespoons plus 2 teaspoons olive oil

2 tablespoons packed fresh dill

2 teaspoons white miso

1 teaspoon rice vinegar

½ teaspoon ground black pepper

TOPPINGS

3 to 4 asparagus stalks, thinly sliced

3 ounces (90 g) torn or shredded mozzarella cheese

Chopped fresh dill

Olive oil

MAKE THE SCALLION SAUCE: Rub the scallions with 1 to 2 teaspoons of olive oil and place on the hot skillet. Return the skillet to the oven and cook until the greens are quite charred and the whites are tender, 1 to 2 minutes. Remove from the oven and let cool.

Transfer the scallions to a food processor. Add the dill, miso, vinegar, pepper, and remaining 2 tablespoons of olive oil. Pulse until well combined. Alternatively, mince the scallions and place them in a jar along with the remaining ingredients, then shake well to combine.

ASSEMBLE THE PIZZA: On a lightly floured surface, stretch one of the dough into a 12-inch (30 cm) circle. Place on a floured pizza peel and spread the scallion sauce over the dough. Top with the asparagus, then sprinkle with the mozzarella cheese.

Transfer the pizza to the pizza stone and bake, rotating the pizza occasionally, until the cheese is bubbly and the crust is golden brown and cooked through, 8 to 12 minutes. Sprinkle the baked pizza with a handful of dill and drizzle with olive oil before serving.

Notes

A couple helpful tips when it comes to the dough, which is arguably the more nuanced part of making pizza. Once I have my three balls of dough, I keep them on a quarter sheet pan that conveniently fits inside a 2-gallon (8 L) ziplock bag that I reuse for this purpose. I live in a dry climate, and keeping the dough from forming a crust is always a battle. As a bonus, these smaller sheet pans fit well in the refrigerator.

Pull the dough out of the refrigerator a short time before shaping as the yeast is still doing its job, just a bit slower. If the dough has been frozen and thawed or stored for an extended period of time, it's helpful to give the yeast a bit more time to wake up. In these cases, I pull the dough out 1 to 2 hours before using.

Leftover pizza will keep in the refrigerator for a few days. To reheat, put pieces on a sheet pan and place in the oven. Turn the heat on to 425°F (220°C). When the oven comes to temperature, the pizza should have melted cheese and a crisp bottom. Alternatively, heat a skillet with a bit of olive oil. Add the pizza slices, cover, and cook until the bottom is crisp and the cheese has melted.

Seasonal Variations: In California I can grow scallions mostly year-round, and their fresh mild flavor can work with a wide array of vegetables, such as thinly sliced zucchini or sweet corn kernels in summer and shredded greens or Brussels sprouts during the cooler months.

Vegan Riff: Omit the mozzarella, then top with a salad, like the Greens with Green Goddess Tahini Dressing (page 207) or with vegan ricotta (see page 201).

Make Ahead: The pizza dough can be made ahead and refrigerated for up to 48 hours or frozen for up to 3 months and thawed in the refrigerator before using. Scallion sauce can also be made ahead and stored in the refrigerator for a few days.

Chipotle-Braised Cauliflower with Pickled Einkorn

Serves 4

Give leftover cooked einkorn grains the pickle treatment to make a punchy topping for smoky cauliflower wedges. Even though the einkorn is small in size, the pickled grain adds a nice bit of texture and a pop of acid.

The beauty of braising vegetables comes from really embracing the two levels of heat. The sear, from high heat, creates a perfect crust on the vegetables while the low, damp heat at the end helps create a perfect, tender texture.

PICKLED EINKORN

1 cup (140 g) cooked einkorn (see page 31)

½ cup (120 ml) rice or apple cider vinegar

½ cup (120 ml) water

2 teaspoons cane sugar

1 teaspoon kosher salt

CHIPOTLE SAUCE

2 chipotles in adobo sauce

½ cup (120 g) crushed tomatoes

¼ cup (60 ml) water or vegetable broth

8 scallions, trimmed and thinly sliced

1 tablespoon cane sugar

2 teaspoons white miso

1 teaspoon kosher salt

BRAISED CAULIFLOWER

1 head (1½ pounds / 680 g) cauliflower

3 tablespoons avocado oil

Fresh cilantro leaves, for serving

MAKE THE PICKLED EINKORN: Place the cooked einkorn in a heat-safe jar or bowl. Combine the vinegar, water, sugar, and salt in a small saucepan. Bring to a boil and let cook for a minute or so until the sugar is dissolved. Immediately pour over the einkorn and let sit for at least 30 minutes.

MAKE THE CHIPOTLE SAUCE: Place the chipotles in a small bowl and mash with a fork. Add the tomatoes, water, scallions, sugar, miso, and salt; stir to combine.

MAKE THE CAULIFLOWER: Trim off the leaves and the bottom of the stem, leaving as much stem intact as possible. Cut the cauliflower into eight wedges, making sure to include part of the core in each wedge. Don't worry if pieces fall off—use them too. Heat the avocado oil in a large skillet over medium-high heat. Add the cauliflower wedges and any loose pieces. Sear until browned, 2 to 3 minutes, flip, and repeat, working in batches to not crowd your pan.

Once the cauliflower has a nice crust on both sides, reduce the heat to low and pour the chipotle mix over the wedges, using the lid to the skillet as a splatter shield if needed. Cover the pan and let the cauliflower cook until tender, 10 to 12 minutes.

TO SERVE: Transfer the cauliflower wedges to a small serving platter and spoon any remaining cooking liquid over the top. Drain the einkorn and sprinkle over the cauliflower, then finish with a hefty sprinkle of cilantro.

Notes

Seasonal Variations: During the cooler months, broccoli, cabbage, and winter squash hold their texture during braising. Look for winter squash that has skin thin enough to eat, such as red kuri, kabocha, or delicata. In the summer, I cut small zucchini in half lengthwise and braise just for a few minutes to keep it from getting mushy.

Make Ahead: Pickled einkorn will keep in the refrigerator in its brine for a few days. Chipotle sauce will keep in the refrigerator for up to a week.

Carrot Soup with Chile-Fried Spelt

Serves 4

A creamy vegetable soup is a meal I feel like everyone should have in their rotation. It's straightforward, can use many different vegetables, and can be a lovely base for fun toppings. For this version, I've paired the sweet carrot flavor with a chile-spiked crunchy spelt—a favorite way to use up leftover cooked grains. The spelt only softens slightly in the soup and offers a crunch with every bite. Just try to not eat all the spelt before serving the soup!

SOUP

3 tablespoons avocado oil

1½ pounds (680 g) carrots, peeled and halved lengthwise

2 medium yellow onions, cut into wedges

4 garlic cloves, smashed and peeled

5 cups (1.2 L) water

2 teaspoons kosher salt, plus more as needed

½ cup (120 ml) heavy cream

3 to 4 teaspoons lemon juice

FRIED SPELT

1 cup (194 g) cooked hulled or pearled spelt (see page 31)

Avocado or other neutral high-heat oil, for frying

2 teaspoons medium-heat ground chile

1½ teaspoons kosher salt

1 teaspoon cane sugar

MAKE THE SOUP: Heat the avocado oil in a large pot over medium-high heat. Add the carrots, onion, and garlic. Cook the vegetables, stirring just a couple times, until everything has a good sear. Add the water and salt, bring to a boil, reduce to a simmer, and cook until the carrots are quite tender, 15 to 20 minutes.

Using a stand or immersion blender, carefully puree the vegetables until you have a soup consistency. Return the soup to the stove over medium heat. Add the heavy cream and heat until the soup is warm. Turn off the heat and stir in the lemon juice to taste, adding more salt if needed.

MAKE THE FRIED SPELT: Add about 1 inch (2.5 cm) of oil to a small saucepan and heat until it reaches 325°F (160°C). Carefully add the spelt and fry for 4 to 6 minutes, until the grains have substantially darkened in color. Use a spider strainer or slotted spoon to remove the spelt from the oil and place in a medium bowl.

Combine the ground chile, salt, and sugar in a small bowl. While the spelt is still hot, sprinkle with the chile mixture and toss until well coated.

TO SERVE: Divide the soup into four bowls. Sprinkle with the fried spelt and a bit of the chile mixture left in the bottom of the bowl.

Notes

Using water instead of broth helps keep the carrot flavor prominent. The right amount of salt and lemon juice are key to brightening the soup without taking over. Play around with balance of flavor and find what works best for you.

Seasonal Variations: This soup is my base recipe for most cream soups. During summer, I like to char paste tomatoes and make a cream of tomato soup; during the colder months, root vegetables like parsnips and rutabagas or cauliflower or winter squash puree well and are great with the crunchy grains.

WHEAT PRODUCTS (BULGUR, FREEKEH, COUSCOUS)

Beyond the wheat grains and flours, I thought it important to mention a few store-bought wheat forms made from cracked grains or wheat flour. These three items are quick cooking and come in handy when I'm trying to get dinner on the table.

BULGUR

A version of cracked wheat, bulgur is common in Middle Eastern and Mediterranean cuisines. It has a convenience factor built in because it is cooked and dried before cracking. This is why bulgur, which is considered a whole grain, can cook in a short amount of time with little preparation. In addition, by cooking the grains before, the starch molecules bind to create a fluffy grain upon cooking at home.

The coarseness of the grain will vary but is often labeled **fine**, **medium**, **coarse**, or **very coarse**, which has an impact on cooking time and the texture of the final product. Most bulgur sold by companies or in bulk bins is medium. The benefit of fine bulgur is that it doesn't require any cooking and can simply be soaked in hot water, then fluffed before serving.

Beyond coarseness, bulgur may be presented as golden or red. **Golden bulgur**, the most common, is traditionally made from durum wheat, while **red bulgur** is made from red hard wheat.

FREEKEH

Freekeh is actually the term for a way to process wheat that dates back thousands of years in the eastern Mediterranean basin, where durum wheat originated. While occasionally these green-tinged berries can be purchased whole, the cracked version is what's commonly sold and what I keep on hand.

The freekeh process takes immature, green ears of durum wheat, then burns off the chaff. Because the wheat still has a high amount of moisture, the berries do not burn and instead take on a bit of a smoky flavor. The heat also stops the development of starch within the seed. Once the grain chaff is charred, the wheat is threshed and dried. From there, the berries can be taken through similar steps to make bulgur, where the berries are parboiled, dried, and cracked.

COUSCOUS

And finally, we come to couscous, which is not a grain at all, but flour rolled and steamed into a grain-like texture. Variations of couscous range in size with the most common being Moroccan (small), pearl (medium), and Lebanese (large). I keep Moroccan on hand most often. Couscous has been steamed and dried again, which means cooking at home is simply a matter of rehydrating.

COOKING WHEAT PRODUCTS

GRAIN	UNCOOKED QUANTITY	WATER	COOKING METHOD	COOKING TIME	COOKED GRAIN YIELD
Bulgur, coarse/ medium	1 cup (160 g)	1¾ cups (420 ml)	Absorption	10 minutes	3 cups (480 g)
Bulgur, fine	1 cup (180 g)	1 cup (240 ml)	Steam	1 minute	4 cups (400 g)
Couscous, Moroccan	1 cup (170 g)	1¼ cups (300 ml)	Steam	1 minute	2 cups (360 g)
Couscous, pearl	1 cup (150 g)	1½ cups (360 ml)	Absorption	10–15 minutes	1½ cups (400 g)
Freekeh	1 cup (160 g)	2½ cups (600 ml)	Absorption	15–20 minutes	3 cups (480 g)

Absorption method: Place the grains and cool water in a saucepan over medium heat. Once the cooking water comes to a rapid simmer, cover the saucepan, reduce the heat to medium-low and cook for the specified time. Remove the saucepan from the heat and let it sit, covered, for 10 to 15 minutes.

Steam method: Fine bulgur and Moroccan couscous only require a quick steam. Place the grains and cool water in a saucepan over medium heat. Once the grains come to a rapid simmer, cover and remove from heat. Let rest for 10 to 15 minutes before fluffing.

Notes: Soaking is not necessary for these quick-cooking processed forms of wheat.

Toasting your grains is a great way to add layers of flavor before cooking (see page 27).

BULGUR, FREEKEH, COUSCOUS RECIPES

Bulgur Breakfast Bowl

Serves 4

I have Korean banchan to thank for my developed love of cooked greens. For most of my life, I never really liked the texture of cooked greens, and it wasn't until I tried *sigeumchi namul*, a cooked and marinated spinach, that I realized I just didn't like poorly cooked greens. Here I take the marinated spinach and pair it with bulgur and a chile-fried egg. I often reach for bulgur when I want a grain-based meal but need a quick-cooking option.

BULGUR

1 cup (160 g) uncooked medium bulgur
2 cups (480 ml) water
1 small yellow onion, cut into wedges
1 teaspoon kosher salt
1 tablespoon unsalted butter
1 tablespoon soy sauce

SESAME SPINACH

6 cups packed (180 g) spinach leaves with stems
2 teaspoons sesame oil
2 teaspoons toasted sesame seeds, plus extra for serving
1 teaspoon rice vinegar
Pinch of salt

CHILE-FRIED EGG

3 to 4 tablespoons unsalted butter
1 bunch scallions, trimmed and thinly sliced, green and white parts kept separate
1 to 2 tablespoons sambal oelek
4 large eggs

MAKE THE BULGUR: Dry toast the bulgur in a small saucepan over medium heat until the bulgur is fragrant, 2 to 3 minutes. Add the water, onion wedges, and salt. Cover, bring to a boil, reduce to a simmer, and cook for 10 minutes. Remove from the heat and let rest for 5 minutes.

Remove the onion wedges and add the butter and soy sauce. Let rest until needed.

MAKE THE SESAME SPINACH: Bring a saucepan of salted water to a boil and place ice water in a small bowl. Add the spinach to the boiling water and blanch for 60 seconds. Immediately strain and transfer to the ice bath. Once cool, remove the spinach from the ice bath and squeeze as much water as possible from the greens. Drain the water from the bowl, dry, and return the spinach to the bowl.

Drizzle the spinach with the sesame oil, sesame seeds, rice vinegar, and salt. Toss until well combined.

MAKE THE EGG: Melt the butter in a medium skillet over medium heat. Stir in the whites of the scallions along with the sambal. Crack the eggs into the pan and spoon some of the butter mixture over the egg whites. Cook until the edges are a bit crisp, the whites are set, and the yolks are to your liking.

TO SERVE: Assemble each bowl with bulgur, spinach, and a fried egg. Finish with the scallion greens and extra sesame seeds.

Notes

The chile is a great way to boost flavor in a fried egg. You can use any kind of chile-based product you might already have, including different kinds of chile paste like harissa (see page 53), gochujang, chile flakes, or chile oil (see page 37).

Seasonal Variations: Kale, chard, or collards are an easy substitute; just remove any tough stems, chop, and blanch a bit longer.

Vegan Riff: Instead of frying an egg in a chile butter, fry tofu slices in a bit of oil and sambal.

Freekeh Chili

Serves 4

When I really dove into vegetarian cooking, my mother told me about an elusive chili recipe she had saved from a magazine in the '90s but had subsequently lost. She could remember a few of the ingredients; most importantly, bulgur stood in for the meat. I started playing around with this idea, and I believe this is my fiftieth iteration (and the best yet, if I do so say myself). Here, freekeh is used instead of bulgur, which I find lends just a hint of smokiness.

Also, over the years, I've developed a love of using lentils in chili. Lentils are quite handy for the days you realize too late you don't have any cooked beans on hand (speaking from experience). I recommend using a green or brown lentil or the small black lentils in place of the beans.

CHILE PASTE

2 teaspoons cumin seeds

1 teaspoon coriander seeds

2 dried mild chiles, such as pasilla

1 dried mild smoky chile, such as ancho

2 teaspoons dried Mexican oregano

¼ to ½ cup (60 to 120 ml) vegetable broth

CHILI

3 tablespoons olive oil

1 large yellow onion, minced

½ teaspoon kosher salt, plus more to taste

3 garlic cloves, minced

3 tablespoons (45 g) tomato paste

⅓ cup (60 g) uncooked cracked freekeh

3 to 4 cups (720 to 960 ml) vegetable broth

1 (15-ounce / 425 g) can crushed tomatoes

1 tablespoon dark brown sugar

1 tablespoon soy sauce

1 ounce (30 g) bittersweet chocolate

1½ cups (270 g) cooked pinto, black, or similar size bean

MAKE THE CHILE PASTE: Toast the cumin and coriander seeds in a small skillet over medium heat until fragrant. Allow to cool slightly, then grind using a mortar and pestle or spice grinder.

Discard the stems and seeds from the dried chiles. Toast the chiles in the skillet used for the seeds over medium heat for about 2 minutes, until the chiles have slightly darkened in color. Remove from heat, then cover with hot water and a lid. Let soak for 20 minutes, then drain and discard the soaking water. Transfer to a blender to puree with the oregano, the ground spices, and a splash or two of the vegetable broth, enough to get the chile peppers mostly smooth.

MAKE THE CHILI: Heat the olive oil in a large saucepan or braiser over medium heat. Add the onion and salt and cook until the onion is tender, 14 to 16 minutes. Stir in the garlic and cook for 2 minutes until fragrant. Add the tomato paste and cook for another 2 minutes until heated. Stir in the freekeh, followed by 3 cups (720 ml) of the vegetable broth, the crushed tomatoes, brown sugar, soy sauce, and chocolate. Bring to a boil, reduce to a simmer, and cook until the freekeh is mostly tender, 10 minutes.

CONTINUES

Freekeh Chili

CONTINUED

TOPPINGS

½ small red onion, minced

¼ cup loosely packed (7 g) fresh chopped cilantro

¼ cup (30 g) roasted and chopped pepitas (see page 186)

Stir in the beans and chile paste and continue to cook for another 10 to 15 minutes until the chili has thickened. As the chili thickens, stir in more vegetable broth as desired. Taste and season with salt as needed. I typically add up to another ½ teaspoon or more, depending on how salty the vegetable broth is.

TO SERVE: Divide the chili among bowls and top with red onions, cilantro, and toasted pepitas.

Notes

I recognize that my love of dried chiles is not practical for everyone, but fear not, the chili can be made without a homemade chile paste. Use 2 to 3 tablespoons of a good chili powder and stir it in with the freekeh. Add more ground cumin and coriander as desired.

Make Ahead: Leftover chili will keep for a few days in the refrigerator or will freeze wonderfully for a few months. In either case, reheat in a saucepan with a bit of extra broth to achieve a consistency you enjoy.

Kale-Bulgur Fritters with Chipotle Sauce

Makes 16 (2 to 3-inch / 5 to 7.5 cm) fritters

I often use bulgur as a quick go-to dinner grain, especially if I'm looking to have dinner on the table in fifteen minutes. However, I often end up with plenty of leftover bulgur, and I have various ways I like to use it the next day. Fritters are a favorite of mine because they are filling and satisfy cravings for crispy/crunchy textures.

CHIPOTLE SAUCE

1 chipotle pepper in adobo sauce

2 tablespoons adobo sauce

½ cup (120 g) plain Greek yogurt or labneh

¼ cup (52 g) mayonnaise (regular or vegan, page 179)

2 teaspoons rice vinegar

½ teaspoon kosher salt

FRITTERS

2 cups packed (120 g) shredded kale leaves

1 teaspoon kosher salt

1 cup (160 g) uncooked medium bulgur

1 cup (240 ml) water

½ small yellow onion, minced

4 ounces (110 g) cheddar cheese, shredded

4 large eggs

½ cup (30 g) Japanese-style panko

Avocado or other neutral high-heat oil, for frying

MAKE THE CHIPOTLE SAUCE: Place the chipotle in a small bowl and mash with a fork. Add the adobo sauce, yogurt, mayonnaise, vinegar, and salt. Stir well to combine and place in the refrigerator until needed.

MAKE THE FRITTERS: Combine the kale and salt in a medium bowl and massage until the kale starts to soften. Set aside.

Combine the bulgur and water in a small saucepan. Bring to a boil, reduce to a simmer, and cook for 10 minutes, until the water is absorbed and the bulgur is tender. Let rest, covered, for 5 minutes.

Transfer the bulgur to a medium bowl and add the onion, cheese, eggs, and panko. Mix well to combine, then fold in the kale.

Place a wire rack over a large plate. Heat a large skillet over medium-low heat and coat the skillet with a thin layer of oil. Wet your hands and take a little over ⅓ cup (80 ml) of the mixture and form into a thick patty. Place in the pan and fry for a minute or two. With the back of a spatula, press down slightly to flatten the patty. Continue to cook for another minute or two until the bottom is golden brown. Flip, press down again until the fritter is less than a ½ inch (1.3 cm) in thickness, and continue to cook for 3 to 4 minutes, until the second side is golden and crisp. Transfer to the rack and repeat the process with the remaining fritter mix.

TO SERVE: Smear a bit of the chipotle sauce in four low bowls and top with four fritters each.

Notes

When dealing with fritters, patience is your friend. Ensure the bottom of the fritter is well cooked and crisp before attempting to flip. Early flipping can lead to broken fritters that, while still delicious, aren't quite what we're hoping to achieve here.

Seasonal Variations: Kale plays a supporting role in the fritters, but there are many options for swapping. Any green, such as spinach or chard, works well in place of the kale. In summer, shredded zucchini is fantastic—just be sure to let it rest for a bit longer with the salt and squeeze out as much moisture as you can. Most members of the brassica family work as well, including shredded cabbage, shredded Brussels sprouts, and finely minced broccoli.

Harissa-Roasted Delicata Squash and Couscous

Serves 4 to 6

Harissa, a North African chile paste, is another recipe I've continued to evolve over the years to suit what chiles I could find (primarily Mexican), my particular taste (a middle-of-the-road heat), and California influence (fennel!).

While I envision this as a beautiful side dish, adding a bit of protein could make this a whole meal. Try adding a cup of cooked beans when you add the harissa paste to the squash or layer fried halloumi on the platter with the couscous.

HARISSA PASTE

2 teaspoons coriander seeds

2 teaspoons fennel seeds

½ teaspoon cumin seeds

¼ cup (60 ml) olive oil, plus more as needed

8 dried mild chiles, such as New Mexico, stemmed and seeded

4 dried mild smoky chiles, such as ancho, stemmed and seeded

1 to 2 dried hot chiles, such as chiles de árbol, stemmed and seeded

3 garlic cloves, sliced

2 tablespoons minced preserved lemon

¾ teaspoon kosher salt

DELICATA SQUASH

1 large (2-pound / 900 g) delicata squash, halved lengthwise, seeded, and sliced on the bias ½ inch (1.3 cm) thick

2 tablespoons olive oil

½ teaspoon kosher salt

FOR SERVING

2 cups (360 g) cooked Moroccan couscous (see page 45)

½ cup loosely packed (14 g) fresh cilantro, chopped

2 ounces (60 g) chèvre (or other soft goat cheese), crumbled

MAKE THE HARISSA PASTE: Toast the coriander, fennel, and cumin seeds in a dry medium skillet over medium heat, shaking the pan occasionally until the seeds are fragrant, 1 to 2 minutes. Grind the spices using a mortar and pestle or spice grinder, then set aside.

Return the pan to medium heat and add the olive oil. When the oil is hot, add the chiles. Cook, flipping the chiles once or twice, until they have browned but not burned. Remove from the heat and stir in the sliced garlic and ground spices. Cover and let rest for 20 minutes.

Combine the chile mixture, preserved lemon, and salt in a small food processor. Puree until the mixture is as smooth as you can get it, adding more olive oil as needed to bring the paste together.

PREPARE THE SQUASH: Preheat the oven to 425°F (220°C). Line a baking sheet with parchment paper.

Place the squash on the prepared baking sheet, toss with the olive oil and salt, and arrange in a single layer. Roast for 20 minutes.

Remove the squash from the oven and spoon enough harissa over the squash to coat. Return the pan to the oven and roast for another 8 to 10 minutes, until the harissa has darkened in color and the squash is tender. Remove from the oven and let rest for a minute or two.

TO SERVE: Spoon the couscous onto a serving platter and layer on the squash. Drizzle with any oil that remains on the pan and finish with the cilantro and goat cheese.

Notes

Many brick and mortar and online stores carry a variety of harissa pastes. Heat levels vary, so be sure to taste it before you use it.

Harissa paste will last for a couple weeks in the refrigerator in an air-tight container with a thin layer of olive oil covering the top.

BARLEY

Barley has been used throughout history, thanks to its ease of growing and link to many delicious fermented beverages and breads. Unlike its wheat cousin, barley contains two different carbohydrates that create a sticky quality, making it great for baked goods, and a gelatinous finish, making barley perfect for stews and risottos.

Whole-grain barley can be hulled or hulless (see page 19). I keep it on hand for use as grain or for grinding into flour. Whole-grain barley is also used to make barley flakes, which you might see at the store.

Most popular, however, is pearled barley, which is whole barley with the bran layer removed. Unlike most other grains, barley has fiber throughout. This means pearled barley still contains a solid amount of nutrients. Pearled barley is great when a tender and quicker-cooking grain is needed.

Barley is also milled into flour, using either whole or pearled forms, and while it can have similar levels of protein to wheat, it does not have the type of protein needed for the development of the gluten. Therefore, barley flour is best used as a supplemental flour or in baked goods that do not require gluten development (such as the pancakes on page 61).

Varieties of whole and pearled barley can have a black or purple hue.

MALTED BARLEY

Most barley for human consumption is turned into malted barley, which is found in powdered and liquid form. Because the process turns starches into sugars, barley malt syrup is often used as a sweetener, most notably in bagels. In commercial baked goods, malted barley is added to aid in browning and create a more tender crumb. I keep malted barley syrup and powder on hand for bagel making.

COOKING BARLEY

BARLEY TYPE	UNCOOKED QUANTITY	WATER	SOAK	SOAKING ADDITIONS	COOKING METHOD	COOKING TIME (SOAKED)	COOKING TIME (UNSOAKED)	COOKED GRAIN YIELD
Pearled	1 cup (190 g)	2½ cups (600 ml)	4 hours (optional)	½ tsp salt 1 Tbsp acid (optional)	Absorption	15-20 minutes	30-35 minutes	3½ cups (600 g)
Whole, hulled or hulless	1 cup (180 g)	Cover with 1 inch (2.5 cm)	8 hours	½ tsp salt 2 Tbsp acid	Pasta	30-35 minutes	50-60 minutes	3 cups (600 g)
Whole grain or pearled, cracked	1 cup (140 g)	3½ to 4 cups (840 to 960 ml)	4 hours (optional)	½ tsp salt 1 Tbsp acid (optional)	Absorption	25-35 minutes	35-45 minutes	3½ cups (740 g)

Absorption method: After any soaking, place the barley water or soaking liquid, if using, in a pot over medium heat. Once the cooking water comes to a rapid simmer, cover the pot, reduce the heat to medium-low and cook for the specified time, checking 5 to 10 minutes before the grain might be done. The barley is done when it is tender and the water has been absorbed. For pearled barley, remove the saucepan from the heat and let it sit, covered, for 10 to 15 minutes. For cracked barley, serve immediately.

Pasta method: Place the whole-grain barley and soaking liquid in a pot and add enough water so that the grains are roughly covered by about an inch (2.5 cm). Cover, bring to a rapid simmer, and until the grains are quite plump with a few that have burst open, using the chart times as a guide. Once the barley is done to your liking, drain, return to the pot off heat, cover, and let rest for 10 minutes.

Notes: You can replace the vinegar in a soak with liquid from a ferment, just double the amount (see page 27).

You can omit the acid or start with fresh water for cooking if desired.

Toasting your grains is a great way to add layers of flavor before cooking (see page 27).

Cracked grains refer to home-cracked grains (see page 25).

BARLEY RECIPES

Cherry and Fennel Smoked-Barley Salad

Serves 4

Many authors paved the way for my exploration of grains, including Ann Pittman and her book *Everyday Whole Grains*. Her book led me down the path of creaming grains, like the Garlicky Millet Cream (page 109); pickling grains (see page 41); and smoking grains, like for this recipe.

I've experimented with many ways to smoke grains, and I've landed on the version in this book (page 28). I don't like a highly pronounced smoky flavor most of the time. Smoking the grains in this manner lends just enough flavor to be a delightful companion to the sweet cherries and anise-y fennel.

1 fennel bulb, trimmed (reserve the fronds) and thinly sliced
2 small shallots, thinly sliced
¼ cup (60 ml) lemon juice
2 teaspoons lemon zest
1 teaspoon kosher salt
¼ cup (60 ml) olive oil
¼ cup loosely packed (7 g) flat-leaf parsley, minced
¼ cup (30 g) roasted and crushed sunflower seeds
2 cups (280 g) pitted fresh sweet cherries, halved
1 cup (200 g) smoked and cooked whole-grain barley (see page 55)

Combine the sliced fennel and shallot in a medium bowl along with the lemon juice, zest, and salt. Toss to coat and let rest for 10 minutes, until the fennel has softened.

Mince the reserved fennel fronds and add to the macerated fennel and shallots. Stir in the olive oil, parsley, and sunflower seeds. Fold in the cherries and cooked barley. Taste and adjust lemon and salt as desired before serving.

Notes

This salad can be made without smoking the barley and still be a great late-spring or early-summer dish. I recommend dropping the kosher salt to a pinch and using some smoked finishing salt to pro-vide just a hint of the smokiness instead.

If you want to make a meal with this salad, it's great spooned over grilled cheese, such as halloumi or panela, or grilled tempeh.

Seasonal Variations: In the fall, this salad is delightful with cubed apples instead of the cherries. During the deep summer, reach for apricots, plums, or peaches.

Make Ahead: While the salad is best enjoyed on the day it is made, the barley can be smoked and cooked ahead of time. Smoked barley will last a few days before beginning to lose its smoky flavor, and the cooked barley will keep for a couple days in the refrigerator.

I recommend making a large batch of the smoked barley and using it in any application you might use a whole-grain barley, such as for the Parmesan Cracked Barley (page 58), as a grain base for the Corn Fritter Bowls (page 132), or in the Barley Navy Bean Soup (page 147).

Parmesan Cracked Barley with Braised Leeks

Serves 4

I often think about how I show love through food, but if I'm being honest, this is the kind of meal when I show love to myself. Using a medium-cracked grain (see page 24) creates a texture that sits between a risotto (for which I use a coarse crack) and a porridge (for which I use a fine crack). Pair that creaminess with the salty cheese and the butteriness of the leeks and it's truly love in every bite.

Cracking pearled barley will result in a much creamier and more tender texture; using whole-grain cracked barley will result in a bit more texture.

BARLEY

1 cup (140 g) medium-cracked pearled or hulled barley

4 cups (960 ml) water

4 garlic cloves, smashed

1 teaspoon kosher salt

1 bay leaf

1 lightly packed cup (50 g) finely grated Parmesan cheese

BRAISED LEEKS

2 large leeks

2 tablespoons avocado oil

½ cup (120 ml) dry white wine

3 cups (720 ml) vegetable broth

1 teaspoon kosher salt

1 teaspoon ground black pepper, plus more for serving

3 thyme sprigs

2 tablespoons unsalted butter

COOK THE BARLEY: In a small saucepan combine the barley, water, garlic cloves, salt, and bay leaf. Bring to a boil, reduce to a simmer, and cook until the barley is soft and creamy, 30 minutes for pearled barley or up to 1 hour for hulled barley. If at any time the barley looks dry, add more water as needed. Remove from the heat and stir in the Parmesan.

BRAISE THE LEEKS: Trim the dark-green tops and roots off of the leek then cut the leek in half lengthwise. Place in a shallow bowl and cover with water. Gently lift up the layers of the leek halves and rinse with the water to remove any dirt. Remove the leeks from the water and pat dry. Cut each half in half lengthwise.

Heat the avocado oil in a small pan over medium-high heat. Add the leeks, cut side down, and sear until charred. Flip and repeat the sear on the opposite side. Flip the leeks to the cut side, turn the heat to medium, add the wine, and cook for a few minutes, until the wine evaporates. Add the vegetable broth, salt, black pepper, and thyme. Let simmer over medium heat, occasionally spooning broth over the leeks, until the leeks are tender and only a small bit of liquid is left, 20 to 25 minutes.

Remove the pan from the heat, remove the thyme sprigs, and stir in the butter.

TO SERVE: Divide the barley between four bowls, top with the leeks and butter left in the pan, and sprinkle with black pepper.

Notes

I always like to mention that Parmesan is not technically a vegetarian-friendly cheese due to the use of animal rennet. There are a couple of non-Italian brands that make Parmesan-like cheese with vegetarian-friendly rennet. The package will say or have the ingredient labeled as "microbial rennet."

Seasonal Variations: In the spring, I relish braising spring onions for their tender and light oniony taste. Scallions and shallots also work.

Vegan Riff: Use your favorite nondairy butter, and instead of the Parmesan cheese, mix in a bit of nutritional yeast. I recommend not adding miso to the barley—miso reacts in creamy grain dishes (such as polenta and cracked grains) and creates a looser, possibly undesirable texture.

Summer Squash Barley Bake

Serves 4

This bake is a bit influenced by the Midwestern casseroles of my youth and my love of an Italian baked ziti with ricotta and tomato sauce. Here I mix the ricotta and tomato sauce with a combination of cooked barley and summer squash (because what is summer without an abundance of squash?).

This is one of my favorite meals to take to families that might be in need of a hot meal as it stores well, is full of flavor, and will fill you up. I'll often include a salad with a citrus vinaigrette, like the one on page 175, to balance the richness of this meal.

MISO CREAM TOMATO SAUCE

2 tablespoons olive oil

1 large yellow onion, diced

½ teaspoon kosher salt

4 garlic cloves, minced

2 tablespoons tomato paste

1 (15-ounce / 425 g) can crushed tomatoes

2 teaspoons dried oregano

3 tablespoons (45 ml) heavy cream

2 tablespoons red miso

GRAIN BAKE

2 cups (280 g) cooked whole-grain or pearled barley

1 medium summer squash, diced

1 medium zucchini, diced

1½ cups (360 g) whole-milk ricotta

1 large egg

2 to 3 tablespoons julienned basil

¼ teaspoon kosher salt

TOPPING

½ cup (60 g) shredded mozzarella cheese

¼ cup (25 g) grated Parmesan cheese

MAKE THE SAUCE: Heat the olive oil in a medium saucepan or braiser over medium heat. Add the onion and salt. Cook until the onion begins to soften, about 6 minutes. Reduce the heat to medium-low and cook until the onion is golden and quite soft, stirring occasionally and ensuring the onion remains in a thin, even layer, about 20 minutes. Add the garlic and cook until fragrant, about 2 minutes. Stir in the tomato paste and cook until it deepens in color, about 2 minutes. Add the crushed tomatoes and oregano. Adjust the heat to medium and cook until the mixture thickens slightly, about 8 minutes. Whisk together the heavy cream and miso in a small bowl. Remove the sauce from the heat and stir in the heavy cream mixture.

Preheat the oven to 375°F (190°C).

COOK THE GRAIN BAKE: Put the cooked barley in an 8-inch (20 cm) square pan along with the summer squash and zucchini. In the bowl you used for the heavy cream, whip together the ricotta, egg, basil, and salt. Add to the pan with the barley and vegetables, stirring until well combined. Cover with the pasta sauce and bake for 20 minutes. Remove from the oven, sprinkle with the cheeses, and return to the oven for 10 to 15 minutes, until the cheese has melted and lightly browned.

Notes

Even though tomato paste is technically cooked, the umami goodness of tomato paste is not unlocked until it's directly in contact with the heat. I like to make sure the tomato paste has a bit of color (caramelization) to it before I add more ingredients.

Seasonal Variations: This is a year-round meal for me. During the cooler months, I add shredded greens, roasted squash, or steamed broccoli. In summer, I add sweet peppers and chiles, caramelized eggplant, and grilled Romano beans.

Vegan Riff: Omit the cream from the sauce and use a vegan ricotta alternative, such as the Almond Ricotta on page 201.

Make Ahead: The preassembled bake can be made a day in advance and stored in the refrigerator. It can also be frozen, unbaked, for up to 3 months.

Buttermilk Barley Pancakes with Roasted Black Raspberries

Makes 8 to
10 (4-inch /
10 cm) pancakes

The wild black raspberries that grew around my parents' house defined summer for me. I'd layer protective clothes from head to toe in the heat to traverse thick patches, eating two berries for every one that went into the bucket. This was also when I started cooking, especially breakfast, so black raspberries were a staple atop pancakes.

My pancakes have changed a bit since then, primarily with a variety of whole-grain flours. Barley is a bit of an underdog flour since it lacks gluten-developing ability, but it makes for an amazing baking flour. The batter will be thick, but resist the urge to add more liquid right away. With the buttermilk and leavening agents, the batter will spread. Cook one pancake first and adjust with more buttermilk if needed.

ROASTED BLACK RASPBERRIES

2 cups (240 g) black raspberries

1 tablespoon cane sugar

Pinch of salt

PANCAKES

2 tablespoons maple syrup

1 tablespoon unsalted butter

1 cup (140 g) whole-grain or pearled barley flour

1¼ teaspoons baking powder

¼ teaspoon baking soda

¼ teaspoon kosher salt

1 cup (240 ml) buttermilk

1 large egg

Butter or neutral oil, for frying

TOPPING

Unsalted butter, at room temperature

Maple syrup

Preheat the oven to 450°F (230°C).

PREPARE THE BLACK RASPBERRIES: In a shallow roasting pan, toss the raspberries with the sugar and salt. Roast until the berries are quite tender and juicy, 20 to 30 minutes.

MAKE THE PANCAKES: Combine the maple syrup and butter in a small saucepan. Heat until the butter is melted and let cool slightly.

In a medium bowl, combine the barley flour with the baking powder, baking soda, and salt. In a separate bowl, whisk together the buttermilk, egg, and cooled butter mixture. Stir into the dry ingredients, just until combined.

Heat a skillet or griddle over low to medium-low heat. When the skillet is hot (if you flick water onto the skillet, it should sizzle), add butter and pour a scant ¼ cup (60 ml) of batter onto the skillet. Cook for 1 to 2 minutes, until the pancake begins to bubble slightly and the edges have a nice golden crust. Flip and cook for another 1 to 2 minutes, until the pancake is cooked through. Repeat until all the batter is used.

TOP THE PANCAKES: Divide the pancakes among plates and spread on butter, if desired. Finish with the roasted black raspberries and maple syrup.

Notes

Buttermilk pancakes are tender because the buttermilk and the baking soda react, creating carbon dioxide, which causes an airy texture.

Seasonal Variations: Many different fruits roast well, including stone fruits, apples, and pears. The strawberry compote on page 226 can also be used, or simply top your pancakes with a bit of jam.

RYE

Rye is the grain that started it all for me, the little seed that ignited my curiosity about everything I'm sharing in this book. I grew up in a small midwestern town with a large Swedish population, including my own grandfather. Rye's ability to grow in cooler climates made it popular in Scandinavian and Eastern European countries.

Similar to barley, rye contains higher levels of a carbohydrate that can cause a bit of stickiness in the grain and flour. This can make rye a bit troublesome to mill but aids the flour when used in breads.

FORMS OF RYE

Whole rye berries: The seeds that come directly from the plant are dried, threshed, and winnowed to become rye berries. This version of the grain is not super popular but can be found in bulk bins at co-ops and natural food stores. I keep rye berries on hand and process then into cracked grains (see page 25) and flour (see page 26) as needed. Malted rye berries are whole rye berries that have been taken through the malting process (see page 26) and used as a base for fermented beverages, such as beer and whiskey.

Cracked rye: Exactly what the name implies: cracked rye is commercially cracked pieces of rye.

Rye flakes: Similar to rolled oats, rye flakes are whole rye berries that are steamed and then pressed into flakes. These flakes are great for porridges and granolas.

Rye flour: The most popular form of rye for the home cook is rye flour. Flour made from rye can have a wide range of protein levels, but is unable to form a strong gluten network. However, rye can still be used to make unique, dense breads or to add a distinctive flavor to wheat-based breads.

Rye flour is sold in many types, depending on the amount of bran and germ included. **White rye** and **light rye** refer to flour milled from grains that have had the bran and germ removed, although light rye may contain a trace of bran. **Medium rye** has partial bran removal and **whole rye flour** includes all parts of the grain. Occasionally rye flour is marketed as **dark rye**, which could be whole grain or not. **Pumpernickel** is often thought of as coarsely ground rye flour and could be whole grain or not.

COOKING RYE

RYE TYPE	UNCOOKED QUANTITY	WATER	SOAK	SOAKING LIQUID ADDITIONS	COOKING METHOD	COOKING TIME (SOAKED)	COOKING TIME (UNSOAKED)	COOKED GRAIN YIELD
Cracked grains	1 cup (140 g)	3 to 4 cups (720–960 ml)	4 hours (optional)	½ tsp salt 1 Tbsp acid (optional)	Absorption	25–35 minutes	35–45 minutes	3½ cups (740 g)
Whole grain	1 cup (180 g)	Cover with 1 inch (2.5 cm)	8 hours	½ tsp salt 2 Tbsp acid	Pasta	30–35 minutes	50–60 minutes	3 cups (420 g)

Pasta method: Place the whole-grain rye and soaking liquid in a pot and add enough water so that the grains are roughly covered by about an inch (2.5 cm). Cover, bring to a rapid simmer, and cook until the grains are quite plump with a few that have burst open, using the chart times as a guide. Once the rye is done to your liking, drain, return to the pot off heat, cover, and let rest for 10 minutes.

Absorption method: Place the rye and cool water or its soaking liquid, if using, in a pot over medium heat. Once the cooking water comes to a rapid simmer, cover the pot, reduce the heat to medium-low and cook for the specified time, checking 5 to 10 minutes before the grain might be done. The rye is done when they are tender and the water has been absorbed. For cracked rye, serve immediately.

Notes: You can replace the vinegar in a soak with liquid from a ferment, just double the amount (see page 27).

You can omit the acid or start with fresh water for cooking if desired.

Toasting your grains is a great way to add layers of flavor before cooking (see page 27).

Cracked grains refer to home-cracked grains (see page 25).

RYE RECIPES

Pumpkin-Rye Bread

Makes 1 (8-inch / 20 cm) loaf

One of my hopes is that through the smattering of flour-based recipes in this book, you'll see that flours can add unique and delightful flavors as well as structure.

After many iterations of this one-bowl pumpkin quick bread, I believe this rye version is my favorite. The rye adds a rustic flavor and creates a tight, moist crumb. However, with 100% rye flour, this bread is quite dense. If you're looking for something slightly lighter, use a mix of soft wheat or all-purpose flour with the rye flour.

1½ cups (360 g) pumpkin puree

½ cup (100 g) cane sugar

½ cup (120 ml) maple syrup

½ cup (120 ml) walnut oil or other neutral oil

2 large eggs

2 teaspoons ground cinnamon

2 teaspoons ground ginger

¼ teaspoon ground cloves

1 teaspoon baking soda

½ teaspoon kosher salt

1¾ cups (190 g) whole-grain rye flour

½ cup (60 g) roasted and crushed pecans or walnuts (see page 185)

Preheat the oven to 350°F (180°C). Line an 8-inch (20 cm) loaf pan with parchment paper and grease with a bit of oil.

In a medium-large bowl, combine the pumpkin puree with the sugar and stir until the pumpkin is smooth. Stir in the maple syrup, oil, eggs, cinnamon, ginger, cloves, baking soda, and salt. Stir in the flour and nuts until the batter is combined. Pour into the prepared pan.

Bake until the top of the loaf springs back when lightly pressed and a knife comes out clean if entered into the center, 45 to 55 minutes.

Let the loaf cool in the pan for 5 to 10 minutes. Turn out onto a wire rack and let cool completely before slicing. If sliced too soon, the bread will be gummy.

Notes

You can make this bread with pumpkin puree from roasted sugar pie pumpkins. To roast pumpkins, cut in half and place cut side down in a roasting pan with ¼-inch (6 mm) of water. Bake at 425°F (220°C) until the pumpkin halves begin to collapse, 30 to 40 minutes. Let cool, remove the seeds, scoop the pumpkin out, and use as the puree. This also works for other winter squash, including kabocha, acorn, and butternut squash.

Store leftover quick bread at room temperature, loosely covered, and only move to a sealed container if it begins to dry out. Bread will last up to 3 days with this method. For longer storage, freeze for up to 3 months.

Ras El Hanout Carrot Galette

Makes 1 (8-inch / 20 cm) galette

A galette, which is a rustic tart, makes a stunning vegetarian main dish. You can stack it high with vegetables and come out with a savory pie worthy enough for a decadent dinner or roadside picnic. Hot or at room temperature—they are equally delicious.

Opt for whole-grain rye as its slightly nutty, earthy flavor is perfect with the spices and slightly sweet carrots. If all you can find is light rye, use all rye flour instead of mixing it with all-purpose.

RYE CRUST

¾ cup (90 g) all-purpose flour

½ cup (60 g) whole-grain rye flour

¼ teaspoon kosher salt

½ cup (110 g) cold unsalted butter, cut into small pieces

¼ cup (60 ml) ice cold water

Egg, for finishing

RAS EL HANOUT CARROTS

2 large carrots

¾ teaspoon kosher salt

½ teaspoon ground coriander

½ teaspoon ground cumin

½ teaspoon ground ginger

¼ to ½ teaspoon ground chile

¼ teaspoon ground allspice

¼ teaspoon ground cinnamon

Small pinch ground cloves

WHIPPED FETA

3 ounces (85 g) feta, at room temperature

¼ cup (60 g) labneh or Greek yogurt

Zest of ½ lemon

MAKE THE CRUST: Combine the all-purpose and rye flours and salt in a bowl and stir to combine. Add the butter to the flours. Using your hands, rub the butter into the flour, leaving the butter in flat, paper-like pieces. Add enough of the cold water to bring the dough together in a shaggy ball that is not too firm and not too sticky. Form into a loose ball, place in a bowl, cover, and refrigerate for 20 minutes

MAKE THE CARROTS: Using a mandoline, slice the carrots into strips, as thinly as possible. Place in a bowl along with the salt. Let rest for at least 10 minutes. Drain any water and then add the coriander, cumin, ginger, chile, allspice, cinnamon, and cloves, tossing to evenly coat the carrots.

MAKE THE WHIPPED FETA: Combine the feta, labneh, and lemon zest in a food processor. Blitz until well combined. Alternatively you can mash and whip together in a small bowl.

Preheat the oven to 425°F (220°C). Line a baking sheet with parchment paper.

MAKE THE GALETTE: On a lightly floured surface, roll the prepared dough into a 12-inch (30 cm) circle and transfer to the prepared baking sheet. Place an 8-inch (20 cm) plate, upside down, gently on the dough to leave an indentation to guide the inner circle. The goal is to leave at least 2 inches (5 cm) around the edge of the dough. Use a sharp knife to cut slits every 3 to 4 inches (7.5 to 10 cm) along the dough border, then carefully remove the plate.

Spread the feta mixture evenly over the center circle. Layer the carrot mixture evenly on top of the whipped feta.

In a small bowl, whisk the egg until frothy. Take one of the border sections of dough and fold it over the filling. Brush with the egg, then repeat with the next section of dough, overlapping it slightly with the previous section. Continue in this fashion all the way around the dough border.

Bake the galette for 22 to 24 minutes, until the crust is crisp and golden. Let cool for 10 minutes.

CONTINUES

Ras El Hanout Carrot Galette

CONTINUED

PISTACHIO SPRINKLE

¼ cup loosely packed (7 g) fresh flat-leaf parsley

1 tablespoon roasted pistachios (see page 185)

Zest from ½ lemon

Pinch of kosher salt

MAKE THE PISTACHIO SPRINKLE: Put the parsley, pistachios, lemon zest, and salt in a small pile on the cutting board. Chop back and forth until the mixture is well combined and the pistachios are crushed.

TO SERVE: Cut the galette into six wedges and top with the pistachio sprinkle before serving.

Notes

Don't be tempted to skip letting the carrots rest in the salt. This pulls out water from the carrots, which is crucial for the texture of the carrots and prevents adding moisture to the galette.

The cooked galette will keep in an airtight container for up to 3 days in the refrigerator. To reheat, place on a sheet pan in a 375°F (190°C) oven and bake until the filling is warm and the crust is crisp, 10 to 15 minutes.

Seasonal Variations: A galette is truly a great way to showcase seasonal produce and while carrots are year-round here, I like to play around depending on the season. During the cooler months, use roasted sweet potatoes, Yukon gold potatoes, beets, and parsnips. For summer, use sliced sweet peppers, sweet corn, or a mix of both.

Vegan Riff: Swap the butter in the crust for your favorite vegan alternative, use a soft vegan cheese or a nut cream as the base, and skip the egg wash.

Braised Celeriac with Chile-Miso Sauce and Basil-Rye Berries

Serves 4

Celeriac is a bit of an underdog in the vegetable world, but get past the gruff exterior, and the reward is a luxurious vegetable with a slightly nutty taste and a hint of celery. The gentle flavor of braised celeriac can pair with quite a few flavor combinations. Here I've paired it with a chile-spiked pan sauce made from the braising liquid and herby dressed rye berries.

BRAISED CELERIAC

2 to 3 tablespoons avocado oil

2 pounds (900 g) celeriac, peeled and sliced ½-inch (1.3 cm) thick

2 cups (480 ml) water

2 vegetable bouillon cubes

PAN SAUCE

¼ cup (56 g) unsalted butter

2 tablespoons white miso

1 teaspoon ground chile

1 teaspoon sweet paprika

BASIL-RYE BERRIES

¾ cup loosely packed (36 g) basil

2 small garlic cloves, minced

2 teaspoons lemon zest

½ teaspoon kosher salt

3 cups (420 g) cooked rye berries (see page 63)

PREPARE THE CELERIAC: Heat enough of the avocado oil to thinly coat the bottom of a large pan with a good-fitting lid over medium-high to high heat. Add the celeriac and cook until seared on one side. Flip and repeat. Reduce the heat to low. With the lid in hand to protect yourself from splatter, add the water and bouillon cubes. Cover, reduce the heat to low, and cook until the celeriac is tender but still has texture, 15 to 20 minutes. Any longer and the celeriac will begin to fall apart.

MAKE THE PAN SAUCE: Remove the celeriac from the pan, place on a plate, and set aside. Return the heat to medium-high and cook until the remaining liquid in the pan has reduced to a thick consistency. Reduce the heat to low, add the butter, miso, ground chile, and paprika, and cook until the butter has melted into the reduced liquid. Turn off the heat, return the celeriac to the pan, and spoon the sauce over the celeriac.

PREPARE THE RYE BERRIES: Place the basil on a cutting board and top with the minced garlic, lemon zest, and salt. Chop the mixture until combined and minced well. Transfer to a medium bowl and add the rye, tossing to combine.

TO SERVE: Divide the rye between four plates and top each with celeriac. Drizzle with the pan sauce and serve.

Notes

Timing on the braising is really important. I recommend checking the texture of the celeriac occasionally with a knife to feel how easily it pierces as any variance in thickness can change the amount of time it will need.

Also, you can swap the bouillon cubes and water for 2 cups (480 ml) vegetable broth; however, I find the use of the concentrated cube to be more impactful in the pan sauce.

Seasonal Variations: Slabs of cauliflower, slices of winter squash, or even onions can be used in place of the celeriac during the cooler months. During the summer I use halved paste tomatoes; they only need 5 or so minutes for braising.

Roasted Red Pepper Rye Risotto

Serves 4

I often advise people wanting to eat more vegetarian meals to start with what they know and make small changes. The same holds true for cooking with more grains. My favorite example of this is risotto. While traditional risotto uses arborio rice, cracked rye can also make a great creamy base.

Beyond the cracked rye, I also like to use a cream-based item to take risotto to the next level of comfort. Here it's a balance of cream cheese and roasted red peppers, but any creamy goat cheese, farmer cheese, or mascarpone cheese works.

RISOTTO

6 to 7 cups (1.4 to 1.6 L) vegetable broth

2 to 3 tablespoons olive oil

1 cup (140 g) coarsely cracked rye

4 garlic cloves, smashed

ROASTED RED PEPPER CREAM

2 red bell peppers, roasted, peeled, and seeded

2 ounces (30 g) cream cheese

1 teaspoon nutritional yeast

1 teaspoon kosher salt

1 teaspoon rice vinegar

FOR THE TOPPING

1 red bell pepper, roasted, peeled, seeded, and minced

¼ cup (60 ml) olive oil

1 to 2 teaspoons smoked finishing salt

1 teaspoon sweet paprika

MAKE THE RISOTTO: Heat the vegetable broth to a simmer in a saucepan. Heat a thin film of oil in a medium braiser or skillet over medium heat. Add the cracked rye and garlic. Toast until the rye has golden sheen and the garlic is fragrant, 3 to 4 minutes.

Ladle in enough broth to cover the rye. Reduce the heat to medium-low. Cook the rye, stirring occasionally, until most of the liquid has been absorbed. Add a few more ladles of the broth and continue in this pattern until the rye is plump and tender, 50 to 60 minutes.

MAKE THE ROASTED PEPPER CREAM: Combine the roasted peppers, cream cheese, nutritional yeast, kosher salt, and rice vinegar in a food processor and puree until smooth; set aside.

MAKE THE TOPPING: Place the roasted red pepper in a small bowl. Heat the olive oil in a small saucepan until warm. Pour over the roasted red peppers and let sit until cool.

TO SERVE: When the rye is tender, decrease the heat to low, remove the garlic, and stir in the roasted red pepper cream. Continue to cook until the risotto is creamy and thick. Divide between four bowls and top with the roasted red peppers in oil, smoked salt, and a sprinkle of sweet paprika.

Notes

Without soaking the rye ahead of time, the grain will have a bit more bite but is still a lovely risotto base. For a more tender risotto, I recommend cracking and toasting the rye, then doing a short, acidulated soak (see page 63) before continuing on with the recipe.

You can buy roasted red peppers in a jar instead of roasting your own, just be mindful of any salt they bring to the dish.

Leftover risotto will keep for a day or two. Reheat with enough vegetable broth to ensure a creamy consistency.

Vegan Riff: I like using cream cheese in recipes because there are readily available vegan cream cheeses on the market. A nut cream or pureed silken tofu can stand in for the cheese and help add a bit of creaminess too.

RICE

In the diet culture of white America in the 1990s, rice, specifically white rice, was vilified. If you had to eat rice, it was brown rice, but really all rice was bad. My journey with rice has only taken hold upon moving to California.

The thing I love most about rice is how ingrained this tiny seed is in cultures across the globe. This outlook, fueled by over 100,000 varieties, has allowed rice to perch atop the grain pedestal, and for good reason. And just to note, white rice has no business having any sort of bad reputation. White rice still contains good nutrients that are foundational to many diets around the world.

I've tried to put into words why rice is so special and honestly, Michael W. Twitty in his book *Rice* says it best: "Rice dances with everything."

RICE VARIETIES

Japonica and indica rice varieties are the two most commonly grown rice varieties.

Japonica rices are mostly short- and medium-grain rices. They have higher levels of amylopectin, a starch that gives it the waxy, glutinous, or sticky texture and allows it to cook in less water and in less time. After cooking, these rice grains stay softer for longer. Japonica varieties of rice are primarily grown in temperate climates and include Mediterranean and Japanese rice.

Indica rices tend to be elongated and thinner (medium and long grain) and typically grow in the tropics and subtropics, including many Southeast Asian varieties. These varieties of rice stay distinct and separate from each other; however, they need more water and longer cooking times. As the rice cools, it begins to harden.

COLORS

Rice comes in a variety of colors controlled by polishing or presence of anthocyanins, water-soluble pigments.

Brown rice: A whole-grain rice. Only the husk is removed, leaving the entire bran layer intact. It does not include pigments.

White rice: Created to be more shelf-stable and easier to cook, white rice has been milled and polished, removing the bran and husk.

Pigmented rice: Types of rice high in anthocyanins can be a shade of red, purple, blue, or black. These colors can be present in many different rice varieties and lengths of rice. Pigmented rice is also sold as whole grain and partially milled—the package should say as this will impact cooking time.

LONG AND MEDIUM-GRAIN RICE

Long-grain rice: Basmati, a type of aromatic long-grain rice, is most commonly sold in brown and white and has a flavor that is a bit nutty and grassy. Basmati has higher amounts of amylose, which contributes to the cooked grains staying separate. **Jasmine**, another type of aromatic rice, is often just a bit shorter and plumper than basmati, has more sweet and floral notes, and is somewhat more starchy. Jasmine rice is often found in red, brown, and white. **Carolina Gold** is an American variety of long-grain golden rice. It is a nutty and flavorful grain and has a slight cling upon cooking. This variety has made a comeback as an heirloom variety but is also the basis for most of the long-grain rice found in the United States.

Medium-grain rice: Medium-grain rice can be used as an all-purpose rice or for risotto or paella. **Calrose** is a California-grown medium-grain rice that is known for being plump with a nice cling and mild flavor upon cooking. This can work in place of either long or short-grain varieties. Calrose comes in brown and polished white.

Arborio, the go-to mild-flavored Italian rice for risotto, is medium-grain in size but has high levels of the starch that creates the creamy base sought after in a good risotto. It is typically found in polished form. **Bomba**, a Spanish rice often known as paella rice, has slightly more starch, creating a medium-grain rice that exhibits a bit of firmness and separation compared to arborio. It is typically found in polished form.

SHORT-GRAIN RICE

Short-grain rice is used for making sushi, as well as sake and vinegar. **Japanese short-grain rice (uruchimai)** is short-grain rice prized for its plump, sticky texture and mild flavor. This is a category of rice that includes varieties grown in Northern California, such as koshihikari, akitakomachi (often labeled as just "sushi rice"), and tamaki gold (a combination of koshihikari and yumegokochi).

GLUTINOUS RICE

Japanese short-grain sweet or glutinous rice (mochigome): Known for its short, plump size and extremely sticky texture upon cooking, this rice is used for foods that rely on the stickiness, such as mochi. This rice has a hint of sweetness and a mellow flavor. Glutinous rice contains no gluten and can be safely eaten by those who avoid gluten.

Thai sticky rice: A medium- to long-grain variety, Thai sticky rice is a bit of an anomaly because of its length and high levels of starch. The rice cooks up quite sticky, and it is also the rice used to make rice powder (page 75).

GABA RICE

This is any length of brown rice that has gone through germination; it has a slightly sweeter flavor and briefer cooking times.

WILD RICE

Wild rice is not a true rice. As the name implies, this rice, which is still a grass, is primarily harvested from wild rice that grows in wetlands and marshes, primarily around the Midwestern United States and Canada. Wild rice can also be found in California since it was brought here in the 1970s. This grain can be used in similar ways as rice but has a more pronounced, nutty flavor.

I use wild rice sparingly, primarily due to personal preference. However, I recommend it in soups, such as the Barley Navy Bean Soup on page 147, as the base for a grain pilaf, or as a base for stewed or braised vegetables.

PREPARING RICE FOR COOKING

RINSING

Rinsing is by far the most important part when dealing with most white rice. During the polishing process, starch gets loose and deposits a light dusting on all the grains. That starch, when left on the rice, creates a gummy consistency (not to be confused with the delightful sticky qualities of glutinous rice). By rinsing the rice, you are helping ensure even cooking and the intended texture of the style of rice.

To rinse, with your rice in a bowl, cover the grains with water. Swish around for 10 seconds, then drain. Repeat the process until the water runs mostly clear. And if you feel bad about using that much water—save it to water plants, use it as a slight thickening base for a stew, or even add it to compost (in dry climates compost can typically use the added moisture).

Do not rinse arborio rice for risotto and bomba rice for paella because starch is what we like.

SOAKING

Part of my trust in my rice cooker is due to spending time understanding the process of how the machine cooks the rice. There are three stages and the first is soaking. While it doesn't soak for long, the process of soaking happens every time.

Rice can be cooked without soaking, but certain rice varieties do better with a short 30 to 60 minute, water-only soak. Medium and long-grain brown rice is better with an acidulated soak.

COOKING RICE

First and foremost, given the sheer number of rice varieties, I recommend referring to the package or company website for directions. However, not all rice comes with instructions; use this chart as a starting guide for rice cooking based on type.

RICE TYPE	UNCOOKED QUANTITY	WATER	SOAK	SOAKING LIQUID ADDITION	COOKING METHOD	STOVETOP COOKING TIME (SOAKED)	STOVETOP COOKING TIME (UN-SOAKED)	RICE COOKER SETTING	COOKED GRAIN YIELD
Black rice	1 cup (180 g)	2½ cups (600 ml)	4 hours (optional)	None	Absorption	25–30 minutes	35–40 minutes	Brown rice	3 cups (600 g)
Brown rice, long-grain	1 cup (180 g)	Cover with 1 inch (2.5 cm)	8 hours	½ tsp salt 1 Tbsp acid (optional)	Pasta	25–30 minutes	40–45 minutes	Brown rice	3 cups (580 g)
Brown rice, medium-grain	1 cup (180 g)	Cover with 1 inch (2.5 cm)	4 hours (optional)	½ tsp salt 1 Tbsp acid (optional)	Pasta	25–30 minutes	40–45 minutes	Brown rice	3 cups (580 g)
Brown rice, short-grain	1 cup (180 g)	1¾ cups (420 ml)	4 hours (optional)	None	Absorption	25–30 minutes	40–45 minutes	Brown rice	3 cups (580 g)
White rice, long-grain/basmati	1 cup (180 g)	1¾ cups (420 ml)	1 hour (optional)	None	Absorption	10–15 minutes	15–20 minutes	White rice	3 cups (480 g)
White rice, medium-grain	1 cup (190 g)	1½ cups (360 ml)	30 minutes (optional)	None	Absorption	10–15 minutes	20–25 minutes	White rice	3 cups (570 g)
White rice, short-grain	1 cup (200 g)	1¼ cups (300 ml)	30 minutes (optional)	None	Absorption	10 minutes	20 minutes	White rice	3 cups (600 g)
Wild rice	1 cup (180 g)	3 cups (720 ml)	4 hours (optional)	None	Absorption	25–30 minutes	40–45 minutes	Brown rice	3½ cups (560 g)

STOVETOP COOKING

Absorption method: Place the rice and cool water or its soaking liquid, if applicable, in a saucepan over medium heat. Once the cooking water comes to a rapid simmer, cover the saucepan and reduce the heat to low so the rice is just simmering. Cook undisturbed for the specified time, until the water has been absorbed. Remove the pot from the heat and let it sit, covered, for 10 to 15 minutes before serving.

Pasta method: Place the rice and soaking liquid, if using, in a pot and add enough water so that the grains are roughly covered by about an inch (2.5 cm). Cover, bring to a rapid simmer, and cook until the rice is quite plump and tender, using the chart times as a guide. Once the rice is done to your liking, drain, return to the pot off heat, cover, and let rest for 10 minutes.

Notes: If you use a rice cooker, follow the manufacturer's instructions with the chart as a guide.

You can replace the vinegar in a soak with liquid from a ferment, just double the amount (see page 27).

You can omit the acid or start with fresh water for cooking if desired.

Toasting your rice is a great way to add layers of flavor (see page 27).

Most rice should be rinsed before soaking and cooking (see page 73).

RICE PRODUCTS

Beyond the rice grain, I keep a few rice products on hand at all times. Some I make, some I buy.

Rice flour: Made from grinding any type of rice. I use regular rice flour in tempura batters and to shape bread loaves. Sweet (sometimes called glutinous) rice flour, which is high in starch, can be used as a thickening agent akin to corn and potato starch. I typically grind what I need, but rice flour is found in most stores—just be sure you know which kind you're after as regular rice flour and sweet/glutinous rice flours will give very different results.

Toasted rice powder (*khao khua*): Made from sticky rice that's been toasted, either in a skillet or oven, until it's a deep golden brown. From there, the rice is ground into a coarse flour. Toasted rice powder is mainly found in dishes from Thailand and Laos, but I like to sprinkle it in salads and use it to lend a bit of texture to all kinds of sauces. In this book I used it in the Tamarind Tofu Skewers on page 180.

Rice noodles: Noodles made from rice flour come in various thicknesses and can be made from white or brown rice. I typically keep them on hand for making Vietnamese and Thai recipes.

Vietnamese rice paper: Rice flour, water, and starch are combined to make sheets that become pliable when wet and are easy to use as a wrapping. I love making fresh spring rolls, usually with the tofu from my Tofu Brown Rice Bowls (page 80).

Brown rice syrup: The method for making this syrup is similar to that of barley malt syrup. Brown rice is sprouted, then cooked to create a thick, sweet syrup. I find brown rice syrup to have a good level of sweetness without an intense flavor.

Rice bran oil: Made from the bran of brown rice, rice bran oil has a high smoke point. I use it in rotation with avocado oil when I need a neutral higher heat oil.

RICE RECIPES

Zucchini and Olive Paella

Serves 4

Paella is one of my favorite meals to make in the summer when friends stop for a visit. This vegan version of the traditional Spanish dish shines with plenty of olive oil, good-quality smoked paprika, and saffron. I love a punchy side salad for this. Try my Green Goddess Tahini Dressing (page 207).

SOFRITO

6 tablespoons (90 ml) olive oil

2 medium yellow onions, diced

2 red bell peppers, diced

1 tablespoon kosher salt

12 garlic cloves, minced

¼ cup (60 g) tomato paste

PAELLA

Pinch of saffron

1 cup (180 g) uncooked bomba rice

1 (28-ounce / 794 g) can crushed tomatoes

3 cups (720 ml) vegetable broth, plus more as needed

1½ cups (270 g) cooked chickpeas, drained

2 teaspoons smoked paprika

2 medium zucchini, thinly sliced

½ cup (80 g) pitted green olives, sliced

FOR SERVING

Minced fresh flat-leaf parsley

Olive oil

Lemon wedges

MAKE THE SOFRITO: Heat the olive oil in a 14-inch (36 cm) cast-iron skillet or paella pan over medium heat. Add the onions, bell peppers, and salt. Cook, stirring occasionally, until the onions are translucent, 10 to 12 minutes. Reduce the heat to medium-low and continue to cook until the mixture is golden and quite tender, 10 to 15 minutes. Stir in the garlic and continue to cook for a few more minutes, until fragrant. Finally, add the tomato paste and cook another 2 to 3 minutes.

MAKE THE PAELLA: Place the saffron in a small bowl. Cover with a few tablespoons of warm water and let soak for 10 minutes.

Add the rice to the pan and stir to coat the rice in a bit of oil. Stir in the crushed tomatoes, increase the heat to medium-high, and simmer until most of the liquid has cooked off, 2 to 3 minutes. Leave the tomatoes mostly undisturbed during this time so that they brown just a bit.

Reduce the heat to medium. Stir in the saffron mixture, broth, chickpeas, and paprika. Bring the mixture to a simmer, reduce the heat to low, and cook, uncovered, for 10 minutes.

After 10 minutes, there should still be a bit of broth. If the rice has absorbed most of it, add ½ cup (120 ml) or so, without stirring it into the rice. Layer the zucchini slices in an overlapping spiral over the entire paella. Use your cooking spoon to gently press down on the zucchini so that broth covers the zucchini slightly. Scatter the olives over the top, then let the paella cook, undisturbed, until the broth has been absorbed and the rice is tender, 15 to 20 minutes.

Once the rice is cooked, turn the heat to medium-high and cook for 1 to 2 minutes to create the *socarrat*, a crispy, flavorful crust at the bottom of the pan. Remove from the heat, cover, and let rest for 5 minutes.

TO SERVE: Sprinkle with parsley and olive oil. Serve with lemon wedges.

Notes

If you'd prefer to use fresh tomatoes, bring a saucepan of water to a boil. Score an X at the bottom of 2 to 3 pounds (900 g to 1.4 kg) tomatoes. Boil for 1 minute, until the skin begins to loosen. Transfer to an ice bath and let cool. Remove the skins, then, using your hands, crush the tomatoes into a bowl.

Seasonal Variations: Green beans are a lovely summer addition, along with eggplant. Artichokes, fennel, peas, and mushrooms can be added during the cooler seasons.

Unagi-Inspired Eggplant Onigiri

Makes 6
onigiri

As I pack more and more school lunches, I'm constantly on the lookout for ideas and inspiration that don't revolve around sandwiches, but can hold together when an eight-year-old slings their lunchbox around. Enter *onigiri*. These Japanese rice balls are an equal-opportunity base that are easily vegetarian and can be packed with fresh or cooked vegetables, tofu, or tempeh. This version is heavily inspired by *unagi*, eel that is basted in a sweet sauce, but instead of fish, the eggplant is seared and tossed in a sweet sauce.

When I make onigiri for myself, I typically pair it with a marinated and grilled tofu, pickles, and some kind of greens, either fresh or cooked like the spinach on page 47.

EGGPLANT UNAGI

1 or 2 small Japanese eggplant, peeled
1 tablespoon soy sauce
1 tablespoon mirin
2 teaspoons sake
1 teaspoon dark brown sugar
1 teaspoon vegetarian oyster sauce
2 teaspoons avocado oil

ONIGIRI

3 cups (420 g) cooked short-grain white rice (see page 74)
1 tablespoon toasted white sesame seeds
1 tablespoon toasted black sesame seeds
Medium-heat ground chile (optional), for garnish
6 (1½ by 4-inch / 4 by 10 cm) nori rectangles

PREPARE THE EGGPLANT: Bring a few inches of water to a boil in a saucepan fitted with a steamer basket. Put the eggplant in the basket and steam for 8 to 12 minutes, until tender. Cut in half lengthwise and lightly mash, but keep the halves intact as much as possible.

Combine the soy sauce, mirin, sake, sugar, and oyster sauce in a skillet over medium heat. Add the eggplant, mashed side down, and cook until the sauce thickens and only a bit is left, about 4 to 5 minutes. Add the oil and cook for 2 to 3 minutes, until the eggplant is caramelized. Let the eggplant cool, then transfer to a cutting board and chop.

MAKE THE ONIGIRI: Wet your hands and take about ½ cup (120 ml) of the cooked rice. Pat the rice into a thick circle and add about 1 tablespoon of the eggplant. Form the rice around the filling and shape into a triangle, keeping your hands damp as needed. Alternatively, and my preferred way, is to use an onigiri mold. Press ¼ cup (60 ml) of the rice in the bottom, add 1 tablespoon of filling, top with another ¼ cup (60 ml) of rice, and press.

Combine the sesame seeds and ground chile, if using, on a small plate. Roll the outer edges of the onigiri in the sesame mixture. If serving right away, wrap in the nori squares and serve. If serving later, wrap in waxed paper and keep in the refrigerator up to a day. Wrap in nori right before serving.

Notes

Get an onigiri mold! They are relatively inexpensive, make the process much easier, and are a great way to get kids involved in making their own lunches.

Seasonal Variations: For fall and winter, I replace the eggplant with slices of kabocha or delicata squash. In spring, I swap in broccoli or hakurei turnips. Any of these vegetables will steam and sear well with the sauce.

Tofu Brown Rice Bowls

Serves 4 Mention California and vegetarian, and people assume I only eat brown rice bowls. While this book shows that's not true, I felt like being a bit cheeky and including my rendition of a stereotypical California brown rice bowl (which I do not-so-secretly love).

TOFU

12 ounces (340 g) firm or extra-firm tofu

¼ cup (60 ml) regular soy sauce

2 tablespoons avocado oil, plus extra for grilling

2 tablespoons balsamic vinegar

2 tablespoons maple syrup

2 garlic cloves, minced

PEANUT SAUCE

¼ cup (64 g) creamy peanut butter

2 tablespoons maple syrup

2 tablespoons soy sauce

1 tablespoon lime juice

1 tablespoon rice vinegar

2 teaspoons sambal oelek

2 teaspoons minced fresh ginger

Kosher salt, to taste

CABBAGE SLAW

4 cups (280 g) shredded purple cabbage

6 scallions, trimmed and thinly sliced with some greens reserved for garnish

¼ cup (60 ml) lime juice

1 teaspoon kosher salt

¼ cup (30 g) roasted and crushed peanuts, plus extra for serving

FOR SERVING

3 cups (580 g) cooked brown rice, any type (page 74)

2 baked sweet potatoes, cut into wedges

1 ripe avocado, sliced

PREPARE THE TOFU: If the tofu feels overly moist, press the tofu between two paper towel-lined plates for 30 minutes. You can add a bit of extra weight to the top in the form of cans.

In a small storage container with a tight lid, combine the soy sauce, oil, vinegar, maple syrup, and garlic. Cut the tofu into ½-inch (1.3 cm) thick slices and add to the container. Seal and shake, then let the tofu marinate, shaking a couple times more, for 30 minutes.

MAKE THE SAUCE: Combine the peanut butter, maple syrup, soy sauce, lime juice, vinegar, sambal oelek, and ginger. Whisk to blend. Add water to thin the sauce enough that it can be drizzled. Taste and add salt, if needed. Set aside.

MAKE THE CABBAGE SLAW: In a medium bowl, combine the cabbage with the scallions, lime, and salt. Massage the cabbage until it softens, then stir in the crushed peanuts.

COOK THE TOFU: Heat a grill pan or griddle over medium heat and brush with avocado oil. Remove the tofu from the marinade and place on the grill pan. Cook, brushing with any leftover marinade, until the first side is seared, 1 to 2 minutes. Flip, continue brushing, and cook the other side for another 1 to 2 minutes.

TO SERVE: Divide the rice between four bowls. Add the tofu, sweet potato wedges, cabbage, and avocado slices. Drizzle with the peanut sauce. Finish with the reserved scallion greens and extra crushed peanuts.

Notes

When I make grain bowls such as this, I'm often thinking about color as being an important consideration. While something that is all brown can be equally as delicious as something with color, I believe having a mix of colors can be even more enticing (and also a bit of a pat on the back—look at all those colorful vegetables I'm eating!). I urge you to play around with the vegetables, thinking about texture, flavor, and color as the ultimate grain-bowl trinity.

Seasonal Variations: During the spring season, I like to swap sweet potatoes for grilled asparagus or charred snap peas. During the summer, my California bowl is all about fresh tomatoes and roasted green beans in place of the cabbage.

Kimchi and Rice Omelet

Makes 2 large omelets

Occasionally, I wake up feeling like I need a big, sturdy breakfast. Sometimes, this might be pancakes (page 61), or a large bowl of Cream of Wheat (page 33). And then, there are mornings when only a large omelet will do. Here, I've taken my inspiration from kimchi fried rice and just changed the proportions. The kimchi and rice are folded into the egg to create an extremely hearty omelet packed with flavor.

While I typically go with short-grain rice for kimchi fried rice, I make this omelet with leftover medium-grain rice when I have that on hand. I recommend reheating previously cooked rice before adding it to the omelet so that the rice loses some of the hardness that can develop on cooling.

OMELET

¼ cup (56 g) unsalted butter

6 scallions, trimmed and thinly sliced with some greens reserved for garnish

1 cup kimchi (240 g), chopped

1 cup (200 g) cooked medium-grain white rice, such as Calrose

6 large eggs

¼ cup (60 ml) heavy cream

1 teaspoon kosher salt

1 ounce (30 g) cheddar cheese, shredded

FOR SERVING

2 tablespoons unsalted butter

2 tablespoons soy sauce

MAKE THE OMELETS: Heat an 8-inch (20 cm) omelet pan over medium heat. Add the butter, let it melt, and add the sliced scallions. Cook for 1 to 2 minutes until softened. Add the kimchi and continue to cook until hot and tender, 3 to 4 minutes. Stir in the rice.

Whisk the eggs, cream, and salt in a small bowl. Spoon half of the kimchi mixture out of the pan and set aside. Add half of the egg mixture to the pan and cook until the bottom begins to set, about 30 seconds. Lift up the edges as needed to allow the uncooked egg to flow to the edges of the pan, until the majority of the omelet is set. Flip, add half the cheese to the cooked side, fold, and transfer to a plate. Return the reserved kimchi mix to the pan and repeat the process for the second omelet.

TO SERVE: Wipe out the pan and return the pan to medium heat. Add the butter and soy sauce. Heat together until combined and bubbling, then immediately pour over the omelets. Scatter the reserved sliced scallion greens over the omelets and serve.

Notes

I'm not a confident flipper of eggs even though I've practiced and practiced. I like to employ the help of a plate. To do this, loosen the omelet and slide it directly onto a plate that is larger than the skillet. Drizzle the top of the omelet with any butter that might be left in the pan then turn the skillet over and place over the omelet. Holding the handle of the skillet with one hand, pick the plate up from the bottom with the other hand and firmly and quickly flip so the plate is on top, then remove the plate. Return the skillet to the heat and continue.

Also, note that kimchi is not traditionally vegetarian and you should use your preferred style.

Ancho-Tomato Braised Green Beans with Panela and Rice

Serves 4

There are a few vegetables that if asked about, I'll jump on my box and talk about at length. During the summer, it's green beans. They are amazingly versatile. In my house we eat them steamed, grilled, fried, and braised like this. I was inspired by a recipe featured in *Food and Wine* magazine some time ago for *loubieh*, Lebanese tomato-braised green beans. However, given my love of both fried cheese and dried chiles, I took a bit more of a Mexican spin with this dish.

I pair these green beans with basmati rice because I adore long-grain rice paired with rich tomato-based sauces, most likely related to my love of Indian curries. Also, the aromatic nature of basmati provides a hint of nuttiness to go with the warm ancho-tomato sauce.

ANCHO-TOMATO SAUCE

2 dried mild smoky chiles, such as ancho

¼ cup (60 ml) avocado oil, divided

1 yellow onion, peeled and cut into 4 wedges

4 garlic cloves, smashed

1 (15-ounce / 425 g) can crushed tomatoes

1 teaspoon sweet paprika

1 cup (240 ml) vegetable broth

½ teaspoon kosher salt

8 ounces (240 g) green beans, trimmed

FRIED CHEESE

10 ounces (280 g) panela cheese, cut into slices

FOR SERVING

Cooked basmati rice (see page 74)

MAKE THE TOMATO SAUCE: Bring a small pot of water to a boil. Meanwhile, heat a large skillet over medium heat. Add the chiles to the dry pan and toast until they are soft and starting to brown, 1 to 2 minutes per side. Let the chiles cool slightly, then remove the stems and seeds. Add the chiles to the pot of hot water off heat, cover, and allow to soak for 20 minutes.

Return the skillet to medium-high heat and add 2 tablespoons of the oil. Add the onion wedges and garlic cloves. Toast, turning once or twice, until the onion and garlic are charred, about 2 minutes per side.

Drain and transfer the chiles to a blender along with the onion, garlic, crushed tomatoes, paprika, vegetable broth, and salt. Puree until smooth. Return the sauce to the skillet.

Add the green beans to the tomato sauce. Bring to a boil, reduce to a simmer, cover, and cook until they are quite tender, 15 to 20 minutes.

FRY THE CHEESE: Meanwhile, heat the remaining 2 tablespoons of avocado oil in a medium skillet over medium heat. Add the cheese and fry on each side until golden brown, 2 to 3 minutes per side.

TO SERVE: Divide the rice between four bowls. Top with the panela, green beans, and any remaining sauce.

Notes

You can use ground chiles in place of the whole chiles; start with 2 to 3 teaspoons and increase as desired. Or swap the ancho for two chipotles in adobo, which don't need to be toasted or rehydrated. Add the ground chile or chipotles straight to the blender with the rest of the sauce ingredients.

If you are unable to find panela cheese, substitute halloumi or paneer. Give paneer a sprinkle of salt after frying.

Seasonal Variations: For the cooler months, use chopped cauliflower or cubed winter squash, in place of the green beans.

Vegan Riff: Tempeh or tofu can replace the panela.

CORN

All the corn we consume in its dried state is **field corn**, as in corn grown in a field, as opposed to sweet corn, which we eat green. Within the field-corn family there are a few varieties.

Dent corn: Named for the small dent in the kernel, dent corn is often ground into cornmeal and corn flours and used in the production of cornstarch because of its endosperm, which is softer than that of flint corn.

Flint corn: Used in similar ways to dent corn but is harder and a bit tougher to mill. However, flint corn can be stored for longer periods of time and often has a shorter growing season, which are positives for growers in cooler climates.

Flour corn: The endosperm of this variety is nearly all soft starches with lower amounts of proteins and oils. As the name implies, this corn is often used for flour.

Popcorn: A type of flint corn with a harder pericarp that traps the existing moisture inside the grain better than other varieties. The pressure build up is what causes the sudden pop!

CORN COLOR

All the colors of corn have different flavor attributes, ranging from sweet and delicate (white varieties) to the corn flavor most of us think of when we think of corn (yellow). Corn can also have mineral, floral, and citrusy notes (something I didn't really think too much about until I started using products from Anson Mills).

CORN PRODUCTS

Corn flour: Typically made from flour corn, corn flour is the finest milled product, which is great for corn-based pastries and breads.

Cornmeal: Comes in varying levels of coarseness, and most commercial cornmeal has had the germ and bran removed to make it more shelf-stable. Look for stone-ground cornmeal, which means all parts of the corn are included. I typically keep medium-coarse cornmeal on hand for adding texture to breads and muffins.

Grits: Typically coarser than cornmeal, grits come in varying levels of coarseness and wholeness. Quick grits have the germ and bran removed, while whole-grain grits include all parts of the corn. Traditionally grits are made from dent corn to allow a creamy, soft porridge but they can be made from flint corn as well.

Grits made from whole grains take a fair amount of time to cook and, depending on the brand, can benefit from an overnight soak. I always recommend referring to the package or miller's instructions.

Polenta: Traditionally made from a specific variety of flint corn that has now taken on the name of polenta corn, the grains are reductively milled (the grain goes through the mill multiple times, decreasing in size each time), which ensures uniform size; the low-heat milling also preserves flavor.

Polenta is often more finely ground than grits, but that's up to the miller, so coarseness can vary. Because it comes from flint corn, polenta has what is described by Glenn Roberts of Anson Mills as a "beading texture and palate grip" and often more subtle flavors.

Cornstarch: Made from the extracted starch of dent corn, cornstarch is often used as a thickening agent. It provides a nice crisp coating when dusted on tofu and fried.

Corn syrup: An enzymatic process converts the complex sugars of cornstarch into simple sugars.

NIXTAMALIZATION

Nixtamalization is the process by which whole dried corn is steeped and cooked in alkaline water. This is achieved by adding items such as wood ash and calcium hydroxide (pickling lime) to water to create a pH above 7.

Dried corn can be and is often used without going through this process. However, as shown in much of Mexican, Central, and South American cuisines, there is quite a benefit to nixtamalized corn. For starters, the solution aids in loosening the hard pericarp, allowing easier access to the good starches of the endosperm. In addition, carbohydrates found in the plant cell walls are alkaline soluble. The breakdown of the cell walls and the presence of calcium allow the pectin molecules to form the basis of a network that's later developed through kneading. It's a bit like the gluten network without the need for the gluten proteins.

One note: Any grain or bean can be nixtamalized, and the internet is awash with people who have taken this and run. It's a worthy search if you're interested.

Hominy is nixtamalized corn that goes through rinsing to leave a whole, plump nixtamalized corn kernel that can be used as is, often in soups and stews like pozole (page 91). Hominy is sold dried, or for convenience, cooked and canned. Occasionally some companies will sell hominy grits as well, which is dried, cracked hominy intended for porridges.

Masa is nixtamalized corn that is not rinsed and instead passed through a grinder to create a dough. That dough can be used in a myriad of ways, as seen in cultures throughout the Americas. The masa can also go through one more process: drying and grinding to become **masa harina** (great to have on hand for homemade tortillas; see page 88).

COOKING CORN

CORN TYPE	UNCOOKED QUANTITY	WATER	SOAK	SOAKING LIQUID ADDITION	COOKING METHOD	COOKING TIME (SOAKED)	COOKING TIME (UNSOAKED)	COOKED GRAIN YIELD
Corn grits, stone-ground	1 cup (140 g)	4½ cups (1.1 L)	4 hours (optional)	1 tsp kosher salt	Absorption	40–45 minutes	60–70 minutes	4 cups (1 kg)
Hominy	1 cup (260 g)	Cover with 2 inches (5 cm)	8 hours	N/A	Pasta	2 hours	N/A	4 cups (720 g)
Polenta, medium coarseness	1 cup (140 g)	3½ to 4 cups (840–960 ml)	4 hours (optional)	1 tsp kosher salt	Absorption	20–25 minutes	30–35 minutes	4 cups (740 g)

Pasta method: I follow the instructions from Steve Sando of Rancho Gordo: After soaking, drain and transfer to a pot along with a chopped onion and 2 inches (5 cm) of water. Boil for 5 minutes, then lower the heat, cover, and simmer until the kernels open up, typically after about 2 hours of cooking.

Absorption method: After any soaking, place the grits/polenta and cool water or their soaking liquid, if using, in a pot over medium heat. Once the cooking water comes to a rapid simmer, reduce the heat to medium-low and cook for the specified time, stirring often, until creamy and mellowed in flavor. Once cooked, add-ins such as butter can be stirred in before serving.

Notes: Leftover grits and polenta can be saved and fried using the instructions on page 29.

CORN RECIPES

Spoon Pudding with Greens

Serves 4

When it came to holidays, as a child I wasn't excited by most of the offerings except one: my family's recipe for corn casserole. And by *recipe*, I mean cornbread mix combined with sour cream and creamed corn. The combination of these ingredients resulted in a casserole with a texture that sits in between a cornbread and a soufflé. It was perfect in every way.

I wanted to make a recipe that gave a bit of a nod toward that holiday corn casserole, using cornmeal as the base. The closest in resemblance is spoon pudding, which, depending on who is making it, is nearly identical to the casserole of my youth or more akin to a soufflé. I prefer the soufflé approach, which has a light and creamy texture.

SPOON PUDDING

2 tablespoons unsalted butter

2 large egg whites

¾ cup (180 ml) vegetable broth

¼ cup (60 ml) heavy cream

⅓ cup (45 g) stone-ground cornmeal

1 cup (165 g) fresh or frozen corn kernels

1 ounce (30 g) cheddar cheese, shredded

1 tablespoon cane sugar or maple syrup

½ teaspoon kosher salt

GREENS

2 to 3 handfuls baby arugula

1 tablespoon olive oil

1 teaspoon lemon juice

½ teaspoon finishing salt, such as Maldon salt

½ teaspoon ground black pepper

Preheat the oven to 350°F (180°C). Butter a 1-quart (1 L) casserole dish.

MAKE THE SPOON PUDDING: Using a hand mixer, whip the egg whites in a clean bowl until stiff peaks form. Place in the refrigerator to hold.

Combine the vegetable broth and heavy cream in a medium saucepan over medium-low heat. Whisk in the cornmeal and cook until the mixture thickens, 1 to 2 minutes. Remove the saucepan from the heat and stir in the corn, cheese, sugar, and salt.

Fold the egg whites into the corn mix. Transfer the batter to the prepared dish and place in the oven. Bake until the center of the corn pudding does not jiggle and is a golden brown across the top, 30 to 35 minutes.

PREPARE THE GREENS: When the spoon pudding is just about done, put the arugula in a medium bowl. Add the olive oil, lemon juice, salt, and pepper. Toss until the arugula is evenly coated.

TO SERVE: The spoon pudding can be served immediately for a softer and creamier texture, but I prefer the pudding to rest until just warm. The consistency is more akin to the corn casserole of my youth. Serve with the greens on the side or piled on top.

Notes

I like the consistency that a medium-ground cornmeal lends to this spoon pudding. However, if you have fine-ground or even corn flour, that can work. I recommend avoiding more coarsely ground cornmeal, which doesn't cook as evenly and occasionally leaves deposits of hard bits, which is unpleasant at best.

Tostadas with Salsa Negra Tempeh and Quick Curtido

Serves 3 to 4

During the extended stay at home in 2020, I challenged myself to really learn the nuances of my favorite items. On that list: the corn tortilla. The difference between a freshly cooked tortilla and that of a store-bought one is night and day (not to mention the difference of using home-milled masa—a step I'm still quite new to).

These tostadas are a bit of a mash-up between two inspirations: *salsa negra* and *curtido*. The salsa negra is inspired by Nixtaco, one of my favorite Sacramento-area restaurants, while the curtido came into rotation after being inspired by learning more about Salvadoran cooking.

TORTILLAS

½ cup packed (75 g) masa harina

½ cup (120 g) warm, 100°F (38°C) water, or as needed

½ cup (120 ml) avocado oil or other neutral high-heat oil for frying

SALSA NEGRA

2 dried medium-heat chiles, such as mulato, stemmed and seeded

1 to 2 dried hot chiles, such as chiles de árbol, stemmed and seeded

8 to 10 garlic cloves, smashed

1 tablespoon white sesame seeds

1 tablespoon dark brown sugar

2 teaspoons rice vinegar

1½ teaspoons kosher salt

TEMPEH

4 ounces (115 g) tempeh

1 tablespoon avocado oil or other neutral high-heat oil

MAKE THE TORTILLAS: In a medium bowl, combine the masa harina and warm water. Stir and knead until well combined and smooth, cover, and let rest for 5 minutes.

Preheat a cast-iron skillet or comal to medium heat. Divide the dough into eight pieces and shape into balls. Using a tortilla press (or something similar if you're feeling crafty), press one ball into a 4-inch (10 cm) tortilla.

Transfer the tortilla to the preheated surface and cook for 20 seconds, then flip and cook for another 20 seconds. Flip once more, allowing the tortilla to puff, then transfer to a plate. Repeat with the remaining balls of dough.

Pour the avocado oil into an 8-inch (20 cm) skillet over medium heat. Once the oil is hot, add one tortilla and fry until crisp and golden, about 45 seconds per side. Drain on a wire rack and repeat with the remaining tortillas. Set aside.

MAKE THE SALSA: Add the chiles to the same skillet with the remaining oil from frying the tortillas. Cook over medium heat until starting to brown, 1 to 2 minutes. Turn off the heat and add the garlic and sesame seeds. Let cool slightly. Transfer to a blender or food processor. Add the sugar, vinegar, and salt and puree. Set aside.

PREPARE THE TEMPEH: Bring a few inches of water to a boil in a saucepan fitted with a steamer basket. Put the tempeh in the steamer basket and steam for 10 minutes. Remove from the steamer, let cool enough to handle, then crumble.

Heat the oil in a medium skillet over medium heat. Add the crumbled tempeh and fry, stirring occasionally, until golden, 3 to 4 minutes. Stir in a few spoonfuls of salsa and set aside.

CONTINUES

Tostadas with Salsa Negra Tempeh and Quick Curtido

CONTINUED

CURTIDO

2 cups (140 g) shredded purple cabbage

1 medium carrot, shredded

2 scallions, thinly sliced

1 teaspoon dried Mexican oregano

1 teaspoon kosher salt

3 tablespoons (45 ml) rice vinegar

FOR SERVING

2 large avocados

Lime wedges

MAKE THE CURTIDO: Combine the cabbage, carrot, scallions, vinegar, oregano, and salt in a medium bowl and massage until the cabbage is slightly wilted.

TO SERVE: Peel and pit the avocados and smash in a small bowl. Spread a bit of avocado onto each of the fried tortillas, then layer with spoonfuls of the tempeh. Finish with a bit of the curtido and serve with lime wedges.

Notes

When working with masa harina, the most important thing you can do is explore hydration. Don't assume you have it correct—it's very much a feel kind of thing. The brand of masa harina, water temperature, humidity, and the earth's rotation (I jest) can change the level of hydration.

When the ball of dough is pressed in your hands, the edges should remain smooth with few, if any, cracks. If you see cracks, return

the ball to the dough and add a bit more water. If, on the other hand, you find the tortillas are sticking to the press, return the ball to the dough and add a small amount of masa harina. The more you make and observe, the faster this process will go each time.

Also, I keep a cut-apart ziplock bag for lining the tortilla press. As long as the hydration is correct, the tortillas peel off easily.

Not ready to tackle this? Enjoy corn in its store-bought tortilla or tostada form. There's no shame— there are plenty of good options on the market!

Make Ahead: The tortillas, if not fried, will last for a couple days sealed at room temperature or frozen for an extended time; the salsa negra can be made up to 5 days in advance and refrigerated.

Pozole Verde

Serves 4 While I'd had pozole a few times in my life, it wasn't until my friend Emma gifted me Steve Sando's *The Rancho Gordo Pozole Book* and some RG hominy that I made pozole from dried hominy. It was a game changer—the flavor and texture were unmatched. Over the years, I've made Steve's pozole verde many times, but as with most things, I've adapted it over time to suit my cooking style.

SAUCE

2 pounds (900 g) tomatillos

4 poblano peppers

4 jalapeño peppers

¼ cup (60 ml) olive oil

2 medium onions, cut into wedges

8 garlic cloves

6 cups (1.4 L) vegetable broth

½ cup (60 g) roasted pepitas (see page 186)

½ cup packed (24 g) minced fresh cilantro leaves and stems

2 teaspoons cane sugar

2 teaspoons dried oregano, preferably Mexican

POZOLE

2 tablespoons mushroom powder

2 tablespoons white miso

4 cups (720 g) cooked and drained hominy (see page 85)

1 pound (450 g) gold potatoes, such as Yukon gold, diced into ¼-inch (6 mm) pieces

FOR SERVING

Thinly sliced radishes

Minced fresh cilantro leaves and stems

Lime wedges

Avocado slices

Red onion slices

Shredded cabbage

MAKE THE SAUCE: Preheat the broiler. Remove the husks from the tomatillos and place on a sheet pan along with the poblanos and jalapeños. Broil until the tomatillos have released their juice and there is a nice char across everything. This takes 2 to 3 minutes, but start checking on it after 1 minute. Let cool. Peel the skin from the poblanos and remove the stems and seeds from all chiles.

While the tomatillos char, heat the olive oil over medium-high heat in the pot you will use to cook the pozole. Add the onion wedges and garlic cloves, turning as needed to get a sear on all sides, 30 to 60 seconds per side.

Once the onions and garlic have a good sear, add the vegetable broth. Bring to a boil, reduce to a simmer, and cook the broth for 5 minutes. After 5 minutes, turn off the heat and use a slotted spoon to transfer the onions and garlic to a blender or food processor.

Add the tomatillos, chiles, roasted pepitas, cilantro, sugar, and oregano to the blender. Puree until a sauce forms with no large pieces of poblano left.

COOK THE POZOLE: Whisk the mushroom powder and miso into the broth, then add the tomatillo sauce, hominy, and diced potatoes. Bring to a boil, reduce to a simmer, and cook until the potatoes are tender, 20 to 25 minutes. Taste and add more miso, mushroom powder, or salt if desired.

TO SERVE: Divide the pozole among bowls and top with your desired toppings. I typically overload my bowl and use everything I've listed.

Notes

Potatoes cooked in an acidic base will not break down very much and will result in a firmer texture. If you prefer a more tender potato, I recommend cooking in the vegetable broth until mostly tender, then adding the tomatillo mixture.

Make Ahead: Pozole will keep in the refrigerator for 4 to 5 days. Reheat with extra vegetable broth as needed.

Grits with Smoky Roasted Squash

Serves 4

When writing my first book about flours, I did a lot of research into companies selling quality grains. Finding Anson Mills became a game changer for working with grits and polenta. The care that goes into every part of the process results in a product that cooks well, is beautiful, and most importantly, tastes amazing.

Grits were not on the menu in many places when I was growing up in the Midwest. The majority of restaurants trended toward polenta. However, I've come to really respect and appreciate the creaminess grits provide, especially when paired with something rich and hearty.

These grits and squash can easily stand on their own as a meal, but sometimes I like to add a cup of cooked beans to the mix depending on what else I'm serving. The beans provide a boost of protein, transforming this into a one-bowl meal, perfect for those cold winter nights.

GRITS

4½ cups (1.1 L) water

1 teaspoon kosher salt

1 cup (140 g) stone-ground coarse white grits

¼ cup (56 g) unsalted butter

SQUASH

3 tablespoons (45 ml) avocado oil

1 small yellow onion, minced

3 tablespoons (45 g) tomato paste

½ cup (120 ml) water

3 tablespoons (63 g) molasses

2 tablespoons apple cider vinegar

2 tablespoons soy sauce

1 tablespoon vegan Worcestershire sauce

2 teaspoons stone-ground mustard

2 teaspoons smoked paprika

2 teaspoons kosher salt

1 teaspoon medium-heat ground chile

1½ pounds (675 g) red kuri squash, seeded and cut into ½-inch (1.3 cm) wedges

MAKE THE GRITS: Bring the water and salt to a boil in a medium saucepan. Once the water is hot, slowly add the grits while whisking constantly. Reduce the heat to low and continue to cook, whisking every few minutes to avoid scorching on the bottom. Grits will be done when they achieve a texture that pleases you. I typically cook for about 1 hour, until the grits have thickened and have a smooth texture. Once the grits are to your liking, remove from heat and whisk in the butter.

Preheat the oven to 425°F (220°C).

PREPARE THE SQUASH: Heat the oil over medium heat in a dutch oven, braiser, or oven-safe skillet with a lid. Add the onion and cook until quite tender, 14 to 16 minutes.

Stir in the tomato paste and cook for another minute or two, until the tomato paste is hot. Add the water, molasses, vinegar, soy sauce, Worcestershire sauce, mustard, paprika, salt, and ground chile. When the sauce is hot, add the squash and flip to coat. Turn off the heat, cover with the lid, and transfer the pot to the preheated oven.

Bake for 25 to 30 minutes, until the sauce is a bit thick and the squash tender. Watch closely—overcooking will result in the sauce becoming too thick.

TO SERVE: Divide the grits between four bowls and top with a few wedges of squash and a spoonful or so of the remaining sauce.

Notes

I typically cook with Anson Mills coarse stone-ground white grits, which are best soaked in water for up to 8 hours for a creamy texture with a shorter cook time. Other varieties, depending on milling and grinding techniques, will possibly have different cook times. Refer to the package for instructions, and when in doubt, cook and taste until you're happy.

I use vegan Worcestershire sauce, but feel free to use standard if that's what you have on hand.

Seasonal Variations: Any other hearty vegetable will work in place of the red kuri squash. Use sweet potatoes, cauliflower, an alternative winter squash, or mushrooms.

PSEUDOGRAINS (AMARANTH, QUINOA, BUCKWHEAT)

Pseudograins are not true grains, because they don't come from the grass family, but that doesn't stop us from using them in similar ways.

AMARANTH AND QUINOA

Quinoa and amaranth are both members of the same family, Amaranthaceae, that make up a wide variety of flowering herbs and shrubs including spinach. Quinoa seeds can range in color from red to ivory to black while cultivated amaranth seeds tend to be ivory.

Quinoa is slightly larger than amaranth, but both are powerhouses when it comes to nutrients. They are both complete proteins, providing all the essential amino acids, among other nutrients, which is in part what led to their drastic rise in popularity.

A couple key notes: Amaranth has a high amount of amylopectin starch, which means that no matter what ratio you use, the grains will end up with a sticky consistency.

As for quinoa, many instructions will tell you that rinsing quinoa is a must because it's coated in saponin. However, most growers have machines that handle this for us now. I'd only recommend rinsing if you're getting it from a local farmer or growing it yourself.

Often eaten as whole grains, amaranth and quinoa can both be ground into flour and have become popular in flour blends for gluten-free baking. However, use a bit of caution and go slow if you decide to mill your own amaranth: some home mills have issues with the smaller grains—they can bring the mill to a halt.

BUCKWHEAT

A grain with big flavor, buckwheat has two main varieties: common, which is considered to be more sweet, and tartary, which has a deeply bitter quality. Today, common buckwheat is grown and used worldwide. Tartary buckwheat is grown and used in more limited applications even though it tends to be more frost tolerant and grinds a bit more easily.

The fibrous pericarp on the buckwheat must be removed before cooking as a whole grain but can be left if the buckwheat is ground into flour. The pericarp on the buckwheat grain is often referred to as the hull or husk, but technically it's more akin to the shell of a sunflower seed.

Buckwheat also contains a small amount of a polysaccharide that is highly absorbent and also lends a bit of stickiness, which can be helpful when working with buckwheat flour. This is most evident in Japanese soba noodles, which can be made from 100% buckwheat flour.

FORMS OF BUCKWHEAT

Whole buckwheat, with the pericarp still attached, is not as prevalent, but is often sold through seed companies, including for microgreens. Once the pericarp is removed, buckwheat comes in two forms: raw or toasted groats. The toasted groats are occasionally labeled as kasha and can also be sold as ground kasha.

Buckwheat flour comes in two forms: light and dark. Light buckwheat flour is ground from the hulled buckwheat so that the dark pericarp is removed to create a subtle-flavored, fine flour. Dark buckwheat flour is ground from the whole buckwheat grain, creating a slightly darker and more robust flour.

COOKING PSEUDOGRAINS

GRAIN	UNCOOKED QUANTITY	WATER	COOKING METHOD	STOVETOP COOKING TIME	RICE COOKER SETTING	COOKED GRAIN YIELD
Amaranth	1 cup (190 g)	3 cups (720 ml)	Absorption	20 minutes	Quick cook	3½ cups (875 g)
Buckwheat, cracked	1 cup (140 g)	2½ cups (600 ml)	Absorption	10-15 minutes	Quick cook	3½ cups (600 g)
Buckwheat, whole	1 cup (180 g)	2 cups (480 ml)	Absorption	15 minutes	Quick cook	3 cups (520 g)
Quinoa	1 cup (180 g)	2 cups (480 ml)	Absorption	12 minutes	Quick cook	3 cups (550 g)

STOVETOP COOKING

Absorption method: Place the grains and cool water in a saucepan over medium heat. Once the cooking water comes to a rapid simmer, cover the saucepan, reduce the heat to medium-low, and cook for the specified time. The grains are done when they are tender and the water has been absorbed. Remove the saucepan from the heat and let it sit, covered, for 10 to 15 minutes.

Notes: You can also cook pseudograins in your rice cooker on the "quick cook" setting.

Toasting your grains is a great way to add layers of flavor before cooking (see page 27).

AMARANTH, QUINOA, AND BUCKWHEAT RECIPES

Ginger-Rhubarb Amaranth Porridge

Serves 4

The taste and texture of amaranth can be a bit of a surprise to people who are exploring their way through grains. Often people cook amaranth for the first time expecting something light, fluffy, and mellow on flavor and instead get porridge with a grassy flavor (which is a bit cheeky on amaranth's part given it's not a grass).

The key to working with amaranth is to lean into these characteristics that make it so unique. For starters, amaranth is an amazing base for porridge. Little effort is needed to make something creamy and delicious. In terms of flavor, I like to pair the grassy notes with something equally as bold. In this case, tart rhubarb and warm ginger.

AMARANTH

1 cup (190 g) uncooked amaranth

1½ cups (360 ml) whole milk

1½ cups (360 ml) water

Pinch of kosher salt

RHUBARB COMPOTE

1 pound (450 g) rhubarb, diced

6 tablespoons (90 ml) maple syrup, plus more as needed

2 tablespoons cane sugar

2 tablespoons minced fresh ginger

1 teaspoon ground cinnamon

Pinch of kosher salt

FOR SERVING

Heavy cream

Roasted and crushed pistachios (see page 185)

COOK THE AMARANTH: Heat a small saucepan over medium-low heat. Add the amaranth and toast until fragrant and golden, 1 to 2 minutes. Watch the amaranth closely, any longer or higher heat and the risk of popping the amaranth increases. Add the milk, water, and salt. Bring the mixture to a boil, reduce to a simmer, cover, and let simmer for 20 minutes. Remove from the heat and let sit for 5 to 10 more minutes to thicken.

MAKE THE COMPOTE: Combine the rhubarb, maple syrup, sugar, ginger, cinnamon, and salt in a small saucepan. Heat over medium until the rhubarb has mostly broken down and formed a sauce, about 15 minutes. Taste and add additional maple syrup if desired.

TO SERVE: Divide the amaranth between four bowls and stir in the rhubarb compote. Drizzle with heavy cream and sprinkle with crushed pistachios.

Notes

To take this porridge up a notch, I'll occasionally make a maple-sweetened pistachio milk (see page 188) that I'll use in place of the milk, water, and cream. The slightly floral pistachio with the amaranth is a fun combination. This also makes the porridge vegan.

Seasonal Variations: Keep the ginger and pair it with blueberries or raspberries during summer and pears during the fall.

Spring Salad with Toasted Buckwheat

Serves 4

There comes a time, typically in early spring, when I'm done eating winter produce and require all my meals to be fresh for a period of about a week—it feels a bit like coming out of hibernation. Living in California, this typically happens toward the end of February and into early March.

My favorite way to do this is to make a big crispy and crunchy salad full of all the spring produce. Beyond just relying on the fresh vegetables, I like to bring in grains to add an additional layer of texture. Toasting raw buckwheat enhances its nutty side while reducing some of the bitterness. From there I like to crush the buckwheat and use it to finish salads, soups, and grain bowls.

TOASTED BUCKWHEAT

1 cup (180 g) raw buckwheat groats

SALAD

2 small fennel bulbs, trimmed, bulb shaved and fronds chopped

3 tablespoons (45 ml) rice vinegar

1 tablespoon lemon juice

2 teaspoons kosher salt

12 radishes, shaved

4 cups (520 g) fresh peas, shelled and blanched if needed

1 cup loosely packed (24 g) fresh flat-leaf parsley, coarsely chopped

½ cup (60 g) roasted pistachios (see page 185), crushed

½ cup (120 ml) olive oil

2 teaspoons ground black pepper

2 heads butter lettuce

Preheat the oven to 400°F (200°C).

TOAST THE BUCKWHEAT: Spread out the buckwheat on a baking sheet. Toast in the oven until the buckwheat deepens in color and has a nutty aroma, about 8 minutes. Let cool, then use a mortar and pestle to crush the buckwheat into a texture resembling coarse sand.

MAKE THE SALAD: Combine the shaved fennel in a medium bowl with the vinegar, lemon juice, and salt. Stir to coat and let rest for 5 minutes. Add the fennel fronds, radishes, peas, parsley, pistachios, olive oil, and pepper. Toss to combine.

TO SERVE: Wash and tear the lettuce into bite-sized pieces and add to the bowl with the fennel mixture. Add about two-thirds of the buckwheat and toss until everything is well incorporated. Finish with the remaining buckwheat and serve.

Notes

Using fennel, especially in raw form, can be a bit polarizing, but I've found that when people are on the fence, allowing it to mellow in acid and salt helps convince those who are unsure. I swear by this when using raw shallots in dishes as well.

Çilbir (Turkish Eggs) with Herbed Quinoa Pilaf

Serves 4

When I'm not testing new recipes or ideas, I'm a creature of habit, especially in the mornings. Bagels, breakfast burritos, and eggs of all kinds are in heavy rotation. *Çilbir* is definitely on that list. The tangy labneh paired with the rich chile butter and egg hits all the flavors. An herby grain pilaf brings this meal together and adds protein from the quinoa.

This meal can also be made from whatever you have on hand. The herbs can easily be swapped for other tender herbs. And if you'd prefer a different grain, go for it.

LABNEH

2 garlic cloves

1 teaspoon kosher salt

1⅓ cups (320 g) labneh or Greek yogurt, at room temperature

QUINOA PILAF

⅔ cup (120 g) uncooked quinoa

1⅓ cups (320 ml) water

½ medium onion, peeled

1 teaspoon kosher salt, plus more as needed

¼ cup loosely packed (6 g) minced fresh dill

¼ cup loosely packed (7 g) minced fresh flat-leaf parsley

¼ cup loosely packed (7 g) minced fresh chives

2 tablespoons fresh lemon juice

CHILE BUTTER

6 tablespoons (85 g) unsalted butter

2 teaspoons Calabrian chile flakes or dried red pepper flakes

2 teaspoons white sesame seeds

1 teaspoon sweet paprika

1 teaspoon lemon zest

FOR SERVING

4 large eggs, soft-boiled

Fresh dill

PREPARE THE LABNEH: Grate the garlic into a small bowl using a Microplane. Add the salt and allow it to rest for 5 minutes. Stir in the labneh, cover, and set aside.

MAKE THE QUINOA: Combine the quinoa, water, onion, and salt in a small saucepan. Bring to a boil, reduce to a simmer, cover, and cook for 15 minutes. Remove from the heat and let rest for 5 minutes.

Discard the onion and transfer the quinoa to a medium bowl. Add the dill, parsley, chives, and lemon juice. Toss to combine, taste, and add more salt as desired.

MAKE THE CHILE BUTTER: Melt the butter over medium-low heat in a small saucepan. Add the chile flakes and sesame seeds and cook for 1 to 2 minutes, until both are toasted. Remove the butter from the heat and stir in the sweet paprika and lemon zest.

TO SERVE: Divide the labneh into four dishes and spread across the bottom. Peel the eggs, slice each into halves or quarters, and place on top of the labneh. Drizzle a bit of the chile butter over the labneh and egg, then spoon the quinoa pilaf on the side. Finish with a sprinkle of dill before serving.

Notes

Traditionally this dish is served with a poached egg, but I prefer the texture of 7-minute soft boiled eggs. They are a bit easier to make and I'm usually making them in batches anyway. You can of course make this dish with poached or even fried eggs.

Seasonal Variations: During the summer months, I make a basil-quinoa pilaf, which is just as wonderful with the chile butter and garlic labneh.

Make Ahead: I like to make the components for this dish the night before so that breakfast comes together rather quickly. The pilaf, butter, and labneh can be saved in the refrigerator for a couple of days. In the morning, I leave the pilaf and labneh at room temperature for 30 minutes to take the chill off, cook the eggs, then melt the butter again to finish.

Buckwheat Crepes with Burnt-Honey Butter

Makes 10 to
12 (8-inch /
20 cm) crepes

There are two things that make these crepes: the buckwheat flour and the buttermilk. The toasted buckwheat flour is nutty and a bit earthy in the best way while the buttermilk gives the thin crepes a bit of lift. I suggest playing around with the batter thickness as well. If the batter is too thick, you get something like a flat pancake; too thin and the crepe may stick to the pan. I like a batter that has a thick, heavy cream consistency.

BURNT HONEY BUTTER

2 tablespoons water

¼ cup (80 g) honey

½ cup (110 g) unsalted butter, at room temperature

½ teaspoon finishing salt, such as Maldon salt

BUCKWHEAT CREPES

1 cup (140 g) buckwheat flour, toasted

1 cup (240 ml) buttermilk

1 large egg

2 tablespoons avocado or other neutral oil

1 tablespoon cane sugar

Pinch of kosher salt

½ to 1 cup (120 to 240 ml) water

Butter, if needed

MAKE THE BURNT HONEY: Measure the water into a small bowl and set aside. Heat the honey in a small saucepan over medium-high heat. Cook, stirring occasionally, until the honey turns a deep amber color as it bubbles. Once this happens, the honey will begin to smoke. Remove from heat and whisk in the water, using caution as the honey will spatter. The whole process will take only a few minutes. Cool the honey to room temperature.

Combine the butter in a small bowl with the cooled burnt honey and finishing salt. Stir vigorously using a spoon until the butter is lighter in texture. Set aside.

Preheat the oven to 175°F (80°C) with a sheet pan or heat-safe large plate on an oven rack.

MAKE THE CREPES: Whisk together all the ingredients for the crepes in a medium bowl, adding enough water so the batter has the thickness of a slightly thick heavy cream.

Heat a 10-inch (25 cm) well-seasoned cast-iron skillet over medium heat, adding a small amount of butter if the skillet has not been oiled recently. Once the skillet is hot, stir the batter again and add a splash of water if it seems thick.

Using a ladle, pour about ¼ cup (60 ml) of batter into the skillet. Use the back of the ladle or, my preference, a small icing spatula to spread the batter into a thin 8-inch (20 cm) circle. As long as the skillet is hot enough, the crepe should begin to bubble immediately. Cook for 30 to 60 seconds, until the bottom is browned, then flip and cook for another 60 seconds.

Transfer the crepe to the sheet pan in the oven and repeat the process with the remaining batter.

TO SERVE: Fold crepes into triangles and layer three triangles on each plate. Top with a spoonful of the burnt honey butter before serving.

Notes

Make Ahead: Cooked crepes will keep in the refrigerator for 2 to 3 days but can be frozen for extended storage. Separate the crepes with parchment paper when freezing to make it easy to retrieve a few at a time.

CEREAL GRAINS (OATS, MILLET, SORGHUM, TEFF, FONIO)

This catch-all category includes a few cereal grains I use in my kitchen on a more infrequent basis. However, these grains are just as important and useful as the grains previously mentioned. Along with corn and rice, these cereal grains make up the grains that fall into the gluten-free category.

I keep a smattering of all these whole grains as well as a large supply of rolled oats for granola and oatmeal.

OATS

Oats are unique in the many ways they are processed. Whole oats, known as groats, go through a heating process to stave off rancidity and help the grain maintain a bit of integrity during processing, given this grain is much softer than most of the other cereal grains.

Post-heating, oats can be cut or ground into pieces, labeled as **steel-cut** and **Scottish oats**, respectively. Whole oats can also be steamed and rolled into various forms and thicknesses including **thick rolled oats**, **regular rolled oats**, and **quick oats**. Oats are also milled into **flour** and the **bran** can be separated into its own product.

Similar to barley, oats are marketed as hulled or hulless (see page 19). Oats are also higher in fats compared to other grains, which means they have a chance to go rancid at a more rapid rate. Also, oats contain water-soluble fiber, which gives oats their gummy texture.

MILLET

This category is a bit of a catch-all within my catch-all category because, while the varieties of millet share the base name, they are all different species. Millet typically refers to small-grained cereal seeds including pearl, foxtail, and proso or common millet. In some writings and cultures, sorghum, fonio, and teff fall under the millet umbrella, but for the purposes of this book and my cooking, I'll talk about them separately.

While pearled millet is the most widely grown variety worldwide, **proso** or **common millet** is the primary millet sold in the United States for both birdseed and in its "hulled" form for human consumption (the hull in this case is actually the bran layer).

While not as popular (yet) in the United States, millet is commonly ground into a flour and used in cuisines throughout Africa, India, and China. I like to use millet as a whole grain, pureed into a cream (page 109), and cracked and made into a porridge or polenta-like dish.

SORGHUM

Sorghum, occasionally called great millet due to its similarities to millet, has four categories: grain, forage, sweet, and grassy. Humans consume mostly grain sorghum, and the stalks of the sweet sorghum plant are used to make **sorghum syrup**.

Whole sorghum can be cooked in the style of the large whole grains (page 105), and I enjoy using this slightly chewy grain as a base for bowls and grilled vegetables. Sorghum can also be nixtamalized for use in both breads and tortillas, or popped.

Fermented sorghum is used in cuisines throughout Africa, including as a substitute for teff in *injera*, the staple flatbread. **Sorghum flour** makes for an excellent gluten-free flour with a sweet, mild flavor. Sorghum is also often malted and used as a base for gluten-free beer.

TEFF

My first encounter with teff was actually with an American grower, Maskal Teff out of Idaho, which is a long way from the horn of Africa, where teff originated. However, this introduction left an impressionable mark.

Unlike most grains, teff is teff is teff—nothing is processed or removed from the grain (which is good because the small size would make it nearly impossible). While teff is grown in pockets around the world, the seed is still primarily grown in Ethiopia and Eritrea and used in injera.

Teff's forms are limited. You'll find the seed in **ivory**, which has a slight mellow flavor and pale color. **Brown teff** is nuttier in flavor and has a light brown color. Both varieties of teff are ground into flour as well. Teff typically has more fiber than other grains, primarily because the bran layer is thick.

FONIO

Finally, fonio is the newest grain addition to my pantry thanks to Pierre Thiam, who, beyond being a renowned chef and cookbook author, cofounded Yolélé, a company created to support biodiverse and regenerative farming communities in West Africa. The company has a wide swath of products, but being a grain lover, I gravitated toward fonio.

Like common millet, fonio has a short life cycle in arid conditions but can also be grown in wetter conditions and will tolerate most soil conditions. Fonio has two cultivated species: **white fonio** and **black fonio**, which, according to Thiam, is closer to a light tan color. The primary difference is the region in which they are grown.

Fonio really stands out among grains primarily for its extremely quick cook time. On the stove, fonio can be done in under 10 minutes, which is a bit unheard of for any whole grain. The grain fluffs into a light texture, making it a solid choice for most any grain-based meals.

COOKING CEREAL GRAINS

GRAIN	UNCOOKED QUANTITY	WATER	SOAK	SOAKING LIQUID ADDITIONS	COOKING METHOD	COOKING TIME (SOAKED)	COOKING TIME (UNSOAKED)	COOKED GRAIN YIELD
Fonio	1 cup (180 g)	3 cups (720 ml)	None	None	Absorption	N/A	5 minutes	3½ cups (610 g)
Millet, for pilaf	1 cup (200 g)	2 cups (480 ml)	4 hours (optional)	None	Absorption	15–20 minutes	20–25 minutes	3 cups (520 g)
Millet, for porridge	1 cup (200 g)	3 cups (720 ml)	4 hours (optional)	½ tsp salt 1 Tbsp acid (optional)	Absorption	15–20 minutes	20–25 minutes	3½ cups (720 g)
Oat groats	1 cup (180 g)	Cover with 1 inch (2.5 cm)	8 hours	½ tsp kosher salt 2 Tbsp acid	Pasta	30–35 minutes	40–50 minutes	3 cups (420 g)
Oats, rolled	1 cup (90 g)	2 cups (480 ml)	None	None	Absorption	N/A	10–20 minutes	2 cups (420 g)
Oats, steel-cut	1 cup (160 g)	3½ cups (840 ml)	4 hours (optional)	½ tsp salt 1 Tbsp acid (optional)	Absorption	20–25 minutes	25–30 minutes	3½ cups (780 g)
Sorghum	1 cup (190 g)	Cover with 1 inch (2.5 cm)	8 hours	2 Tbsp acid ½ tsp kosher salt	Pasta	25–30 minutes	45–55 minutes	3 cups (540 g)
Teff, for pilaf	1 cup (190 g)	1½ cups (360 ml)	None	None	Absorption	N/A	10 minutes	2 cups (360 g)
Teff, for porridge	1 cup (190 g)	4 cups (960 ml)	4 hours (optional)	½ tsp salt 1 Tbsp acid (optional)	Absorption	15 minutes	25 minutes	3 cups (760 g)

Pasta method: Place the grains and soaking liquid, if using, in a pot and add enough water so that the grains are covered by about an inch (2.5 cm). Cover, bring to a rapid simmer, and cook until the grains are quite plump with a few burst open, using the chart times as a guide. Once the grains are done, drain, return to the pot off heat, cover, and let rest for 10 minutes.

Absorption method: Place the grains and cool water or their soaking liquid in a pot over medium heat. Once the cooking water comes to a rapid simmer, cover, reduce the heat to medium-low, and cook for the specified time. The grains are done when they are tender and the water has been absorbed. Remove from the heat and let rest, covered, for 10 to 15 minutes.

Notes: You can replace the vinegar in a soak with liquid from a ferment, just double the amount (see page 27).

You can omit the acid or start with fresh water for cooking if desired.

Toasting your grains is a great way to add layers of flavor before cooking (see page 27).

CEREAL GRAIN RECIPES

Savory Kabocha Teff Porridge

Serves 4

There are certain ways I look at food that are most likely tied to my middle-America upbringing. The one I held on to the longest: grain porridge is sweet. What changed is that I had congee, a creamy rice porridge with savory toppings. It was basically with the first bite that my savory-porridge aversion ended.

I've taken my inspiration from congee toppings and applied them to one of my other favorite grain porridges: teff. Teff has a milder flavor than some of the smaller cereal and pseudocereal grains, which makes it a perfect vessel for all the toppings and flavors. Here the teff and the roasted kabocha mingle to create a savory, slightly vegetal combination. It feels rich without needing an abundance of ingredients, and makes for a perfect savory breakfast on its own.

TEFF PORRIDGE

1 kabocha squash (about 2 pounds / 900 g)

1 cup (190 g) uncooked teff

4 cups (960 ml) vegetable broth, plus more as needed

1 yellow onion, peeled and halved

½ teaspoon kosher salt, plus more if needed

FOR SERVING

Garlic-chile oil (see page 152)

Roasted and crushed peanuts (see page 185)

Crispy shallots

MAKE THE PORRIDGE: Cut the squash in half and place it cut side down in a roasting pan with ¼-inch (6 mm) of water. Bake at 425°F (220°C) until the squash halves begin to collapse, 30 to 40 minutes. Let cool, remove the seeds, scoop the squash out, and mash. You should have about 1½ cups (500 g) of puree.

Heat a small saucepan over medium-low heat. Add the teff and toast until fragrant, 1 to 2 minutes. Add the vegetable broth, kabocha mash, onion halves, and salt. Cover, bring to a boil, reduce to a simmer, and cook, stirring occasionally, until the teff is creamy, about 25 minutes.

Remove the lid, stir once more, and add more vegetable broth if needed for your desired porridge consistency. Taste and add more salt if needed.

TO SERVE: Discard the onion and divide the porridge between four bowls. Drizzle with chile oil and finish with a flourish of crushed peanuts and crispy shallots.

Notes

Any squash that can be pureed can be used here—and this includes pumpkin puree from a can if you're not feeling like tackling a whole squash. Roasted sweet potato puree is another good alternative.

You can thinly slice and fry your shallots in a neutral oil until golden, or just buy them fried. I can usually find these at Asian markets.

Garlicky Millet Cream with Charred Bok Choy

Serves 4

One of my main hopes for this book is that you will see one of these ingredients and feel a sense of creativity. All the ingredients featured in this book have so much exploration beyond their simple cooked self.

Take millet, for example. When cooked with the normal ratio of water and time, millet is a fluffy grain for pilafs and salads. However, cook it with extra water and a little more time and the grain breaks down, allowing it to take a run in a blender to become a luscious cream that can serve as a base for grain bowls, legumes, or, as in the case of this recipe, perfectly charred vegetables.

ROASTED GARLIC

1 medium garlic bulb

1 to 2 tablespoons olive oil

¼ teaspoon kosher salt

MILLET CREAM

¼ cup (55 g) uncooked millet

1 cup (240 ml) water

¼ cup (60 ml) olive oil

½ teaspoon kosher salt

½ teaspoon nutritional yeast

BLACK PEPPER-MISO COMPOUND BUTTER

¼ cup (56 g) unsalted butter, at room temperature

2 tablespoons white miso

1 teaspoon ground black pepper, plus extra for serving

1 teaspoon cane sugar

1 teaspoon rice vinegar

Preheat the oven to 400°F (200°C). Line a small baking dish with a piece of parchment paper large enough to fold over the garlic.

MAKE THE ROASTED GARLIC: Cut off enough of the garlic top to expose the majority of garlic cloves. Put the garlic in the prepared baking dish. Drizzle with olive oil, sprinkle with salt, and fold the parchment over the garlic, tucking loose ends under to secure.

Bake the garlic until the whole bulb is soft to the touch and the top is golden, around 40 minutes. Remove and let cool enough to handle.

MAKE THE MILLET CREAM: While the garlic is roasting, combine the millet and water in a small saucepan. Bring to a boil, reduce to a simmer, cover, and cook for 30 minutes. The millet should be quite soft.

Transfer the millet with any leftover water to a blender or food processor. Squeeze the garlic cloves from the peel and add to the millet cream. Add the olive oil, salt, and nutritional yeas and puree until smooth. Transfer to a jar and place in the refrigerator until you are ready to serve. As the millet cools, it will set more; simply stir it with a spoon as needed.

MAKE THE COMPOUND BUTTER: Combine the butter, miso, black pepper, sugar, and vinegar in a small bowl and stir vigorously to combine. Set aside.

CONTINUES

Garlicky Millet Cream with Charred Bok Choy

CONTINUED

CHARRED BOK CHOY

2 tablespoons avocado oil

4 heads baby bok choy

Water

PREPARE THE BOK CHOY: Heat a medium skillet over medium-high heat. Cut the baby bok choy in half lengthwise and submerge in water to rinse out any sand or dirt. Pat dry and place in the skillet. Press down on the bok choy with the spatula until the bulbs have charred, 1 to 2 minutes.

Reduce the heat to low, add a couple tablespoons of water, cover, and cook until the bulb of the bok choy is tender, 6 to 8 minutes. Once tender, flip the bok choy over. Turn up the heat and let any remaining water evaporate.

Remove the skillet from the heat and add the compound butter to the pan. As the butter melts, spoon it over the bok choy.

TO SERVE: Spread the millet cream onto a serving platter and top with the bok choy. Drizzle with any remaining butter and finish with a few cracks of black pepper.

Notes

This is another time you might think to yourself: this cream needs miso! Don't do it. The miso creates a reaction with the starches, effectively rendering them useless. This is why the compound butter has the miso, because I adore the umami it adds, just not in the millet cream.

Seasonal Variations: The millet cream and the black pepper compound butter are friends to nearly all vegetables, so really your imagination is the limit. Grill asparagus, braise winter squash (see page 209), steam broccoli wedges, or roast eggplant wedges depending on the season.

Make Ahead: Millet cream will keep in the refrigerator for a few days. If it begins to separate, simply use a spoon to vigorously stir it back together. The butter will last upwards of a week.

Charred Brussels Sorghum Gratin

Serves 4

In my house, there are typically only two acceptable ways to prepare Brussels sprouts: raw and shaved into a salad or charred until the outer leaves are crispy and any loose ones turn into chips. For this gratin, I use well-roasted sprouts. The Brussels sprouts get a nice color to them before being paired with a creamy cheesy filling.

The sorghum adds just a bit of texture and heft so that the whole dish doesn't disappear into cream, which can be a goal, just not for this gratin. Plus, the mellow, slightly sweet flavor of sorghum adds just enough to be noticeable while supporting the flavor of the Brussels sprouts and cheese.

1 pound (450 g) Brussels sprouts, trimmed and quartered
2 tablespoons olive oil
½ teaspoon kosher salt
1 cup (180 g) cooked sorghum (see page 105)
2 ounces (60 g) aged gouda or cheddar cheese, shredded, divided
1 teaspoon ground mustard
1 teaspoon kosher salt
1 teaspoon ground black pepper
1 cup (240 ml) heavy cream

Preheat the oven to 425°F (220°C).

Put the Brussels sprouts in a 2-quart (2 L) casserole dish and drizzle with olive oil and salt. Roast until the sprouts are browning and quite tender, about 30 minutes.

Remove the dish from the oven and add the cooked sorghum, half of the shredded cheese, the ground mustard, salt, and pepper. Stir to combine everything, then pour in the heavy cream. Top with the remaining cheese.

Return the casserole to the oven and bake for another 15 minutes, until the cream is bubbling and the cheese has melted. Let cool for a few minutes, then serve.

Notes

The cheese is where you can manipulate the flavor a bit. I am an aged-cheese person as I want the salty crystals that form during the aging process. However, a non-aged cheese or even a mildly flavored cheese would work here. The goal is really just to melt.

Vegetables belonging to the brassica family are really the winners for this recipe. Swap the Brussels sprouts for roasted broccoli, cauliflower, or cabbage.

MAKE AHEAD: The roasted Brussels sprouts and sorghum can both be made a day or two ahead of time and stored in the refrigerator.

Sweet-Corn Oats with Halloumi and Basil-Almond Cream

Serves 4

When making a whole-grain pilaf, I like to pair the grains with a solid creamy base. This is for two reasons: I find it's a nice texture balance, and, because the whole grains stay quite separate, the cream acts as a binder, helping get the grains from the plate to your mouth (because there's nothing like going for a bite and having everything fall back to your plate!).

I often keep oat groats on hand to mill into flour and flake into rolled oats, but occasionally I like to use the grassy, soft grain whole. The whole grains cook up plump, a bit chewy, and with just a hint of the oat flavor.

PILAF

2 tablespoons olive oil

2 teaspoons fennel seeds

2 small shallots, minced

1 cup (180 g) uncooked oat groats, soaked overnight (see page 105)

2½ cups (600 ml) water

½ teaspoon kosher salt

Kernels from 4 ears sweet corn (about 3 cups / 650 g)

2 teaspoons rice vinegar

BASIL-ALMOND CREAM

½ cup (70 g) slivered almonds

½ cup (120 ml) hot water

¼ cup packed (24 g) fresh basil

2 tablespoons olive oil

2 teaspoons white miso

1 teaspoon rice vinegar

½ teaspoon stone-ground mustard

Kosher salt (optional)

FOR SERVING

2 tablespoons olive oil

8 ounces (230 g) halloumi, cut into ¼-inch (6 mm slices)

Julienned basil

MAKE THE PILAF: Heat the olive oil in a medium saucepan over medium heat. Add the fennel seeds and shallot and cook until both are fragrant, 2 to 3 minutes. Drain the oats and add to the saucepan along with the 2½ cups (600 ml) water and salt. Bring to a boil, reduce to a simmer, cover, and cook until the oats are tender; about 30 minutes.

When the oats are tender, remove the lid, turn the heat to high, and cook, stirring frequently, until all the extra liquid has evaporated. Remove from the heat and stir in the sweet corn kernels and rice vinegar.

MAKE THE CREAM: Combine the almonds and water in a small food processor or high-speed blender. Puree until mostly smooth. Add the basil, olive oil, miso, vinegar, and mustard. Puree until well combined, taste, and add salt if needed.

TO SERVE: Heat the olive oil in a large cast-iron skillet or similar-size pan over medium heat. Add the halloumi and fry, flipping at least once, until both sides are golden, 2 to 3 minutes per side.

Spread the basil almond cream on a small platter and layer the halloumi and pilaf on top. Finish with a flourish of julienned basil before serving.

Notes

Typically, I would blanch basil to retain the green color in a sauce. However, the nut cream dilutes the basil's color enough that it's not worth the extra step.

Seasonal Variations: I like to maintain the vegetable-herb balance and keep the fennel flavor year-round. During spring, I replace the corn with fresh peas and the almond cream with a dill cream. During the colder months, I like to use quartered and roasted Brussels sprouts with a sage-based cream.

Tortang Talong (Filipino Eggplant Omelet) with Fonio

Serves 4

A bit of a mix between an omelet and a fritter, this Filipino dish is traditionally made with egg and cooked pork. Obviously, no pork here, but I use a combination of tofu and cooked fonio to create a flavorful and slightly crispy layer. Fonio is a phenomenal grain. It cooks fast, fluffs easily, and is right at home in the omelet and as the base, which would typically be rice.

TORTANG TALONG

4 small eggplants, 4 to 5 ounces (115 to 140 g) each, peeled

5 tablespoons (75 ml) avocado or other high-heat neutral oil, divided

2 small shallots, minced

4 garlic cloves, minced

6 ounces (170 g) firm or super-firm tofu, drained

2 tablespoons soy sauce

1 tablespoon vegetarian oyster sauce

1 teaspoon ground black pepper

4 cups (700 g) cooked fonio (see page 105), divided

4 eggs

½ teaspoon kosher salt

SAUCE

¼ cup (68 g) ketchup

2 tablespoons vegetarian oyster sauce

2 tablespoons vegan Worcestershire sauce

1 tablespoon cane sugar

MAKE THE TORTANG TALONG: Bring a few inches of water to a boil in a saucepan with a steamer basket. Steam the eggplants for 8 to 12 minutes, until tender. Remove and place on a plate to cool.

Meanwhile, heat 1 tablespoon of the avocado oil in a small skillet over medium heat. Add the minced shallots and garlic. Cook until they begin to brown, 5 to 6 minutes. Crumble the tofu into the skillet and continue to cook, letting the moisture evaporate. If the tofu begins to form a crust on the skillet, use a wooden spatula or spoon to scrape.

Once the tofu has crisped a bit, turn off the heat and add the soy sauce, oyster sauce, and black pepper. Stir and scrape any stuck bits from the bottom of the pan. Finally, stir in ¼ cup (45 g) of the cooked fonio. Transfer to a small bowl.

Crack the eggs into a wide, shallow bowl, add the salt, and whisk. Pour about three-quarters of the eggs over the tofu mixture and stir.

Preheat a large skillet over medium heat with 1 tablespoon of the avocado oil. Take each eggplant and flatten so that it's ¼ to ½ inch (6 mm to 1.3 cm) thick. Working with one eggplant at a time, dip into the bowl with the remaining egg and place directly onto the heated skillet.

Spoon one-quarter of the tofu-egg mixture on top of the eggplant in the skillet. Once the first side is golden brown, flip and cook the side with the tofu until golden brown, 1 to 2 minutes per side. Transfer to a plate and repeat with the remaining eggplants, adding 1 tablespoon of oil before frying each one.

MAKE THE SAUCE: While waiting for the eggplant to cook, combine the ketchup, oyster sauce, Worcestershire sauce, and sugar in a small bowl and stir to combine.

TO SERVE: Divide the remaining fonio between four bowls. Top each with an eggplant and serve with a drizzle of the sauce.

Notes

I use vegetarian oyster and vegan Worcestershire sauces, but feel free to use standard if that's what you have on hand. If you want to be a bit more traditional in flavor, opt for banana ketchup, a fruit-based ketchup that is made in a style similar to tomato-based ketchup.

LEGUMES

By now, you've most likely heard something along the lines of "Eat beans! Save the planet!"—a rallying cry in our effort to combat the climate crisis. And while I do firmly believe eating less meat is crucial for our planet, I also hold the belief that legumes are magical.

We're not sacrificing anything to eat beans, because beans, along with lentils, chickpeas, and soybeans are the ultimate food we can grow, cook, and share with one another (just don't tell grains I said that; my love for them is different and wonderful).

What makes legumes magical?

For starters, legumes are often used as cover and rotational crops in home gardens and commercial farms and everything in between. Unlike many crops which take and take from the soil, legumes give back in the form of nitrogen, helping to keep soil biomes balanced.

Legumes also provide fresh vegetables. Green beans! Peas! Edamame! These fresh green vegetables are grown year-round in my garden.

But of course, seasons eventually change and the plants die back. However, and feel free to say it with me now, beans are magic: we're left with a dry (often beautiful and colorful) shelf-stable item to get us through the year to eat and replant, starting the cycle over again.

WHAT IS A LEGUME?

Legumes encompass all plants, seeds, and fruits that belong to the Fabaceae family. This includes common dried beans, fresh green beans, peas (fresh and dried), lentils, broad beans, peanuts, soybeans, the clover that covers our grounds, and the vetch that is currently running rampant in my garden.

Many of these legumes also have uses outside our kitchens, including for cooking oil, cover crops, animal feed/forage, and fuel.

Pulses are a broad category of edible legumes, harvested as dry crops around the world, such as dried beans and lentils, but do not include peanuts, soybeans, or legumes only used for cover crops or oil.

LEGUME FORMS

Just like with grains, legumes are found and used various forms.

Whole: These legumes are simply removed from their dried pod and left with their seed coat intact. This includes the majority of dried beans, chickpeas, and lentils.

Spilt: Any legume that has the seed coat removed, allowing the two sides of the seed to fall apart, often referred to as "split." By removing their rigid seed coat, the legumes cook faster and do not hold their shape as well.

Flour: The ground form of either whole or split legumes. I've drastically reigned in my enthusiasm around bean flours for various reasons, including my concern that these flours can contain toxic lectins. I primarily stick to legume flours lower in these lectins, such as chickpea and soy.

BUYING AND STORING LEGUMES

As small food businesses continue to open, your options for finding heirloom legumes expand (see the list on page 230). I find it a bit easier to track harvest dates and legume age from small producers.

The age of the legume is quite important as fresh is best (a running theme among all the pantry ingredients listed in this book). A year from harvest is good, two years is okay, and anything after that might be okay on a case-by-case basis. Beans will begin to deteriorate over time, primarily due to moisture loss, and can cook unevenly if old.

Once you have legumes in hand, check for any irregular beans and discard them. This includes discolored, shrunken, or overly dirty beans. Also check for mold! Legumes not properly dried can have excess moisture that will lead to mold growth over time.

Keep legumes in an airtight container in a cool, dry area for optimal storage.

CANNED BEANS AND CHICKPEAS

While this is book mostly focuses on dried pantry ingredients, it's also a book on ingredients we have in our pantry that come from the dried seed. As such, I believe canned, cooked beans fit into this book.

Ninety percent of the time, I cook legumes from the dried form because I like the flavors I can add and the control I have over the entire process. However, and this is a big *however*, I recognize this is not for everyone. It takes time! And planning! And mental capacity to even think about this process.

Grab those canned beans from the store and use them without hesitation in these recipes. I always have a can or two of beans on hand because even with the best laid plans, things can go sideways. In recipes that feature heirloom legumes, I've also noted alternatives, all of which can be found canned.

A NOTE ON FERMENTED LEGUMES

Legumes have a long history of fermentation, such as for *douchi* (fermented black beans) in Chinese cuisine; *idli* (fermented rice and lentil cakes) and *papadam* (fermented wafer made from gram flour) in Indian cuisine; and a host of fermented soy products (see page 173).

COOKING DRIED LEGUMES

What follows is an in-depth look at everything I think about when cooking legumes. They are not hard to cook, but there are a few steps that can make or break the end product. Specific cooking instructions can be found in the individual legume sections.

Rinsing

I make about two batches of beans and at least one batch of lentils a week, and they all start with a quick rinse. While most store-bought legumes are processed and cleaned well, there's a possibility of dust, dirt, or even debris (I've found a couple of rocks in beans before). This is also an excellent time to catch if any of your beans are moldy. I rinse and do a quick check. It's optional, but I like to be proactive, and rinsing the beans takes little time.

Soaking

I am pro-soaking, as long as it's done correctly. It's important to acknowledge the role that sodium plays in turning legumes from hard seeds into the soft, creamy beans we want. And while there are many who still say salt negatively impacts bean cooking, the science is firm. Similar to grains, we're working against certain carbohydrates and proteins that want to keep the seed safe and intact.

However, unlike grains, legumes have more storage proteins that are primarily water-salt soluble, which means we are only left to tackle the fiber. Luckily for us, salt helps there too.

SOAKING WITH SALT (BRINING)

In the book *The Science of Good Cooking* by America's Test Kitchen, they illustrate that by brining beans for up to 24 hours, the sodium ions replace the calcium and magnesium ions that were protecting the pectin (the glue holding the cell walls together). As the salt does its magic, the pectin, a water-soluble fiber, begins to melt away. All of this leads to a creamy, well-cooked bean.

SOAKING WITH BAKING SODA

Similar to salt, baking soda can also play a role in breaking down pectin and often shows up in hummus recipes as a way to achieve a silky smooth texture. Baking soda can be added to the sodium brine as well, typically at ¾ teaspoon per cup of dried legumes.

However, be forewarned: You can have too much of a good thing. If you're looking for beans that still hold their texture, I recommend sticking to a salt-only brine.

SOAKING AND OLIGOSACCHARIDES

Beyond just legume tenderness, flatulence may be on your mind. Legumes contain oligosaccharides, which are complex carbohydrates that our bodies don't have the enzymes to break down until they reach our colon. While our colon does have the enzymes needed for breakdown, the process produces a large amount of gas, which can cause discomfort.

Fortunately, these carbohydrates are water soluble, so a soak helps dissolve the troublemakers.

Many cultures also reach for ingredients such as epazote, kombu, and asafoetida when soaking and cooking legumes to increase tenderness and decrease gassiness.

QUICK SOAKING

What happens if you decide to soak your legumes but remember only an hour before you should be cooking them? A quick soak can still be beneficial. This is done by bringing everything to a boil for 1 minute, turning off the heat, covering the saucepan, and soaking for 1 hour.

THE SOAKING LIQUID: TO DRAIN OR NOT TO DRAIN

Finally, after soaking, you have a saucepan of water that you will need to decide to keep for cooking or drain and start fresh. On one hand, if you used baking soda, you might want to drain that off before cooking. Or, if you're trying to reduce oligosaccharides that have now dissolved into the water, draining the soaking liquid is a good idea. However, there's no need to rinse.

On the other hand, if it's just salt, and you're trying to preserve nutrients that might have also dissolved into the soaking liquid, cooking the beans in the soaking liquid is just fine.

As a personal preference, I choose to drain the beans and use fresh water. This allows me to start fresh and use aromatics to shape the flavor of the beans without anything that might be left in the soaking liquid. I figure that if I'm eating a balanced diet, I don't need to be so worried about preserving all the nutrients all the time.

Cooking

Once you get past the initial rinsing and soaking process, the fun part happens. I love cooking a pot of legumes on the stovetop; the fragrance, the sound, and the warmth—it's a sensory delight!

AROMATICS

The biggest thing you can do for your legumes is to act as though you're making a flavorful broth and use plenty of aromatics. This includes the addition of alliums (onions, garlic, leeks, scallions), vegetables (carrots, celery, fennel), woody herbs (bay leaves, rosemary, oregano, sage, thyme, marjoram), spices (cumin, coriander, fennel seeds), and olive oil.

I usually toss in the aromatics, lose them in the pot, and remove them as best I can at the end of cooking. For additional flavor, sear the alliums and vegetables in oil before adding the beans and water. If you want a cleaner bean broth, wrap the aromatics in cheesecloth so they are totally removable.

COOKING LEGUMES

Once aromatics are decided, the next step is to determine how to best cook the legume. For the most part, legumes are quite forgiving in their cooking. Specific cooking instructions can be found on page 123 (beans), page 149 (chickpeas), and page 161 (lentils), but I have a few words of wisdom for your overall legume-cooking journey.

Boil, then simmer: Beans and chickpeas need a good 10- to 15-minute boil at the beginning of cooking to neutralize the lectins (see page 21) but after that, they should be simmered over low heat.

This is particularly important for the legumes that are meant to stay intact. The low cooking temperature allows any water-soluble or salt-water-soluble proteins and fiber to dissolve evenly, helping the legumes stay intact.

To intensify the flavor of the legumes and the broth, let the legumes simmer without a lid. The flavor is much better as the liquid concentrates, like in making any broth. Lids decrease cooking time, but I'd rather have more flavorful beans.

Skimming: Recipes call for skimming off the foam that forms on top of the beans while cooking. Skimming isn't a must, but it does help keep the bean liquid clean and your beans within sight. If a lot of foam builds up, I skim. If it's just a little, I leave it be.

Baking soda in the cooking liquid: As with the soaking liquid, baking soda can also be added to the cooking liquid. Keep amounts low to avoid a slight metallic taste, no more than ½ teaspoon baking soda per cup of dried beans, and know that your beans will be quite soft.

JUDGING WHEN LEGUMES ARE DONE

The estimated time on any legume cooking chart is just that, an estimate. Much can change based on how old the beans are, how much you boil versus simmer, and how long you soak your beans. While I've provided estimates in each legume category, I recommend getting intuitive with your cooking. Once you suspect your beans might be close to done, start tasting. Cooked legumes should be soft but remain intact. If the beans begin to fall apart, that's a sign they've been overcooked. Overcooking doesn't hurt the bean; it means if

you had plans to use them in salads or grain bowls, they might not be as firm as you like. After cooking dried beans a few times, you'll find a rhythm.

FINISHING TOUCHES: ACID / DRIED CHILES / TENDER HERBS

Just as I flavor at the start of cooking, I also save some flavor ingredients for the end of cooking.

Acid: Save adding anything acidic until your beans are done to avoid potentially toughening the beans and also so the flavors don't get lost. Citrus, vinegar, and tomato products should all wait.

Chiles: I also love adding different varieties of chiles into the mix. I typically rehydrate chiles on their own, turn them into a paste with the help of a bit of bean broth, and then add the puree to the pot.

Tender herbs: Cilantro, parsley, tarragon, dill, mint, chives, and basil are all herbs I add at the end of cooking. Their flavor is delicate and gets lost after an hour of cooking (or even becomes bitter). Mince a few herbs and toss in at the end.

OTHER COOKING METHODS

Most of the time, I cook legumes on the stovetop. However, it's helpful to have these other cooking techniques in your back pocket when you want to cook legumes over the workday, realize you require beans 45 minutes before dinner, or just want a hands-off method.

Slow cooker: Using a slow cooker is similar to cooking on the stovetop. Start by boiling on the stovetop to remove lectins (especially for kidney and cannellini beans). Once you've hit a boil for 15 minutes, transfer to the slow cooker and heat on low for anywhere from 5 to 8 hours (depending on the variety and size of the legumes).

Pressure cooker/instant pots: This is great for quick beans but not so great for bean texture or flavorful broth. However, if you're in a pinch, cooking in a pressure cooker will work. There's no need to soak or preboil; add everything to the pressure cooker with enough water to cover by 4 inches (10 cm). Let come to full pressure before timing; then cook for around 20 minutes for the smaller beans and upwards of 40 minutes for the larger, heartier beans. Let the pressure release naturally and check. If your beans aren't tender after that, you can finish cooking on the stovetop.

Oven-baked beans: According to America's Test Kitchen, baking your beans is the best way to achieve the perfect texture (it's that low and slow heat). For oven-baked beans, soak them, drain them, and add to a dutch oven with 2 inches (5 cm) of water and salt (1 teaspoon per cup of dried beans). Bring to a boil for 10 to 15 minutes, then cover, transfer to a 300°F (150°C) oven, and bake until the beans are tender: about 1 hour for small beans, such as navy, and over 2 hours for large, such as cannellini.

STORING COOKED LEGUMES

I always store my beans in their liquid and lentils dry because they tend to lose their texture a bit more in the storage liquid. The bean liquid is a delicious broth at this point, and many of my recipes start with doing a second cooking of the beans in their liquid, like brothy beans or soups. The bean liquid is always great for use in soups or pasta sauces. Plus, the beans get the added benefit of lingering in all that flavor you just created.

The first step in storing cooked legumes is cooling them properly. If I make a larger batch, I transfer it to multiple containers, allowing the beans to cool more quickly.

I keep beans for up to about a week in the refrigerator. Most people will say no more than 5 days, but I use my nose. If the beans smell fine, they are fine. If they smell funky, toss them.

FREEZING COOKED LEGUMES

You can freeze legumes in or out of their liquid, but the texture can become a bit mealy after being frozen and thawed, and beans easily take on freezer burn.

BEANS

For much of my life, beans sat in the background. They'd be paired with meat and cornbread my grandmother would occasionally serve, cans of baked beans would be stocked in the cupboard, and at least once a summer, there'd be a potluck with a many-variety bean salad. I didn't think much about beans until I became vegetarian.

Soon, black bean tacos became a norm, and I managed to take some favorite flavors traditionally associated with meat and make them bean-friendly; for example, I ate a lot of chickpeas tossed in Frank's RedHot. My bean intake increased, but my way of cooking was still quite rooted in meat-centric cooking.

Finally, as I became a more experienced cook, I shed my initial understanding of beans. This allowed me to creatively explore beans, which led to satisfying and delicious meals, and eventually I became a bean evangelist, a bearer of bean wisdom.

There are hundreds of varieties of dry beans grown around the world and they all have slightly different personalities—making exploring and playing quite fun. I've attempted to provide recipes for varieties that I use frequently, that are sold by the bean companies I patronize, that I grow, and that I think are absolutely delightful.

Bean varieties fall into a few categories:

Common beans: Common beans are the dried beans we often think of when someone mentions beans. This category includes pinto, black, cranberry, and a whole host of heirloom varieties. When growing, these beans resemble a classic green-bean shape and grow as either a short bush, making them bush beans, or they climb and need a support structure, making them pole beans. Common beans come in a range of sizes from small through large.

Runner beans: These beans, for the most part, are identified as being larger than the largest common bean and, when growing, have pods that are flatter and longer. Most notably, these beans include larger white beans like corona, the ayocote family, and scarlet runner beans.

Tepary beans: Tend to run smaller than the smallest common bean. These beans are known for their drought resistance and ability to grow in hot climates. A few varieties include blue speckled, pinacate, and Sonoran white.

MY BEAN USAGE

Different beans have different personalities and behaviors in the kitchen. For example, does the bean hold its shape well or fall apart when cooking? Is the skin thin or thick? Is the texture dense or creamy? Does the flavor shine or does it take a back seat? Are we in it for the broth?

A bean is never just a bean! Many of the small bean sellers, whether local farmers or companies, now have notes about the individual bean that answer many of these questions and make buying choices a bit easier.

However, I've found as I've cooked with more and more varieties that I cook most often based on size and density.

LARGE, "MEATY" BEANS

These beans take up space and make themselves known to the eater. They are best for hearty and bean-bold recipes where bean texture is important. No matter the size, these beans are meant to be the star. I keep these varieties on hand:

Kidney: Red kidney beans and cannellini (white kidney beans) are great large beans easily found dried and in cans. Offshoots of the kidney family include a few standout speckled heirloom varieties, such as the cranberry/borlotti bean. Just remember, the kidney family has one of the highest concentrations of lectins (see page 21). Be sure to boil them for 15 minutes before reducing the heat during the cooking process.

Lima: These beans are mild and somewhat buttery in taste. Limas can also be found in various colors, including my favorite, the Christmas Lima, which has beautiful swirls of white and maroon.

Ayocote (ayeócotl): A family of heritage runner beans domesticated from the Tehuacán Valley in Mexico, with about eight hundred known genetic varieties. These beans tend to run a bit larger than the common beans and come in a variety of colors, including *negro* (black), *blanco* (white), *morado* (purple), and *amarillo* (yellow). I've loved every ayocote bean I've tried, and they are all a little different in profile and taste.

Miscellaneous runner: Look for white beans, such as royal corona, gigante, or emergo. Colorful runner beans include scarlet or painted lady.

Mayocoba/Peruano/canary: These yellow beans are mild and meaty. The mild flavor of these beans makes them super versatile.

MEDIUM, "EVERYDAY" BEANS

These are the beans that can do it all! One of my criteria for labeling something as an everyday bean is that it can be used in nearly every way, including but not limited to whole, chopped, mashed, or as a creamy puree. They all have solid, well-rounded flavors that work with other flavors with ease.

Pinto and black: While often used in similar ways, they are different enough that it's worth keeping both on hand, either dried or canned. For example, the Smash Burger (page 129) is only really solid with black beans, while the creaminess of the pinto beans is key in the Corn Fritter Bowl (page 132). The Chipotle Pinto Bean Stew (page 126), however, would work just as well with a wide array of varieties.

Great northern: An all-around solid white bean that is smaller than the cannellini bean. It's not too large and has a creamy texture with the ability to retain its shape once cooked but also makes a delightful white bean puree.

Hidatsa shield: A variety from the Hidatsa tribe of North Dakota, this bean has a distinct place on the Ark of Taste, a project from the Slow Food Foundation to preserve heritage food and biodiversity. The bean has a creamy texture and mellow flavor; it is a favorite of mine to grow in the garden.

Zuni gold: From from the Pueblo region of the Southwest, this bean has golden speckles and a soft and slightly sweet flavor.

Ojo de cabra: A Northern Mexico variety. This is a thin-skinned, creamy bean that soaks up flavor. Looks like a goat eye (hence the name).

SMALL "TENDER" BEANS

Sometimes I just want a bean that's soft, supple, and melts into the dish. These beans often have thinner skins, creamy textures, and need a low and slow cooking time to retain their shape.

Most of the beans in this category are great for mashed or pureed bean recipes. Also, because of their creamy texture and need for low and slow cooking, these beans are usually the ones found in baked bean dishes.

Navy: This small white bean is my go-to tender bean from the grocery store. Small in size and mild in flavor, this bean can tuck perfectly into a meal.

Alubia blanca: These beans, with roots in the Americas, are a kindred bean to the navy bean but with slightly more flavor and texture.

Tiger's eye (pepa de zapallo): An ideal creamy bean, these thin-skinned beans with tiger-like markings fall apart when cooked, making them an ideal tender bean.

Yellow eye: A slightly newer variety (and by newer, I mean eighteenth century CE), this is the bean of choice for New England baked beans. It is a relative of the kidney bean and has numerous color variations.

COOKING BEANS

BEAN TYPE	UNCOOKED QUANTITY	SOAK	COOKING LIQUID	COOKING TIME	COOKED BEAN YIELD
Extra-large beans	1 cup (160 g)	5 cups (1.2 L) cool water 2 tsp kosher salt 18 hours	Cover with 2 to 3 inches (5-7.5 cm) water 1 tsp kosher salt	30-60 minutes	2½ cups (400 g)
Large beans	1 cup (170 g)	4 cups (960 ml) cool water 2 tsp kosher salt 12 hours	Cover with 2 inches (5 cm) water 1 tsp kosher salt	30-40 minutes	2¾ cups (415 g)
Medium beans	1 cup (180 g)	4 cups (960 ml) cool water 2 tsp kosher salt 12 hours	Cover with 1 to 2 inches (2.5-5 cm) water 1 tsp kosher salt	25-35 minutes	2¾ cups (435 g)
Small beans	1 cup (190 g)	3 cups (720 ml) cool water 2 tsp kosher salt 8 hours	Cover with 1 inch (2.5 cm) water 1 tsp kosher salt	20-25 minutes	3 cups (450 g)

To cook: Drain your soaked beans and add any aromatics, plus fresh water and salt according to the chart. Bring the beans to a boil and cook for 15 minutes, then reduce the heat so it's as low as it can go while still causing a bit of movement in the broth. Simmer, with the lid off, until the beans are tender, using the times on the chart as a reference.

If you find that as your beans are cooking the liquid stops covering them, add hot water. Adding cool water will disrupt the cooking.

Start tasting your beans for doneness toward the end of the suggested cook time. If they are still firm, continue cooking and check every 10 to 15 minutes. Adequately cooked beans should be soft with no graininess or firmness. If you notice your beans are starting to fall apart, they're overcooked but can still be eaten!

Notes: If using soaking liquid for cooking, decrease salt to ½ teaspoon kosher salt when cooking.

If soaking is skipped, double the amount of water and salt in the cooking liquid. Cooking times will double.

For most beans, I add ½ large onion, a few cloves of garlic, a few sprigs of woody herbs, one bay leaf, and a drizzle of olive oil for every 1 cup of dried beans. I save any tender herbs, chile pastes, or acidic ingredients like citrus, tomato, or vinegar for the end so they don't lose their luster during a long cook or potentially toughen the beans.

The large runner beans are finicky and tend to cook erratically. Start checking at 30 minutes and continue to check often.

BEAN RECIPES

Beans (in Purgatory)

Serves 4

These beans are a direct result of my passion for pizza. When I make tomato sauce, I usually make extra to have on hand the next day for eggs in purgatory. However, I'm not always in the mood for eggs, which is where this bean version comes into play. While you could eat the beans over grains, I often eat this with toast or leftover pizza dough that I've cooked off in the pizza oven.

CHILE-FENNEL TOMATO SAUCE

¼ cup (60 ml) olive oil

2 large yellow onions, diced

1 teaspoon kosher salt

8 garlic cloves, minced

¼ cup (60 g) tomato paste

1 (28-ounce / 794 g) can crushed tomatoes

1 tablespoon ground chile or dried red pepper flakes, plus more to taste

2 teaspoons toasted and ground fennel seeds

BEANS

2 cups (340 g) cooked and drained cannellini beans

FOR SERVING

Olive oil

Fresh basil leaves, thinly sliced

Finishing salt, such as Maldon salt

MAKE THE SAUCE: Heat the olive oil in a medium saucepan or braiser over medium heat. Add the onion and salt. Cook until the onion begins to soften, about 8 to 10 minutes. Reduce the heat to medium-low. Cook until the onion is golden and quite soft, stirring occasionally and ensuring the onion remains in a thin, even layer, about 20 minutes.

Add the garlic and cook until fragrant, about 2 minutes. Stir in the tomato paste and cook until it deepens in color, about 2 minutes. Add the crushed tomato, ground chile, and ground fennel. Adjust the heat to medium and cook until the mixture thickens slightly, about 8 minutes.

HEAT THE BEANS: Add the beans to the sauce and cook until the sauce thickens more and the beans are hot, 4 to 5 minutes. Remove the skillet from the heat.

TO SERVE: Finish with a drizzle of olive oil, basil leaves, and salt.

Notes

Unlike eggs, beans are a bit more forgiving if the tomato sauce isn't thick enough. If you find the tomato sauce isn't thick when the beans are heated, turn the heat to medium-high, stir occasionally, and let the extra water evaporate until the tomato sauce is thick.

I like to swap the ground chile or pepper flakes for a spoonful of chile paste (see page 49), harissa (see page 53), or sambal oelek.

This dish makes a solid landing place for leftover roasted vegetables or greens. Try wilted kale, spinach, roasted sweet potatoes, or asparagus.

Make Ahead: The cooked beans in the sauce can be kept for a few days in the refrigerator and reheated with a splash of water or vegetable broth just to loosen the tomato sauce a bit.

Chipotle Pinto Bean Stew

Serves 4

I say I don't like to play favorites, so let's keep this between you and me: This stew is my favorite. It's my ultimate comfort food. The beans in this stew are the real star because they soak up the flavor of the chipotles while keeping their own personality.

I am rarely without a jar of chipotles in adobo stashed in my refrigerator. While I use dried chiles often, the ease of the canned chipotles is a winner in my book. This stew is loaded with flavor and fairly quick to assemble. If you're not big on heat, I'd recommend starting with one chipotle and adding more as desired.

STEW

¼ cup (60 ml) olive oil

2 large onions, diced

1 teaspoon kosher salt

8 garlic cloves, minced

6 tablespoons (90 g) tomato paste

4 cups (520 g) cooked and drained pinto beans

4 chipotles in adobo sauce, minced, plus ¼ cup (60 ml) adobo sauce

6 cups (1.4 L) vegetable broth

3 tablespoons (16 g) red miso

FOR SERVING

2 ripe avocados

½ cup (24 g) fried shallots

2 red radishes, diced

Olive oil, for finishing

MAKE THE STEW: Heat the olive oil in a medium dutch oven or braiser over medium heat. Add the onion and salt. Cook until the onion has softened substantially, 14 to 16 minutes. If the onion begins to brown, reduce the heat to medium low. Add the garlic and cook for another minute. Stir in the tomato paste and cook for a minute more. Add the beans, chipotles, and adobo sauce. Stir, then add the vegetable broth. Bring to a boil, reduce to a simmer, and cook for 10 minutes.

Place the miso in a ladle and add a bit of broth. Stir to dissolve the miso, holding the ladle over the pot, then add to the stew. Cook for another minute or so, until the stew is hot.

TO SERVE: Divide the stew between four bowls. Top each stew with the sliced avocado. Finish with a sprinkle of fried shallots, radishes, and a drizzle of olive oil.

Notes

If you don't have chipotles in adobo on hand, use 1 to 2 tablespoons of dried chipotle powder and supplement by including a couple teaspoons or so of dried oregano, ground cumin, and sugar along with a splash of vinegar to make up for the flavors in the adobo sauce.

The stew will keep and develop more flavor for a few days but can also be frozen for up to 3 months. The beans in this stew also make a good enchilada or quesadilla filling—cook the broth down a bit and use a potato masher to create a refried bean-like texture and use as such. I've also been known to

thicken the stew slightly by boiling until the broth has reduced, melt some cheese on top, and use it as a dip for tortilla chips.

You can thinly slice and fry your shallots in a neutral oil until golden, or just buy them fried. I can usually find these at Asian markets.

Rosemary Marinated Cranberry Beans

Serves 3 to 4
as a snack

While I like a well-thought-out dinner, I get equally excited for a thrown-together picnic meal–especially if it involves being outside and eating. I have an arsenal of go-to recipes. Topping that list? Marinated beans! They are simple to toss together and only get better with a little cooler time.

Given these beans are a favorite picnic item of mine, I recommend pairing them with a snacky picnic spread that includes a few varieties of cheeses, some fresh bread, dip (such as the kimchi dip on page 166), and pickles. Alternatively, these beans are great as a side dish for pizza (pages 38 and 201) or the Carrot Galette (page 66).

2 cups (355 g) cooked and drained cranberry or cannellini beans
2 tablespoons minced rosemary
2 garlic cloves, minced
1 teaspoon lemon zest
⅓ cup (80 ml) olive oil
1 tablespoon rice vinegar
1 tablespoon lemon juice
1 teaspoon ground black pepper
½ teaspoon kosher salt

Place the drained beans in a medium bowl and set aside. Combine the rosemary, garlic, and lemon zest in a small heat-safe bowl and set aside.

Heat the olive oil in a small saucepan over medium heat until the oil begins to shimmer and is fragrant. Place the end of a chopstick in the oil and if it bubbles, the oil is ready.

Turn off the heat and immediately pour the oil over the rosemary mixture. Stir and let rest until the bubbling subsides. Stir in the rice vinegar, lemon juice, black pepper, and salt while the oil is still warm.

Pour over the beans and toss until well coated. Transfer to a pint jar and slightly press the beans until the oil covers the beans. Allow the beans to rest for at least 2 hours but preferably overnight in the refrigerator. Allow the beans to come to room temperature before serving.

Notes

I recommend starting with only ½ teaspoon of kosher salt even though it might not feel like enough. Depending on how your beans were cooked, they might bring enough salt and the mixture will continue to balance flavors as it sits. However, too little salt and the beans might seem bland, so be sure to taste and adjust before serving (packing a little finishing salt in your picnic is always a good idea).

Make Ahead: The beans will be good for 2 to 3 days stored in the refrigerator but after that I find the flavors have mingled a bit too much and the texture of the beans begins to deteriorate.

Black Bean Smash Burger, In-N-Out Style

Makes 4 double-patty burgers

Upon moving to California, I was often asked if I had been to In-N-Out and if so, what I thought. This California-based fast food restaurant is known for its limited menu of thin, crispy-edged burgers piled with cheese, lettuce, tomatoes, and a special sauce (which is a variation on Thousand Island dressing). Here, I give black beans a similar treatment of thin patties smashed onto a skillet to create those iconic crispy edges.

I'll be up-front: these patties will fall apart. I personally think it's part of their charm. However, there are a few tricks to helping them stay together. First, don't get overconfident and make larger patties; they will let you down upon flipping. Smaller patties are key. Also, don't rush the process, the patty should have some crispy edges forming before you attempt the flip. If you know your pan has a penchant for stickiness, use the best nonstick pan you have. Finally, I recommend not skipping the cheese as it can act as a glue to hold it all together.

THOUSAND ISLAND DRESSING

¼ cup (60 g) mayonnaise (regular or vegan; see page 179)

2 tablespoons ketchup

1 tablespoon sweet pickle relish

½ teaspoon yellow mustard

½ teaspoon rice vinegar

½ teaspoon kosher salt

BLACK BEAN PATTIES

1½ cups (280 g) cooked and drained black beans

6 tablespoons (24 g) Japanese-style panko

1 large egg

2 tablespoons red miso

1 teaspoon kosher salt

½ teaspoon smoked paprika

½ teaspoon garlic powder

CARAMELIZED ONIONS

2 tablespoons avocado oil

1 medium yellow onion, diced

MAKE THE DRESSING: Combine the mayonnaise, ketchup, pickle relish, mustard, vinegar, and salt in a small bowl. Cover and refrigerate until it is needed, at least for 30 minutes.

MAKE THE BLACK BEAN PATTIES: Pulse the black beans in a food processor until the beans have a mashed texture. Transfer to a bowl and add the panko, egg, miso, salt, paprika, and garlic powder. Stir until well combined, then set aside for 20 minutes.

COOK THE ONIONS: Heat the oil in a well-seasoned griddle or cast-iron pan over medium heat. Add the onion and cook, stirring occasionally, until the onion pieces are tender and starting to brown, 14 to 16 minutes. Transfer to a small bowl and set aside.

CONTINUES

Black Bean Smash Burger, In-N-Out Style

CONTINUED

TO SERVE

Avocado or other neutral high-heat oil, for frying

8 thin slices cheddar cheese

8 lettuce leaves

4 thick slices tomato

4 sesame buns

Pickle slices, for serving (optional)

COOK THE PATTIES AND SERVE: Return the griddle to medium heat and drizzle liberally with avocado oil. Lightly wet your hands and form the black bean mixture into eight balls that are slightly larger than golf balls.

Place a black bean ball on the hot griddle. Lay a piece of parchment paper on top, and using the back of a spatula and your hand, press until the patty is flat and only ¼ inch (6 mm) in thickness. Repeat with as many patties as you can fit on your griddle, working in batches as needed. Cook for 2 to 3 minutes on each side, adding oil to the pan as needed to maintain a thin layer for frying. Once the bottom of each patty is quite brown and crisp, flip and add a slice of cheddar cheese. Cook until the second side is brown and crisp. Transfer the patties to a plate and repeat until all patties are cooked, adding more oil if needed.

Lightly toast the buns on the griddle. Spread a small bit of the sauce on the bottom bun, then layer with two patties, lettuce, tomato, onions, and pickles if desired. Spread a bit more sauce on the top bun and add to the burger.

Notes

These burgers showcase a technique I use for burgers and when making fritters: flattening them in the pan. There's just no use getting your hands messy only for the thing to fall apart once it hits the pan. By flattening in the pan, the burger (or fritter) begins cooking, holding together right away, which helps the patty stay together as it

flattens. This is also not a time to skimp on oil. The charm of these burgers is their crispy, slightly greasy bits.

Be patient. As long as you have a decent understanding of the heat on your stovetop, you'll be okay. There's a higher probability you'll flip it too soon than there is that you'll burn it.

Make Ahead: The patties can be frozen and kept for up to 3 months. To do this, sandwich each ball in between pieces of parchment and press down to form the patty. Freeze like this and when you ready to use it, peel off the parchment and place the patty in a hot skillet. The dressing will last up to a week in the refrigerator.

Corn Fritter Bowls with Roasted-Garlic Black Bean Puree

Serves 4

Bean purees make amazing bases for grain bowls, fillings for enchiladas, and dips, such as the Charred Zucchini Bean Dip on page 141. I turned to black bean purees because the average black bean can soften enough to create a creamy, dreamy texture, and there's the added benefit of color: a slight bluish hue (a fun thing, I think).

BLACK BEAN PUREE

1½ cups (390 g) cooked and drained black beans

1 small bulb roasted garlic (see page 109)

1 teaspoon toasted and ground cumin (see page 212)

1 teaspoon rice vinegar

½ teaspoon kosher salt

3 to 4 tablespoons olive oil

CORN FRITTERS

1½ cups (250 g) fresh sweet corn kernels

½ small yellow onion, thinly sliced

¼ cup (35 g) all-purpose flour, plus more as needed

½ teaspoon baking powder

½ teaspoon ground black pepper

½ teaspoon kosher salt

2 large eggs

Avocado or other neutral high-heat oil, for frying

FOR SERVING

2 cups (150 g) shredded red cabbage

½ teaspoon kosher salt

Cooked grains, such as medium-grain rice, pearled barley, or fonio

MAKE THE BLACK BEAN PUREE: Place the cooked black beans in a food processor. Squeeze the garlic from the bulb and add to the beans along with the cumin, vinegar, and salt. Begin to puree the mixture and, with the machine running, drizzle the olive oil in until the puree is smooth.

MAKE THE CORN FRITTERS: Combine the corn in a medium bowl with the onions. Add the flour, baking powder, black pepper, and salt. Toss until the corn is well coated, adding more flour if needed. Crack in the eggs and stir to combine.

Heat a ¼-inch (6 mm) layer of oil in a medium skillet over medium heat and have a plate covered with a wire rack nearby. When the oil is hot, scoop ¼-cup (60 ml) portions of the batter into the hot oil. Press down with the back of the spoon to flatten the fritters. Fry until the fritters are a deep golden, 3 to 4 minutes per side. When crisp, transfer to the rack and repeat frying with the remaining batter.

TO SERVE: Place the shredded cabbage in a bowl, add the salt, and massage until the cabbage has softened a bit. Divide the bean puree among four bowls and smooth with the back of a spoon. Arrange equal parts of the grains, fritters, and cabbage in each bowl and serve.

Notes

It is possible to make a fritter out of many vegetables and greens, for example the Kale–Bulgur Fritters on page 51. Other options that work as a 1:1 swap with the corn include sliced alliums, chopped cauliflower or broccoli, and/or shredded root vegetables, including carrots and parsnips.

Vegan Riff: The best way to make fritters without the egg is to create a paste by mixing more flour with your choice of liquid: water or a plant-based milk/yogurt. Start with ¼ cup (35 g) flour and 3 tablespoons (45 ml) liquid to replace the 2 eggs.

Cabbage Salad with Charred Lime and Jalapeño Dressing

Serves 4 to 6

On occasion I have been known to eat coleslaw as a meal. I'm not proud, but the combination of creamy dressing and crunchy bits of cabbage gets me every time. Sometimes, though, I want that combination in a more substantial meal. This salad is it. The beans and sweet potato bring a solid amount of bulk, while the charred lime and jalapeño dressing does the heavy flavor lifting.

And, if you want more of a meal, this salad makes a stellar addition to tacos. Mash the beans for a base and top with the cabbage (more in slaw form) and the roasted sweet potatoes.

SWEET POTATOES

2 medium sweet potatoes, cut into ½-inch (1.3 cm) cubes

2 tablespoons olive oil

1 teaspoon kosher salt

CHARRED LIME AND JALAPEÑO DRESSING

1 tablespoon avocado oil

1 lime, halved

1 medium jalapeño

4 scallions

¼ cup (60 g) mayonnaise (regular or vegan; see page 179)

¼ cup (60 g) plain whole-milk Greek yogurt

¼ cup packed (24 g) minced fresh cilantro, plus more for serving

1 teaspoon kosher salt

¼ teaspoon MSG

¼ teaspoon sugar

SALAD

6 cups (450 g) shredded red cabbage

3 cups (480 g) cooked and drained pinto beans

6 tablespoons (45 g) toasted pepitas, chopped (see page 186)

Preheat the oven to 425°F (220°C).

PREPARE THE SWEET POTATOES: Arrange the sweet potato cubes in a single layer on a sheet pan. Drizzle with olive oil and toss with the salt. Roast until the sweet potatoes are tender and browning, 25 to 30 minutes.

MAKE THE DRESSING: While the sweet potatoes roast, heat the oil in cast-iron skillet over medium heat. Place the lime cut side down on the skillet. Add the jalapeño and scallions and turn occasionally until charred on all sides. Once everything is well charred, transfer to a plate to let cool slightly. Peel off the loosened skin of the jalapeño, then remove the stem and seeds. Trim the ends from the scallions. Juice the lime into a blender.

Combine the jalapeño and scallions in the blender along with the mayonnaise, yogurt, cilantro, salt, MSG, and sugar. Blend until smooth, taste, and adjust any flavors you might like more of.

ASSEMBLE THE SALAD: Combine the cabbage in a large bowl along with the roasted sweet potatoes, beans, and crushed pepitas. Drizzle with the dressing and toss to combine.

Transfer the salad to a medium serving bowl and garnish with cilantro before serving.

Notes

One of the biggest mistakes I see people make when they roast vegetables, especially ones higher in water content like sweet potatoes, is pulling them out of the oven too early. Sweet potatoes roasted until they are just beginning to brown still have quite a bit of moisture content and once removed from the oven, have a mushy texture. Go beyond this stage and roast until the underside of the sweet potato pieces are quite brown. This will ensure the cubed sweet potatoes hold a bit of shape in the salad and do not turn to mush.

Charred Chimichurri Ayocote Beans over Whipped Ricotta

Serves 4 to 6

I am often trying to break the stigma that vegetarian cooking is limited to a few cooking techniques, when in reality, the possibilities are endless. Take, for example, grilling beans. With the help of a grill basket, beans easily cook over a flame. The outside gets a bit charred while the inside stays creamy—perfect for larger beans.

For this recipe, I embrace the Argentinian tradition of grilled foods with punchy herb-forward chimichurri. Traditionally in chimichurri, the alliums are left raw, which creates a vibrant sauce that cuts through rich meats. Since the beans here aren't as heavy as meat, I like to grill the alliums to tame the bite just a bit.

WHIPPED RICOTTA

1½ cups (370 g) whole-milk ricotta

1 teaspoon lemon zest

½ teaspoon kosher salt

CHIMICHURRI

1 medium shallot

1 small garlic bulb

2 tablespoons apple cider vinegar

1 tablespoon sherry vinegar

1 teaspoon kosher salt

⅓ cup packed (16 g) fresh flat-leaf parsley

⅓ cup (16 g) fresh cilantro leaves

1 tablespoon fresh oregano

½ teaspoon dried red pepper flakes

6 tablespoons (90 ml) olive oil

MAKE THE WHIPPED RICOTTA: Combine the ricotta, lemon zest, and salt in a food processor or blender and puree until mostly smooth. Transfer to a bowl and refrigerate until you are ready to serve.

MAKE THE CHIMICHURRI: Preheat a grill with a vegetable grill basket or grill pan over medium heat. Leave the shallots and garlic intact with the skin on. Place on the grill, over the fire, and cook until charred, 3 to 4 minutes. Move to the outer edge of the grill and continue to cook until softened; you may notice a bit of liquid bubbling from the stem. Remove from the grill and let cool enough to handle.

Cut the shallots and garlic in half and squeeze the flesh from their skins onto a cutting board. Coarsely chop or mash into small pieces. Place in a small bowl along with the cider vinegar, sherry vinegar, and salt. Let rest while you prepare the herbs.

Place the herbs on the cutting board and mince until the herbs are crushed together. Add to the alliums along with the pepper flakes and oil, stir to combine, and let rest for 30 minutes.

CONTINUES

Charred Chimichurri Ayocote Beans over Whipped Ricotta

CONTINUED

BEANS

3 cups (540 g) cooked and drained ayocote (or cannellini) beans

1 tablespoon olive oil

½ teaspoon kosher salt

TO SERVE

2 tablespoons olive oil

4 naans or pitas, for serving

PREPARE THE BEANS: Combine the beans in a medium bowl with the olive oil and the salt and toss to coat. Transfer to the preheated grill basket and cook, shaking the pan occasionally, until the beans have bits of char marks but are still tender; 2 to 3 minutes. Return to the bowl and add the chimichurri. Toss to combine.

TO SERVE: Brush the flatbread with the olive oil and place the bread on the grill. Cook until the bread is warm and has a few grill marks. Flip and repeat on the other side, 30 to 60 seconds per side.

Divide the whipped ricotta among bowls and smooth the top. Spoon the beans over the cheese, drizzling any oil that might remain in the bowl. Cut the bread into wedges and tuck into the bowl before serving.

Notes

I typically work with and prefer a slightly drier ricotta or basket ricotta, which is easily separated from the excess liquid. However, some store brands have a texture more akin to cottage cheese which will make the whipped ricotta too wet. If the ricotta seems overly moist, place the ricotta in a cheesecloth-lined strainer resting over a bowl and refrigerate overnight.

Vegan Riff: While you could easily swap the cheese for a nut puree, my favorite way to make this meal vegan is with a vegetable puree or mash made from zucchini, eggplant (like baba ghanoush), peas, sweet potato, or carrots. Or, make a grain cream such as the millet cream on page 109.

Greens and Beans Gratin

Serves 4

A special place in my heart is devoted to vegetables cooked in heavy cream, thanks in part to hours spent poring over Nigel Slater's cookbooks. His treatment of vegetables greatly inspired me to embrace a level of richness not often associated with vegetarian cooking. Here, that richness takes on the classic greens-and-beans combination.

When I was growing up, my mom would eat fresh baby lima beans with butter, and as such, I've always thought this is how all lima beans should be eaten, covered in butter. While lima beans are obviously delicious in a range of meals, this is my nod to lima beans smothered in something rich and delicious.

RYE BREADCRUMBS

2 slices of rye bread, torn into pieces

2 tablespoons olive oil

½ teaspoon kosher salt

½ teaspoon ground black pepper

GRATIN

2 large leeks, trimmed, halved lengthwise, and cut into half-moons

3 tablespoons olive oil (45 ml), plus more for serving

1 teaspoon kosher salt

1 bunch kale, stems removed and leaves shredded

1 cup (240 ml) vegetable broth or water

2 cups (380 g) cooked and drained large lima beans

⅔ cup (160 ml) heavy cream

2 tablespoons minced preserved lemon

1 teaspoon kosher salt

MAKE THE BREADCRUMBS: Place the bread in a food processor, drizzle with olive oil, and add the salt and pepper. Pulse until coarse breadcrumbs form. Set aside.

MAKE THE GRATIN: Put the leeks in a bowl and cover with cool water. Swish the leeks around to remove any dirt, then let rest for a minute to settle any dirt. Use a slotted spoon to remove the leeks from the water, pat dry, and set aside.

Heat the olive oil in a large oven-safe skillet over medium heat. Add the leeks and salt. Cook for 15 to 20 minutes, until quite tender.

Preheat the oven to 425°F (220°C).

Add the kale and vegetable broth to the leeks and cook until wilted, about 8 minutes. Stir in the beans, heavy cream, preserved lemon, and salt.

Top the gratin with the breadcrumbs and bake for 25 minutes, or until the breadcrumbs are golden and the cream mixture is bubbling. Serve while still hot.

Notes

Kale is easily swapped out for chard or spinach. Beyond greens, small pieces of cauliflower, broccoli, or sweet corn are nice in this dish.

Vegan Riff: To replace the heavy cream, warm 1 cup (240 ml) of soy milk with 4 teaspoons cornstarch and 1 tablespoon nutritional yeast in a small saucepan over low heat. While the soy milk heats, the cornstarch will thicken it, and the nutritional yeast will add rich flavor.

Make Ahead: I find that upon reheating, the texture of the beans isn't quite the same. If you plan to make this ahead, I recommend assembling the gratin up until the addition of the breadcrumbs. Refrigerate, up to a day, then top with the breadcrumbs and bake when ready.

Beans in Tomato-Miso Broth

Serves 4

Around the time I was really into learning about handmade pasta, my son's favorite meal was tomato soup with leftover pasta. I had decided I wanted a grown-up version and landed on cappelletti with a luscious tomato broth. I made these beans one day when I didn't feel like making fresh pasta but needed to use up the broth, and as the story goes, the rest is history.

While it may be bit unconventional, I like to spoon the beans and broth over stale bread, softening it and letting it become part of the broth. Alternatively, if you prefer your bread crisp, toast the bread and dip into the broth, make a cheese toastie (page 218), or serve with fresh bread and butter on the side.

TOMATO BROTH

3 tablespoons (45 ml) olive oil

1 pound (450 g) ripe tomatoes, cut into wedges

¼ cup (60 g) tomato paste

1 tablespoon cane sugar

8 cups (1.9 L) water

4 garlic cloves

1 bay leaf

4 teaspoons kosher salt, plus more to taste

2 tablespoons white miso

2 teaspoons ground black pepper

FOR SERVING

3 cups (560 g) cooked and drained corona or other large beans (see page 123)

4 slices slightly stale bread

Ground black pepper, for serving

MAKE THE BROTH: Heat the olive oil in a medium saucepan over medium-high heat. When the oil begins to shimmer, place the tomatoes cut side down in the saucepan. Sear, turning once or twice, until the tomatoes begin to soften and exude some of their juice, about 2 minutes. Stir in the tomato paste and sugar and continue to cook until you notice some caramelization happening at the bottom of the pan. Turn the heat to low, scrape the bottom of the pan, and add the water, garlic, bay leaf, and salt. Bring to a boil, decrease to a simmer, and use a potato masher to mash the tomatoes into pieces. Simmer for 20 to 30 minutes, until the broth reduces slightly and develops a rounded tomato taste. Remove from the stove and stir in the miso and black pepper.

Pass the broth through a strainer, scraping the inside with a spatula instead of pressing the mixture through—this will prevent the tomato pieces from pushing through. Return the broth to the stove, taste, and adjust the salt and pepper as desired.

TO ASSEMBLE: Once the broth is to your liking, add the beans and simmer for 5 minutes.

Put a bread slice in the bottom of four bowls and top with a few ladles of the broth and beans. Finish with black pepper, as desired.

Notes

As with most broths, the overall flavor is delicate; it's there but can easily be upstaged by something with a lot of flavor. It's rare that I'd tell you a recipe needs home-cooked beans, but this is one of those recipes. The flavor of a well-seasoned bean adds so much to the dish and doesn't outshine the tomato flavor.

If you like a bit of heat in your meals, try adding a chile or two to the broth while it simmers or use a ground chile powder in place of the black pepper.

Make Ahead: The broth will keep up to a week in the refrigerator or in the freezer for up to 6 months. The beans in broth will keep for 5 to 6 days.

Romesco Mayocoba Beans over Polenta

Serves 4

Romesco, a sauce with origins in the Catalonia region of Spain, has a base of tomatoes and charred peppers rounded out with nuts and vinegar. Here, the richness of the romesco makes the large mayocoba beans a star served upon a creamy bed of polenta.

ROMESCO

¼ cup (30 g) raw slivered almonds

¼ cup (35 g) raw hazelnut pieces

5 tablespoons (75 ml) olive oil

2 garlic cloves, smashed

3 tablespoons (45 g) tomato paste

1 large roasted red pepper

2 tablespoons apple cider vinegar

1 teaspoon smoked paprika

1 teaspoon kosher salt

½ teaspoon cayenne pepper

POLENTA

4 cups (960 ml) vegetable broth

1 cup (140 g) uncooked polenta

¼ cup (56 g) unsalted butter

2 ounces (60 g) chèvre (soft goat cheese)

Kosher salt, to taste

BEANS

4 cups (720 g) mayocoba (or cannellini) beans, cooked and drained

¼ cup (60 ml) vegetable broth, plus more as needed

Minced fresh flat-leaf parsley, for serving

Preheat the oven to 300°F (150°C).

MAKE THE ROMESCO: Place the almonds and hazelnuts on a sheet pan. Roast until the nuts are fragrant and golden, 12 to 14 minutes.

While the nuts are roasting, heat 1 tablespoon of the oil in a small skillet over medium-low heat. Add the garlic cloves and let cook until just golden, 1 to 2 minutes. Add the tomato paste, cooking for another minute or so more, until the garlic is a deep golden brown and the tomato paste is fragrant. Remove from the heat.

Grind the nuts in a food processor or crush with a mortar and pestle. Transfer to a bowl. Repeat the process with the garlic mixture, including the olive oil used for cooking and roasted red pepper, grinding or crushing until mostly smooth. Place in the bowl along with the vinegar, smoked paprika, salt, cayenne, and remaining ¼ cup (60 ml) olive oil. Stir until well combined, taste, adjust salt level, and set aside.

MAKE THE POLENTA: Bring the vegetable broth to a boil in a medium saucepan, decrease the heat to a simmer, and whisk in the polenta. Return to a boil, decrease the heat to a low simmer, and cook for about 30 minutes, stirring occasionally. Keep the heat low—the long cook time is to help round out the corn flavor and make a creamy polenta. Once the polenta reaches your preferred texture, stir in butter and goat cheese. Taste and add salt as desired.

PREPARE THE BEANS: Combine the beans, ¼ cup (60 ml) of the vegetable broth, and the romesco in a medium saucepan or skillet. Heat over medium-low heat until the beans and romesco are hot, adding more broth as needed to coat the beans with the sauce.

Divide the polenta among four bowls and top with the romesco bean mixture. Finish with a flourish of parsley before serving.

Notes

The charm of the romesco is in the texture, thanks to finely chopped nuts, pieces of roasted red pepper, and an abundance of olive oil. This is especially important when the soft beans are served on a soft polenta—it needs a bit of texture to balance. As such, I'd urge you to not blitz everything together into a smooth sauce.

Make Ahead: The romesco sauce, the beans tossed in romesco, and the polenta will all last for a few days in the refrigerator. To reheat the beans or polenta, place in a pan and add a splash of liquid to loosen while warming.

Charred Zucchini Bean Dip

Makes 1½ cups (360 ml)

There are some lessons I never learn, even after years of feeling like I should. One of the most notable examples? Planting more than two zucchini plants each summer. I know I shouldn't, but I panic, worried they won't grow, and I'll end up with none! Alas, I'm left to cook my way through the surplus. This dish is inspired by *mutabal kousa*, a Middle Eastern dip with charred zucchini and a tahini yogurt. Here, the beans act a bit like the yogurt would, adding a layer of creaminess to the pureed squash.

---

1 pound (450 g) zucchini (1 medium or 2 small), trimmed and halved lengthwise

3 tablespoons (45 ml) olive oil, divided, plus more for serving

3 garlic cloves

1 cup (180 g) cooked and drained navy or cannellini beans

3 tablespoons (48 g) tahini

2 tablespoons minced preserved lemon

¾ teaspoon kosher salt

¼ teaspoon ground black pepper, plus more for serving

Flatbread, warmed, for serving

Preheat a grill or oven broiler to high. Toss the zucchini with 1 tablespoon of the olive oil to coat. Place on the grill or on a baking sheet under the broiler and cook until the zucchini is very soft and mostly charred all over, 3 to 5 minutes. Let cool slightly.

Heat the remaining 2 tablespoons olive oil in a small skillet over medium heat. Smash the garlic with the side of a knife blade, discarding the skins, and add to the skillet. Cook until golden, turning occasionally, 2 to 3 minutes.

Combine the zucchini, garlic with the cooking oil, beans, tahini, preserved lemon, salt, and black pepper in a blender and puree until smooth. Taste and adjust the flavors as desired.

To serve, transfer the dip to a small bowl and top with a drizzle of olive oil and some black pepper. This is best eaten standing at the counter with warmed flatbread or fresh bread.

Notes

Take inspiration from baba ghanoush and use charred eggplant in place of the zucchini.

Alternatively, grill or broil carrots or winter squash and use in place of the zucchini.

Make Ahead: The dip will keep in the refrigerator for a few days.

Harissa Baked Bean Toast with Salad

Serves 4

Given my love of beans now, it might seem a bit surprising to know that I avoided beans as a child, especially baked beans. I didn't enjoy the texture of the beans, and the idea of a slightly sweet bean was off-putting. These days, during the cooler months, I make a rendition of these beans around once a week. The rich sauce, with the addition of harissa, is the perfect balance of savory and heat, which is all I really want for a hearty meal.

Toast is just the beginning of how to eat these beans. Try them on top of grits (see page 85), millet cream (see page 109), or as the start of a grain bowl, preferably with some nicely charred vegetables.

BEANS

3 tablespoons (45 ml) olive oil

7 to 8 garlic cloves, minced

6 tablespoons (90 g) tomato paste

3 cups (540 g) cooked and drained yellow-eye or navy beans

2 cups (480 ml) vegetable broth

¼ cup (48 g) muscovado sugar or dark brown sugar

¼ cup (60 ml) apple cider vinegar

¼ cup (60 g) harissa (see page 53)

2 teaspoons vegan Worcestershire sauce

FETA DRESSING

¼ cup (28 g) crumbled feta

2 tablespoons mayonnaise

2 tablespoons plain whole-milk yogurt

2 tablespoons whole milk

1 small garlic clove, minced

1 tablespoon minced fresh dill

¼ teaspoon kosher salt

TOAST

1 head of butter lettuce, torn into pieces

3 to 4 tablespoons olive oil

4 thick slices bread

Preheat the oven to 350°F (180°C).

MAKE THE BEANS: Heat the oil in a dutch oven over medium heat. Add the garlic and cook for a minute, until fragrant. Stir in the tomato paste and cook for another minute. Add the beans, broth, sugar, vinegar, harissa, and Worcestershire sauce. Bring to a boil, cover, and transfer the beans to the oven.

Bake the beans for about 45 minutes, then uncover and cook for another 15 to 20 minutes. The sauce should be thickened.

MAKE THE DRESSING: While the beans cook, crumble the feta into a small bowl and add the mayonnaise, yogurt, milk, and garlic. Stir to combine, mashing any large pieces of feta, then stir in the dill and salt.

ASSEMBLE THE TOASTS: Put the lettuce in a medium bowl and toss with the dressing.

Heat the olive oil in a medium skillet over medium heat. Add the bread slices and toast until golden on both sides. Place on plates and top with a couple scoops of the baked beans and divide the salad on top.

Notes

I use vegan Worcestershire sauce, but feel free to use standard if that's what you have on hand.

Vegan Riff: Instead of a tangy feta dressing, make an herby, creamy dressing using your favorite plain nondairy yogurt and vegan mayonnaise. Add more fresh dill or any other tender herbs (parsley, chives, basil) you might have around.

Make Ahead: Both the beans and dressing will keep for a few days in the refrigerator. Reheat the beans on the stovetop with a splash of vegetable broth.

White Bean Pot Pie with Biscuits

Serves 4

As a child, I spent a lot of time with my grandparents, and occasionally my grandmother would buy frozen pot pies for our lunches together. They weren't anything special, but I remember clear as day standing in the kitchen, the smell of pot pie wafting throughout.

As nostalgic as it is, over the years I've become less of a pie person and more of a biscuit person. A creamy sauce and flaky biscuit together are a winning combination. A fun bonus, if you halve this recipe, it fits perfectly in a loaf pan—something I'll occasionally do for a weeknight dinner for two.

BISCUITS

½ cup (70 g) all-purpose flour

½ cup (70 g) rye flour (or use more all-purpose flour)

1 tablespoon baking powder

½ teaspoon kosher salt

¼ cup (56 g) cold unsalted butter, cubed

½ cup (120 ml) whole milk

POT PIE FILLING

¼ cup (60 ml) olive oil

2 large yellow onions, diced

2 to 3 Yukon gold potatoes, cut into ¼-inch (6 mm) cubes

2 to 3 medium carrots, cut into ¼-inch (6 mm) cubes

8 garlic cloves, minced

4 cups (960 ml) vegetable broth

2 cups (270 g) fresh or frozen green peas

2 cups (360 g) cooked and drained alubia blanca or navy beans

⅔ cup (160 ml) heavy cream, plus extra for biscuits

2 tablespoons nutritional yeast

1 heaping tablespoon mushroom powder

2 teaspoons dried sage

2 teaspoons dried thyme

FOR SERVING

Chopped flat-leaf parsley

Maldon salt

MAKE THE BISCUITS: Combine the flours, baking powder, and salt in a medium bowl. Using your fingers, rub the butter into the flour, leaving thin flakes of butter throughout. Add the milk and use a spoon to stir until the dough mostly comes together.

Turn the dough out onto a lightly floured surface and press into a rough rectangle. Complete an envelope fold (folding onto itself in thirds), then press the dough again to a thin rectangle and repeat the envelope fold. Press the dough again to create a rectangle roughly the size of your pan. Cut into four square biscuits, place on a plate, then set aside in the freezer.

Preheat the oven to 400°F (200°C).

PREPARE THE FILLING: Heat the olive oil in a medium skillet or braiser over medium heat. Add the diced onion. Cook the onions for 8 to 10 minutes, until they start to soften. Add the cubed potatoes and carrots. Continue to cook for another 10 minutes, until the onion is quite tender and the potatoes are starting to soften. Add the garlic and cook for another minute or so, until the garlic is fragrant. Add the vegetable broth, peas, beans, heavy cream, nutritional yeast, mushroom powder, sage, and thyme. Bring to a rapid simmer and cook for 6 to 8 minutes to thicken the sauce to a thick cream consistency.

Transfer the filling to a 9-inch (23 cm) square pan or similar-sized baking dish. Layer the biscuits on top and brush with a bit of heavy cream.

Bake for 18 to 20 minutes, until the bean mixture has thickened and the biscuits are baked and golden.

Top with parsley and maldon salt before serving.

Notes

Make Ahead: This recipe can be made ahead of time for a future meal. Prepare the filling, let cool, then freeze before the final bake.

You can bake the pot pie straight from the freezer, with 10 to 15 minutes added to the baking time.

Scallion Miso Beans

Serves 4

This recipe set me on a new path with my cooking journey. When I first made this meal, I thought it was delicious and shared it to my site without thinking that other people would be so excited to eat such a simple bowl of beans. I was quite wrong, and it remains one of the more popular recipes on my site. It's comforting, quick, and serves as a reminder to me that people love good bean cooking just as much as I do.

One note, I have made this dish with all kinds of beans but always end up back with the alubia blanca bean. I like the just-there texture and mouthfeel of the small, tender bean. However, if you want to switch it up and make a statement, make it with a large bean such as corona or cannellini.

3 tablespoons (42 g) unsalted butter
8 scallions, trimmed and thinly sliced
4 cups (960 ml) cooked alubia blanca or navy beans with their broth
Vegetable broth, bean broth, or water (as needed)
2 tablespoons white miso
2 teaspoons lemon zest, or 1 heaping tablespoon minced preserved lemon
Freshly cracked black pepper
4 bread slices, for serving

Melt the butter in a medium skillet over medium heat. Stir in the scallions and cook until tender, 4 to 5 minutes. Add the beans along with their broth. If the broth doesn't cover the beans, add enough extra broth, vegetable broth, or water to reach just to the top of the beans.

Bring to a boil, reduce to a rapid simmer, and cook until the broth has reduced and thickened a bit, 2 to 3 minutes. It will still look a bit brothy, but the beans should be heated through.

Remove the skillet from the heat and stir in the miso and lemon zest or preserved lemon. Taste and adjust as needed. Spoon into bowls and add a generous amount of black pepper. Tuck in the slices of bread and serve.

Notes

If you are using canned beans, I recommend draining and starting with a base of 1½ cups (360 ml) vegetable broth or water with a vegetable bouillon cube. You need a flavorful bean and broth to get the flavor party started here.

Given I make this recipe nearly every week, I've made many variations—some good and some not so good. A few of my favorites include stirring pureed winter squash into the bean broth, to make it just a touch creamier, adding a chile paste to the mix for a bit of heat, or stirring in wilted greens for extra goodness.

Barley Navy Bean Soup

Serves 3 to 4

On occasion I make a meal that tastes how I remember something from my youth tasting. This delicious soup gives me that familiar feeling of eating a hot, slightly umami-based soup with a golden broth and chewy barley.

In terms of the barley, there's a charm in using the pearled grains as they tend to meld into the soup and make it feel just a bit heartier. However, you could use whole-grain barley to retain nutrients. Whole-grain barley will add another 20 minutes or so to the cook time and require a bit more broth.

SOUP

3 tablespoons (36 g) olive oil

1 large yellow onion, finely diced

1 teaspoon kosher salt

1 to 2 celery stalks, diced

1 large carrot, diced

2 garlic cloves, minced

4 to 5 cups (960 ml to 1.2 L) vegetable broth

½ cup (95 g) uncooked pearled barley, toasted

1 tablespoon nutritional yeast

2 teaspoons dried thyme

1 bay leaf

¾ cup (180 g) cooked and drained navy beans

1 tablespoon white miso

¼ cup packed (12 g) fresh flat-leaf parsley, minced

¼ cup packed (12 g) fresh dill, minced

Zest from 1 lemon

¼ teaspoon MSG

FOR SERVING

Olive oil

Freshly cracked black pepper

MAKE THE SOUP: Heat the oil in a medium saucepan or dutch oven over medium heat. Add the onion and salt and cook for 10 to 12 minutes, until the onion is translucent. Stir in the diced celery and carrot; continue to cook for another 10 minutes or so, until the onion is quite tender and the carrots are soft. Add the garlic and cook for another minute or so, until the garlic is fragrant.

Add 4 cups (960 ml) of the broth, the barley, nutritional yeast, thyme, and bay leaf. Bring to a boil, decrease the heat to a simmer, and cook for 20 minutes. Add the beans and continue to cook for another 10 to 15 minutes, until the barley is tender, adding more broth if needed.

Remove the soup from the heat and scoop a bit of broth into a ladle. Add the miso to the ladle and mix together to dissolve the miso. Return the broth to the saucepan and add the parsley, dill, lemon zest, and MSG. Stir well, taste, and adjust flavors as desired.

TO SERVE: Ladle the soup into bowls and drizzle with olive oil and black pepper before serving.

Notes

If you happen to have any Parmesan rinds in your freezer, now is the time to use them. I'll occasionally omit the nutritional yeast and let the rinds simmer in the broth.

Make Ahead: The soup will store for a few days in the refrigerator; for longer storage, the soup can be stashed in the freezer. The barley is a sponge, so be prepared to add more broth when reheating, whether on the stovetop or in the microwave.

CHICKPEAS

Chickpeas are a fascinating little legume to me, having found their way into many uses outside of just a standard cooked bean. Whole and split chickpeas are standard in Middle Eastern and Indian cuisines served whole, pureed into dips and purees (hello, hummus), crisped into snacks, and used as the basis for fermented products, such as miso and tempeh.

Chickpea flour (*besan*) is used to create a myriad of dishes such as *panisse* (chickpea fritters from France), *farinata* (an Italian pancake), *besan chilla* (an Indian pancake), *pakora* (crispy vegetable fritters from India), and shan tofu (page 152).

CHICKPEAS, A TALE OF TWO VARIETIES

Chickpeas are divided into two categories: **desi** and **Kabuli**. The desi chickpea is smaller, darker, and has a tougher seed coat. This chickpea is most often used in India as the basis for **split chickpeas** (*chana dal*) and besan flour. There is also a variety in Italy called **black ceci** that is an heirloom desi variety, in a deep black color.

The Kabuli chickpea, a creamy, plump, and lighter legume, is used predominantly whole in Middle Eastern cuisine and can often be seen on menus across the United States. These chickpeas now grow throughout the United States and Canada and are often labeled as simply chickpea or garbanzo (the Spanish word for chickpea). Flour labeled "chickpea flour" is typically made using this variety and occasionally labeled as garbanzo flour.

AQUAFABA

Through the magic of science, we've learned that the liquid chickpeas are cooked in has a similar chemical composition, specifically the albumin and globulin proteins, to that of egg whites. This is particularly important because this liquid, called aquafaba, can be whipped into a mixture that forms stiff peaks, has stability with added cream of tartar, and provides lift to textures, just like egg whites do.

While all beans, whether cooked or canned at home, produce this magic liquid, canned chickpeas seem to have the correct protein molecules and the right concentrations of protein to make this happen best. Liquid from home-cooked chickpeas can also produce good results but requires cooking the liquid down so that it's more highly concentrated, more akin to what you would find in commercially canned chickpeas. The viscosity of the liquid should be similar to egg whites.

So if you find yourself wanting a decent egg-white substitute, grab your hand mixer and some chickpea liquid, a little pinch of cream of tartar, and whip away.

COOKING CHICKPEAS

CHICKPEAS	UNCOOKED QUANTITY	SOAKING RECIPE	WATER	COOKING TIME	COOKED YIELD
Split	1 cup (200 g)	3 cups (720 ml) cool water 2 tsp kosher salt 8 hours	Cover with 2 inches (5 cm)	20-30 minutes	2 cups (420 g)
Whole	1 cup (200 g)	4 cups (960 ml) cool water 2 tsp kosher salt 12 hours	Cover with 2 inches (5 cm)	30-40 minutes	2 cups (420 g)

To cook: Add any aromatics plus water and salt according to the chart and notes. Bring the beans to a boil and cook for 15 minutes, then reduce the heat so it's as low as it can go while still causing a bit of movement in the water. Simmer, with the lid off, until the beans are tender, using the times on the chart as a reference.

If you find that the liquid falls below the legumes, add hot water. Adding cool water will disrupt the cooking.

Once you suspect your chickpeas might be close to done, start tasting. If they are still firm, keep cooking, tasting every few minutes. Adequately cooked beans should be soft with no graininess or firmness. If the goal is hummus or dal, it's okay to continue to cook until they fall apart.

Notes: If using soaking liquid for cooking, decrease salt to ½ teaspoon kosher salt.

If soaking is skipped, double the amount of water and start with 2 teaspoons kosher salt. Cooking times will double.

For most chickpeas, I add ½ large onion, a few cloves of garlic, a few sprigs of woody herbs, one bay leaf, and a drizzle of olive oil for every 1 cup (200 g) of dried chickpeas I'm cooking. I save any tender herbs, chile pastes, or acidic ingredients like citrus, tomato, or vinegar for the end so they don't lose their luster during a long cook or potentially toughen the chickpeas.

Both whole and split chickpeas have a range of doneness where they can hold their shape or fall apart; time accordingly.

CHICKPEA RECIPES

Chana Masala

Serves 4
generously

Indian cuisine and cookbooks have had a defining impact on my cooking style over the years. This is, in part, because when I was learning to cook, I leaned on fare that was already heavily vegetarian.

As I became a better cook, I also began to appreciate and study the myriad of techniques used to build the flavors prevalent in so many of those recipes. That is why the book has a small section on spice seeds (page 212). Alas, no other recipe brings me comfort like chana masala, and this version is the one I make myself when I want a comforting bowl of chickpeas.

¼ cup (60 ml) avocado oil

2 cinnamon sticks

4 whole cloves

2 black cardamom pods

1 bay leaf

2 large yellow onions, diced

2 teaspoons kosher salt, divided plus more as needed

6 garlic cloves, peeled

2-inch (5 cm) piece fresh ginger, peeled

1 (28-ounce / 794 g) can crushed tomatoes

4 teaspoons garam masala

2 teaspoons toasted and ground cumin

2 teaspoons toasted and ground coriander

2 teaspoons ground chile

3 cups (460 g) cooked and drained chickpeas

2 cups (480 ml) water

2 teaspoons dried fenugreek leaves, crushed

2 tablespoons lemon juice

Cooked long-grain rice, for serving (see page 74)

Heat the oil in a large dutch oven or skillet over medium heat. Add the cinnamon, cloves, cardamom, and bay leaf. Let cook for a minute or so, until the spices are warm and fragrant.

Stir in the diced onion along with 1 teaspoon of the salt. Cook for 16 to 18 minutes, until the onions are golden and quite soft. If the onions start to brown too quickly, decrease the heat slightly as needed.

While the onions are cooking, use a mortar and pestle to pound the garlic, ginger, and the remaining 1 teaspoon salt into a paste. When the onions are done, add the garlic paste to the skillet and cook for 1 to 2 minutes, until fragrant. Stir in the crushed tomatoes, garam masala, cumin, coriander, and chile. Increase the heat to medium or medium-high and cook until the tomatoes have thickened into a thick paste.

Remove the whole spices, then add the chickpeas and water. Bring to a boil, decrease the heat to a simmer, and cook until the sauce thickens to your desired consistency, about 20 minutes. Remove from the heat and stir in the crushed fenugreek leaves and lemon juice. Taste and add more salt as needed.

To serve, divide the rice between four bowls and top with the chana masala.

Notes

Not sure where to find fenugreek leaves? Online is the easiest, but if you live in a larger area, chances are you have an Indian grocery store nearby (mine is actually the closest grocery store I have and the reason I don't try to make paneer at home!).

Seasonal Variations: While I don't stray far from the classic elements of this dish, the same cannot be said for the vegetables I add or eat with it. During the cooler months, I love nestling in wedges of roasted winter squash or adding wilted greens to the mix. In summer, I double up on the beans and will often add steamed green beans to the side.

Pan-Fried Shan (Chickpea) Tofu with Chile-Tomatoes

Serves 4

Having a wide breadth of protein options as a vegetarian is a game changer because it allows for varying flavors and textures throughout the week. Shan tofu is a great item to add to your rotation. This tofu, also known as chickpea tofu, is a Burmese dish that comes from the Shan State in Myanmar and that I was first introduced to by Burma Superstar, a restaurant in San Francisco (which is the recipe I swear by).

Whereas soybean tofu goes through a coagulation stage, this chickpea version is made simply by cooking chickpea flour and water together. The texture of this tofu is more akin to polenta but crisps up nicely and can handle big flavors as companions. Beyond chickpea flour, black bean flour and lentil flour also work for this type of application.

SHAN TOFU

1 teaspoon avocado oil, plus more for frying

1 cup (140 g) finely ground chickpea flour

3 cups (720 ml) water at room temperature, divided

1 tablespoon nutritional yeast

1 teaspoon garlic powder

1 teaspoon ground turmeric

1 teaspoon kosher salt

GARLIC-CHILE OIL

1 garlic clove, minced

2 teaspoons dried red pepper flakes

1 teaspoon sweet paprika

¼ cup (60 ml) avocado oil

½ teaspoon kosher salt

MAKE THE TOFU: Grease an 8-inch (20 cm) square pan with the avocado oil and line with parchment paper, leaving enough hanging over the sides to cover the top of the tofu. Set aside.

Put the chickpea flour in a medium saucepan and whisk in 1 cup (240 ml) of the water. Let rest for 10 minutes to rehydrate the flour. Whisk in the remaining 2 cups (480 ml) water, nutritional yeast, garlic powder, turmeric, and salt until smooth. Turn the heat to medium and continue to whisk or stir so that the mixture does not stick to the bottom for 6 to 7 minutes, until the mixture has thickened to about the consistency of a thick (non-Greek) yogurt. Immediately pour and scrape the tofu into the prepared pan and smooth over the top. The tofu will set quickly once off the heat, so it's best to work fast. Fold the parchment paper over the top and smooth over the top as well.

Let the tofu cool at room temperature for 15 minutes, then transfer it to the refrigerator for another 45 minutes. The tofu should be firm and cool.

MAKE THE CHILE OIL: While the tofu is resting, combine the garlic, pepper flakes, and paprika in a small heat-safe bowl. Heat the oil in a small skillet or saucepan until it begins to shimmer and is quite hot. Immediately pour it over the chile mixture. Stir to combine and as it cools, add the salt.

CONTINUES

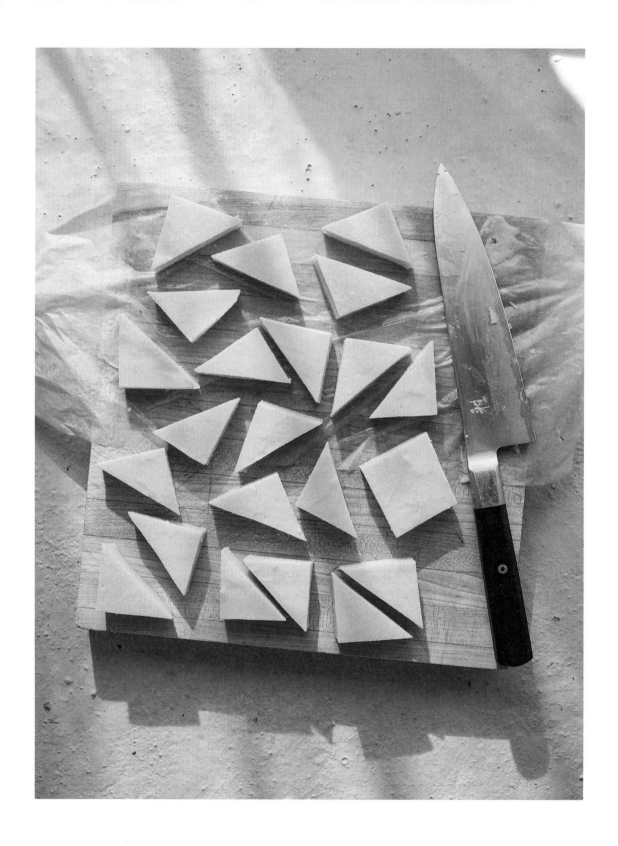

Pan-Fried Shan (Chickpea) Tofu with Chile-Tomatoes

CONTINUED

FOR SERVING

3 cups (450 g) cherry tomatoes

¼ cup packed (16 g) fresh basil, julienned

FRY THE TOFU: Apply a thin coat of avocado oil to a medium pan and turn heat to medium. Cut the tofu into the desired shape. I like triangles for this recipe, cut from 2-inch (5 cm) squares. Transfer the tofu to the heated skillet and fry the two flat, broad sides until they are golden brown and crisp, a few minutes per side. The outer layer may stick if you try to turn the tofu too soon.

TO SERVE: Slice the cherry tomatoes in half and place in a medium bowl. Drizzle and toss with a few spoonfuls of the chile oil and half the basil.

Place the fried tofu on a medium serving plate and spoon on the tomatoes. Drizzle with extra oil, if desired, and finish with the remaining basil before serving.

Notes

A similar dish called *panisse*, from France, often includes oil in the batter, is deep fried, and uses a 2:1 ratio of water to chickpea flour, creating a slightly lighter inner texture. Panisse is often eaten as a snack, but I think this recipe shows there can be a bit of versatility in thickened and cooled chickpea flour as a large part of a meal (or snack)!

Seasonal Variations: During the cooler months, I like to char cabbage, broccoli, or cauliflower to pair with the chile oil. In the spring, I turn to roasted asparagus or fresh snap peas.

Make Ahead: Before frying, shan tofu will last for a few days in an airtight container in the refrigerator or a few months in the freezer. The chile oil can be stored in the refrigerator for up to a week.

Hummus Bowls with Buttered Turnips

Serves 4

I'm probably stating the obvious when I say I love a good bowl meal—a dish that has a few components that all come together to make something hearty. This particular bowl is inspired by one of my favorite Sacramento restaurants, Magpie, that often showcases seasonal vegetables in a hummus bowl with grains. The balance of vegetables with rice, hummus, and egg is easily filling and a combination I could eat for any meal. The black rice I buy is typically a medium-grain, but really any type of rice would work, including wild rice.

HUMMUS

2 cups (320 g) cooked and drained chickpeas (see page 149)
½ teaspoon baking soda
2 garlic cloves
4 to 5 tablespoons (60 to 75 ml) lemon juice
1½ teaspoons kosher salt
⅓ cup (86 g) cup tahini
¼ cup (60 ml) olive oil
Ice water

BUTTERED TURNIPS

1 pound (450 g) hakurei turnips
1 tablespoon avocado oil
6 tablespoons (84 g) unsalted butter
½ teaspoon kosher salt
3 sprigs thyme
1 teaspoon lemon zest

FOR FINISHING

Cooked black rice (see page 74)
4 eggs, soft-boiled or poached
4 slices toast

TO MAKE THE HUMMUS: Combine the chickpeas in a pot with the baking soda and enough water to cover. Bring to a boil, reduce to a rapid simmer, and cook for 15 minutes, stirring occasionally and using a slotted spoon to remove any skins that float to the top. Once the chickpeas are falling apart, drain.

While the chickpeas are cooking, use a Microplane to grate the garlic into a small bowl. Add 4 tablespoons of the lemon juice and salt. Let rest for at least 5 minutes.

Combine the chickpeas with the garlic mixture, tahini, and olive oil in a high-speed blender or food processor. Have a glass of ice water nearby and begin to run the machine. As the mixture comes together, add a couple tablespoons of ice water at a time. Puree, adding more water as needed, until the hummus is smooth and has a whipped consistency. Taste and add more lemon juice or salt, if desired.

COOK THE TURNIPS: Trim the turnips, leaving about an inch (2.5 cm) of the greens on top, then quarter them. Heat the avocado oil in a small skillet over medium-high heat. Place the turnips cut side down in the skillet and sear on each side until browned, 45 to 60 seconds.

Decrease the heat to medium-low and add the butter, salt, and thyme sprigs. As the butter melts, swirl the pan. Continue to cook, swirling the pan occasionally, until the turnips are just tender, 3 to 4 minutes. Remove from heat and add the lemon zest.

ASSEMBLE THE BOWLS: Spread hummus into four shallow bowls. Layer with black rice, turnips, and egg. Tuck in a slice of toast and drizzle any remaining butter left in the skillet over the bowl.

Notes

If you are starting from dried chickpeas, you can soak or cook the chickpeas with the baking soda (see page 149), skipping this second cooking. I prefer to keep a large batch of regular chickpeas on hand for use in salads and meals then re-cook a smaller amount to make hummus.

The classic butter-and-thyme mixture is lovely with many vegetables. Try using pan-seared cauliflower or broccoli, fava beans, asparagus, summer squash, or wedges of cabbage.

Vegan Riff: Omit the egg or swap it for a marinated tofu. Replace the butter with your favorite non-dairy butter product.

Chickpea Deli Sandwich

Serves 4

Living in California has afforded me the opportunity to always be on the go whether that's trips to the beach, hiking, camping, or skiing during the winter. I'm often combining that with food to either cook over a fire or retrieve from a cooler. Food eaten outside always tastes better than food eaten inside. This deli sandwich is definitely a favorite cooler lunch as it can be prepped ahead and assembled on-site.

Not a sandwich person? Forgo the sandwich and eat this straight from the jar with crackers or a flatbread, such as naan.

CHICKPEA DELI SALAD

2 cups (320 g) cooked and drained chickpeas (see page 149)

1 small red onion, minced

2 celery stalks, minced

1½ cups (120 g) mayonnaise (regular or vegan, see page 179)

½ cup (70 g) golden raisins

2 tablespoons sweet pickled relish

2 tablespoons rice vinegar

2 teaspoons stone-ground mustard

2 teaspoons kosher salt, plus more as needed

1 teaspoon ground black pepper, plus more as needed

FOR SERVING

8 slices of bread

4 large slices of tomato

Lettuce leaves

MAKE THE SALAD: Mash the chickpeas in a medium bowl with a potato masher, until all are in pieces of varying size.

Add the red onion, celery, mayonnaise, raisins, relish, vinegar, mustard, salt, and pepper and stir well. Cover and refrigerate for at least 20 minutes.

MAKE THE SANDWICHES: Taste and add more salt and or pepper, if needed. Toast the bread, if desired, and layer with the tomato and lettuce and a scoop or two of the salad.

Notes

The chickpea salad, stored in an airtight container in the refrigerator, is good for 2 to 3 days.

Kale Caesar Salad with Blackened Chickpeas

Serves 4

I made it my mission to make a Caesar dressing I loved but had nary an anchovy in sight. The key is truly the miso and not being shy about the amount of Parmesan cheese you use (it's just a pile of salty goodness). One heads up: traditional Parmesan cheese is not vegetarian; however, at least one cheese maker in the United States has a Parmesan-like cheese made from vegetarian rennet if you prefer to go this route. I find it's not as salty as traditional, and so I add a bit more miso to the mix.

CAESAR DRESSING

1 garlic clove, minced

2 teaspoons lemon juice

½ cup (120 g) mayonnaise, regular or vegan (see page 179)

¼ cup (8 g) grated Parmesan cheese

2 teaspoons white miso

1 teaspoon stone-ground mustard

1 teaspoon vegan Worcestershire sauce

½ teaspoon ground black pepper

¼ teaspoon kosher salt

BLACKENING SEASONING

1 tablespoon dark brown sugar

1 tablespoon smoked paprika

1 teaspoon kosher salt

1 teaspoon onion powder

½ teaspoon garlic powder

½ teaspoon medium-heat ground chile

¼ teaspoon ground allspice

¼ teaspoon ground cinnamon

¼ teaspoon dried oregano

¼ teaspoon dried thyme

Pinch of ground cloves

SALAD

1 cup (160 g) cooked chickpeas

1 tablespoon avocado oil

8 packed cups (510 g) shredded kale

½ teaspoon kosher salt

MAKE THE DRESSING: Combine the garlic and lemon juice in a small bowl and let sit for a couple of minutes to mellow out the garlic flavor. Add the mayonnaise, Parmesan, miso, mustard, Worcestershire sauce, pepper, and salt, stirring until the dressing is smooth. Taste, adjust any of the flavors as desired, and refrigerate until you are ready to use it.

MAKE THE SEASONING: Combine the brown sugar, smoked paprika, salt, onion powder, garlic powder, ground chile, allspice, cinnamon, oregano, thyme, and cloves in a small bowl and stir to combine. Set aside.

Preheat the oven to 425°F (220°C). Cover a baking sheet with parchment paper.

TO MAKE THE SALAD: Rinse and drain the chickpeas and use a tea towel to pat dry. Spread the chickpeas on the prepared sheet pan. Toss with the avocado oil, arrange in a single layer, and roast for 25 minutes. The chickpeas should be browning and nearly crisp. Remove the pan from the oven and toss with the seasoning. Return the chickpeas to the oven and continue to roast for another 4 to 5 minutes. The spices should be browning and the chickpeas mostly crisp. Remove from the oven and let cool completely.

Combine the kale and salt in a medium bowl. Massage the kale until the leaves soften a bit. Add the dressing. Scoot the chickpeas to one side of the pan and fold the exposed parchment over them, then use a rolling pin to crush them.

Toss three-quarters of the chickpeas in with the kale and sprinkle the remaining crushed chickpeas on top before serving.

Notes

When making crispy chickpeas, it is really easy to undercook them, which results in a slightly chewy legume and a sad salad. Before adding the spices, test the chickpeas to ensure they are almost done. The final cook with the spices is really to toast (and not burn) the spices.

I use vegan Worcestershire sauce, but feel free to use standard if that's what you have on hand.

LENTILS

In talking about legumes, I often treat lentils like the third forgotten child in a story. We have the beautiful beans! The multidimensional soybeans! Oh, and there are lentils. That is wholly unfair to these tiny seeds. Lentils often save the day in my meals because they are multifaceted in their uses, ready in under 30 minutes, and are showstoppers in their own way.

LENTIL VARIETIES

I almost always have each of the four main types of lentils stocked. Each one plays a role and opens the door to a different meal every night.

BROWN LENTILS

When it comes to the king of the grocery-store lentils here in the United States, brown lentils are it. If you're buying brown lentils in bags or in bulk bins, there's a high probability that it's the large Brewer variety. This variety cooks fairly quickly (in 20 to 30 minutes), can hold its shape or be quite tender, and has become the standard for a generic brown lentil. The flavor of the brown lentil tends to be mild and earthy, which helps it meld into various recipes.

There are heirloom varieties of brown lentils worth noting, including the small brown Spanish Pardina lentil and the medium light-brown Italian Puglia lentil.

GREEN LENTILS

Often confused with the brown lentils, green lentils are a variety of their own. These lentils often have a thicker seed coat, take longer to cook (30 to 40 minutes), and tend to have a slight peppery flavor. The most notable lentil from this category is the Laird, a large Canadian green lentil, but as with the brown lentils, green lentil varieties vary in size.

One distinction in this category includes the French lentil (*lentilles du Puy*), which is specifically grown in the Puy region of France, known for its volcanic soil. These lentils take on a more pronounced peppery flavor and are most notable for their small size and greenish-grey thick seed coat. Even though this variety is smaller in size, it can still take upward of 30 minutes to cook.

BLACK LENTILS

These lentils, often referred to as beluga lentils, may be small but they can have a rather strong presence in a meal. Black lentils have a medium-thick seed coat, which helps to keep their cook time to 20 to 30 minutes. They don't fall apart and easily retain a bit of texture. I reach for black lentils when I want a solid salad lentil but also love them in stews.

RED, ORANGE, AND YELLOW LENTILS

Red lentils are primarily sold without their seed coat (which could be brown, black, green, grey, or speckled) and are split into their two cotyledons (halves). Most notable is *masoor dal*, a lentil that reveals its orange-red inside when the brown seed coat is removed, and the Red Chief, a larger variety developed by the USDA to combat disease in red lentil crops.

I'd also be remiss if I didn't mention the *macachiados* lentil, which is a large, whole yellow lentil from Mexico that I think is just neat.

COOKING LENTILS

LENTIL TYPE	UNCOOKED QUANTITY	SOAK (OPTIONAL)	COOKING LIQUID	COOKING TIME, SOAKED	COOKING TIME, UNSOAKED	COOKED LENTIL YIELD
Black and Le Puy	1 cup (200 g)	3 cups (720 ml) cool water 2 tsp kosher salt 8 hours	Cover with 1 inch (2.5 cm) water 1 tsp kosher salt	10–15 minutes	25–35 minutes	3 cups / 540 g
Brown, firm	1 cup (180 g)	3 cups (720 ml) cool water 2 tsp kosher salt 8 hours	Cover with 1 inch (2.5 cm) water 1 tsp kosher salt	10–15 minutes	25–30 minutes	2¼ cups / 460 g
Brown, tender	1 cup (180 g)	3 cups (720 ml) cool water 2 tsp kosher salt 8 hours	3 cups (720 ml) water 1 tsp kosher salt	15–20 minutes	30–35 minutes	2½ cups / 440 g
Green	1 cup (170 g)	3 cups (720 ml) cool water 2 tsp kosher salt 8 hours	Cover with 1 inch (2.5 cm) water 1 tsp kosher salt	15–20 minutes	30–40 minutes	2 cups / 440 g
Split (red/orange/yellow)	1 cup (180 g)	None	2½ to 3½ cups (600–840 ml) water 1 tsp kosher salt	N/A	15–25 minutes	2–2½ cups / 450–540 g

To cook: Drain any soaking liquid, then place the lentils in a pot with any aromatics, plus fresh water and salt according to the chart. Bring the lentils to a boil, reduce to a simmer, cover, and cook until the lentils are tender, using the chart as a reference for time.

Notes: For most lentils, I add ½ large onion, a few cloves of garlic, a few sprigs of woody herbs, one bay leaf, and a drizzle of olive oil for every 1 cup (140–180 g) of dried lentils I'm cooking. I save any tender herbs, chile pastes, or acidic ingredients, like citrus, tomato, or vinegar, for the end so they don't lose their luster during a long cook or potentially toughen the lentils.

Given lentils' wide range of possible textures, assume less water / lower cook times for firmer lentils and more water / longer cook times for tender lentils that verge on falling apart.

Lentils are lower in lectins and as such do not require the initial 15-minute boil that beans do.

LENTIL RECIPES

Lentil Sloppy Joes with Spring Slaw

Makes 4 sandwiches

I believe the messier a sandwich is, the more the flavor is amplified. Like, if it's falling apart and there is sauce dripping everywhere, it must be good! That's how I feel with these sloppy joes, which are a staple in our meal rotation. They are great when I'm looking for something hearty for dinner and want to please the whole family.

The key to these sandwiches is a step I think many people miss when using lentils as a filling: crush the cooked lentils. By crushing, the texture changes a bit so that it doesn't feel like you're just eating lentils on a bun and instead feels like you're eating a well-put-together sandwich. It may feel insignificant, but I think it makes all the difference!

SPRING SLAW

1 large carrot, julienned

1 large raw golden beet, peeled and julienned

½ medium red onion, thinly sliced

2 tablespoons rice vinegar

1 teaspoon celery seeds

½ teaspoon kosher salt

LENTILS

1 cup (180 g) dried brown lentils

4 cups (960 ml) water

2 teaspoons kosher salt

½ medium yellow onion

MAKE THE SLAW: Combine the carrot, beet, and red onion in a small bowl. Add the vinegar, celery seeds, and salt. Massage the mixture together and set aside until you are ready to serve.

MAKE THE LENTILS: Combine the lentils with the water, salt, and onion in a medium saucepan. Bring to a boil, reduce to a simmer, cover, and cook until the lentils are quite tender, about 30 minutes. Remove from the heat, discard the onion, then use a potato masher to crush the lentils with the leftover liquid, until about half the lentils are in pieces.

CONTINUES

Lentil Sloppy Joes with Spring Slaw

CONTINUED

SLOPPY JOE SAUCE

2 tablespoons olive oil

½ medium yellow onion, minced

2 teaspoons kosher salt

4 garlic cloves, minced

¼ cup (60 g) tomato paste

½ cup lightly packed (100 g) dark brown sugar

1 (15-ounce / 425 g) can tomato sauce

2 tablespoons vegan Worcestershire sauce

1 tablespoon balsamic vinegar

1 tablespoon stone-ground mustard

1 tablespoon sweet paprika

1 teaspoon ground allspice

1 teaspoon ground black pepper

FOR SERVING

8 semi-thick slices of soft white sandwich bread, toasted

MAKE THE SAUCE: While the lentils are cooking, heat the oil in a medium skillet over medium heat. Add the onion and salt and cook until quite tender, 14 to 16 minutes. Stir in the garlic and tomato paste, cooking for a minute or two more until the garlic is fragrant. Add the brown sugar, tomato sauce, Worcestershire sauce, vinegar, stone-ground mustard, paprika, allspice, and black pepper. Turn off the heat.

Add the sauce to the cooked lentils. The mixture will seem a bit thin. Bring the mixture to a rapid simmer and cook until the sauce has thickened and the lentils soak up the flavor of the sauce, around 10 minutes, depending on how much liquid your lentils had left.

TO SERVE: Divide the lentil mixture and slaw between four slices of the toast, then top with the remaining pieces of toast and slice each sandwich in half.

Notes

Like all legumes, lentils can be a bit finicky when cooked in more acidic bases, especially when the lentils might be older. This is the reason

I don't cook the lentils in the sauce. By cooking separately, you ensure tender lentils every time.

I use vegan Worcestershire sauce, but feel free to use standard if that's what you have on hand.

Caramelized Kimchi Red Lentil Dip

Makes 3 cups (720 ml)

When it comes to making dips from legumes, lentils are usually my last choice. I find they often overpower the delicate flavors of herb-, allium-, or vegetable-based dips. However, I've wanted a red lentil dip in my back pocket since red lentils are the quickest cooking, which would make it a good back-pocket recipe. Enter kimchi, which has no problem dominating with flavor.

I prefer to serve this dip with crackers or toasted bread, but it also works nicely with fresh vegetables, such as carrots, broccoli, and celery.

½ cup (90 g) dried red lentils

1½ cups (360 ml) water

8 scallions, trimmed

6 tablespoons (90 ml) avocado oil, divided

2 cups packed (400 g) kimchi

3 tablespoons cane sugar

2 teaspoons kosher salt

1 tablespoon rice vinegar

½ cup (115 g) plain whole-milk yogurt

Combine the red lentils and water in a small saucepan. Cover, bring to a boil, then reduce to a simmer and cook until the lentils are starting to fall apart, 25 minutes or so. If the lentils still have water left after starting to fall apart, remove the lid, turn up the heat, and let the lentils cook until most of the water has cooked off.

While the lentils are cooking, preheat the broiler. Place the scallions on a sheet pan. Add 1 tablespoon of the oil and coat the scallions. Place under the broiler and let the scallions char until the greens are basically blackened and the whites are quite tender, 2 to 3 minutes. Crush and save some of the charred bits for topping, then run your knife through the rest before placing in a blender.

Heat a medium skillet over medium heat with the remaining 5 tablespoons avocado oil and add the kimchi, sugar, and salt. Cook, stirring occasionally, until the kimchi is quite tender and caramelized, 4 to 5 minutes. Remove from the heat and add to the blender. Return the skillet to the stove over medium heat and add the vinegar and stir to deglaze the pan. Add the vinegar bits to the blender along with the cooked lentils and yogurt.

Puree the dip until smooth, adding a splash of water or yogurt if the dip is too thick to puree. Transfer to a bowl and top with crushed charred scallions before serving.

Notes

This dip is really great if you have some older kimchi that's gone a bit soft or become too sour. The caramelization with the sugar balances the sour notes, and since we're blending it, the softness of the cabbage doesn't impact the dish. Also, note that kimchi is not traditionally vegetarian and you should use your preferred style.

Make Ahead: This dip will keep for a couple days in the refrigerator, which means you can easily make it ahead of time.

Lentil Croquettes with Za'atar and Labneh

Serves 4

I love a good fried snack that can easily double as a meal. These lentil croquettes are soft on the inside, crispy on the outside, and pair perfectly with the earthy za'atar and tangy *labneh*. I like to make a large batch of the croquettes and keep frozen for the days I don't want to think about dinner.

One note, stores carry za'atar, and they carry za'atar. Confusing: yes! Za'atar can refer to the dried herb, but it can also refer to the blended mix that features the herb. I think it's worth seeking out the herb to make the blend yourself. If you have a garden, za'atar is a beautiful herb to grow. However, don't miss this recipe if you can't find it! Swap in a mix of dried thyme, oregano, and marjoram.

CROQUETTES

½ cup (90 g) dried red lentils

1¼ cups (300 ml) water

2 garlic cloves, minced

3 tablespoons all-purpose or soft wheat flour

1 tablespoon nutritional yeast

¾ teaspoon kosher salt

2 large eggs, divided

Avocado or other neutral high-heat oil, for frying

1 cup (60 g) Japanese-style panko

½ teaspoon kosher salt

ZA'ATAR

3 tablespoons (3 g) dried za'atar

1 tablespoon (8 g) sumac

½ teaspoon kosher salt

1 tablespoon (8 g) white sesame seeds, toasted

MAKE THE CROQUETTES: Place the lentils and water in a small pot. Cover and cook over medium–low heat for 15 to 20 minutes, until the lentils begin to break down. Remove from the heat and let cool.

While the lentils are cooling, line an 8 by 4–inch (20 cm by 10 cm) loaf pan with parchment paper.

When the lentils are cool, add the garlic, flour, nutritional yeast, salt, and 1 egg. Stir to combine, mashing the lentils together as you mix. Transfer to the prepared pan and smooth the top. Place in the freezer and chill until mostly frozen, at least 3 to 4 hours.

MAKE THE ZA'ATAR: Using a mortar and pestle, crush the dried za'atar with the sumac and salt. Add the toasted sesame seeds and partially grind until some of the sesame seeds are in pieces. Set aside.

CONTINUES

Lentil Croquettes with Za'atar and Labneh

CONTINUED

FOR SERVING

¾ cup (180 g) labneh or Greek yogurt

Olive oil

COOK THE CROQUETTES: Heat 2 inches (5 cm) of avocado oil in a deep, heavy saucepan to 325°F (160°C). Have a medium bowl and the za'atar ready to use.

Remove the lentils from the freezer, lift out of the pan, and cut into eight 4-inch (10 cm) long bars. If needed, let the lentils sit at room temperature for a few minutes, cut, then return to the freezer until the oil is hot.

Whisk the remaining egg in a small bowl and combine the panko and salt in a separate bowl. Working with a few croquettes at a time, roll in the egg and then the panko. Place directly in the hot oil and fry until the panko is golden brown and crisp, 3 to 4 minutes.

Using a skimmer or slotted spoon, remove the croquettes from the oil, tapping off any excess oil, and place in a medium bowl. Sprinkle and toss with a bit of the za'atar, then repeat with remaining croquettes.

TO SERVE: Spread the labneh in a shallow bowl or platter and drizzle with olive oil. Arrange the croquettes on top and sprinkle with any remaining za'atar before serving.

Notes

I see a lot of recipes that attempt to make dough ready to fry by simply adding enough eggs or breadcrumbs to get it to hold together. While this can work in some scenarios, more often than not it leads to a dry and unappetizing texture.

I prefer to employ freezing when dealing with sticky or soft items to be deep-fried. Then it doesn't matter how sticky the dough is; the outsides begin to crisp while the insides thaw and cook. My recommendation: work in batches, storing the remaining croquettes in the freezer until ready to coat and fry.

Vegan Riff: Given these croquettes are fried from a frozen state, you can easily replace the egg with a mix of ¼ cup (60 ml) cool water and 1 tablespoon cornstarch for dredging. Then, use a nondairy yogurt, grain cream such as the millet cream on page 109, or nut cream (see page 112) for serving.

Make Ahead: The unbreaded croquettes can stay in the freezer for up to 6 months. I like to do the initial freeze, cut, and then return to a freezer-safe container for long storage. Then I can pull out the amount I'd like and fry as needed.

Potato Lentil Stew with Poached Eggs

Serves 4

Don't be fooled into thinking I don't eat lentils in a lot of soups and stews by the fact that this is the only stew in the lentil section. I'll often make the chili (page 49) with lentils, hearty bowls of dal with red lentils, and substitute black lentils in the pinto stew on page 126. There is a lentil for every soup or stew.

When I was developing this recipe, I knew I wanted to make a stew that enlisted the help of warming spices in a rustic way. Be sure to serve it with some good bread to soak up all the last bits of flavor.

¼ cup (60 ml) olive oil, plus more for serving

1 large onion, diced

2 celery stalks, diced

2 teaspoons kosher salt

4 garlic cloves, minced

8 ounces (230 g) gold potatoes, such as Yukon gold, cut into ½-inch (1.3 cm) cubes

1 tablespoon smoked paprika, plus more for serving

2 teaspoons ground cinnamon

½ teaspoon ground allspice

¼ teaspoon ground cloves

½ cup (90 g) green or brown lentils

6 to 7 cups (1.4 L to 1.6 L) vegetable broth

1 (15-ounce / 425 g) can crushed tomatoes

2 tablespoons lemon juice

2 teaspoons lemon zest

4 eggs, poached or fried

Olive oil, for finishing

Heat a medium braiser or saucepan over medium heat with the olive oil. Add the onion, celery, and salt. Cook, occasionally stirring, until quite tender, about 15 minutes. Stir in the garlic and potatoes and cook for a minute more.

Stir in the spices and let cook for a minute more. Add the lentils and vegetable broth. Bring to a boil, decrease the heat to a simmer, and cook until the lentils are tender, around 25 minutes for brown lentils or 35 minutes for green lentils. Stir in the crushed tomatoes and continue to simmer for another 10 minutes, until the potatoes are cooked and the flavors have had time to mingle.

Turn off the heat and stir in the lemon juice and zest. Add salt to taste and divide between four bowls. Top each bowl with an egg. Drizzle with olive oil and sprinkle with a bit of smoked paprika before serving.

Notes

This stew is a perfect example of how I use an acid, in small amounts, to brighten a dish because without it, the stew feels like it's missing something.

The potatoes can be swapped for something similar in texture such as a sweet potato or cubed winter squash.

Make Ahead: This is a stew with flavors that get better with age, at least for a couple days. For longer storage, it will freeze nicely. Just reheat and add eggs before serving.

Sazón-Roasted Kabocha with Cilantro Black Lentils

Serves 4

Sazón is quintessential to Puerto Rican cooking and known for its earthy flavor and bright color thanks to the annatto seeds. Here I've paired the seasoning with thick wedges of roasted kabocha squash and lightly marinated black lentils. Kabocha is great for roasting because no peeling is required—the skin is thin enough to eat. As for the lentils, I prefer the small black lentils for their ability to hold their shape. They also feel a bit like a statement garnish.

SAZÓN

1 tablespoon toasted and ground coriander

1 tablespoon toasted and ground cumin

2 teaspoons kosher salt

1½ teaspoons ground annatto seeds

1½ teaspoons garlic powder

1 teaspoon dried oregano, preferably Mexican

½ teaspoon MSG

SQUASH

1 pound (450 g) kabocha squash, seeded and cut into ½-inch (1.3 cm) wedges

3 to 4 tablespoons olive oil

CILANTRO BLACK LENTILS

1 cup (200 g) cooked black lentils (see page 161)

2 small shallots, minced

½ cup (24 g) minced fresh cilantro

2 tablespoons olive oil

1 tablespoon fresh lime juice

1 teaspoon kosher salt

FOR SERVING

1 cup (240 g) *labneh* or Greek yogurt, at room temperature

Fresh cilantro leaves

Olive oil

MAKE THE SAZÓN BLEND: Combine the coriander, cumin, salt, annatto, garlic powder, oregano, and MSG in a small bowl and set aside.

Preheat the oven to 425°F (220°C). Line a baking sheet with parchment paper.

TO PREPARE THE SQUASH: Arrange in a single layer on the prepared baking sheet and drizzle with enough olive oil so the squash is well coated. Bake for 25 minutes until the squash is tender and beginning to brown.

Remove the squash from the oven, toss with a tablespoon of the spice mixture, return to the oven, and cook for another 5 minutes.

PREPARE THE LENTILS: While the squash is roasting, combine the cooked black lentils, shallot, cilantro, olive oil, lime juice, and salt in a small bowl. Set aside.

TO SERVE: Spread the labneh on a small serving platter. Set the squash on top of the labneh, spoon lentils over the squash, and finish with a sprinkle of cilantro and a drizzle of olive oil.

Notes

The kabocha squash can be swapped for other hearty cool-weather vegetables that wedge well, such as cauliflower, cabbage, other hard squashes, and sweet potatoes.

SOYBEANS

Had you told me a decade ago that eventually I'd be ordering 20 pounds of soybeans each year, and have a mild obsession with this little legume, I would have had a hearty laugh. I'd think back to the unflavored tofu on my college's salad bar, the soybean fields that surrounded my small town grown for oil production, and the soymilk popularity of the 1990s that started the wave of nondairy milks. Beyond that, soy didn't cross my mind.

And yet, here I am today, constantly thinking about soy. If I'm not basing a meal on tofu or tempeh, I am using a variety of fermented soy products. In this section, I'm cheating a little bit by using products made from soybeans rather than making them from scratch, but I wanted to drive home how ubiquitous they are in our foods. And technically you could make all these ingredients with some time and learning. I promise homemade tofu is worth it, but that's another book.

Unlike most of the other legumes in this book, there is concise and well-documented information on soybean-based foods. This is primarily in thanks to William Sheffield and Akiko Aoyagi who wrote about tofu in the 1970s and now have definitive books on soy and a dedicated website called the SoyInfo Center.

As a humble soy enthusiast, I've been on a slow path to grow more soybeans and explore these varieties to make my own tofu, tempeh, miso, and shoyu. In the meantime, I typically source bulk soybeans from Laura's Soybeans and buy soy-based foods from brands I enjoy.

SOY-BASED PRODUCTS

Soy-based products fall into two categories: unfermented and fermented, and both play an important role in my cooking. Below are the soy-products I use most.

TOFU AND TEMPEH

The magic of turning humble seeds into plant-based protein powerhouses is still one of the coolest things about plants for me. Tofu and tempeh can be made at home with a bit of practice and time. If I had 500 pages in this book, I'd provide instructions for making these items but alas, there's only so much space (there are, however, some great resources on tofu and tempeh already—see page 231). For now, I've included a small breakdown of these items so that you can better purchase and use them in recipes.

Tofu: The result of adding a coagulate (typically gypsum or nigiri, which is magnesium chloride) to hot soy milk. This produces curds that are transferred into molds and pressed into blocks to remove whey. The type of soy milk, the type and amount of coagulate, and distribution of weight and time during pressing all factor into the tofu texture.

These textures range from **medium** through **firm**, **extra-firm**, and **super-firm**. The higher the firmness, the more whey was extracted. Most recipes call for extra-firm or super-firm tofu, which holds together best when it is grilled, fried, and the like.

I prefer firm to extra-firm tofu as the bit of moisture left allows me to use the tofu in softer applications or firmer applications.

Silken tofu is made in a slightly different way, keeping the whey and curds together. This creates a soft and quite smooth tofu.

Tempeh: Cakes created from processed soybeans inoculated with spores that create a mycelium network, holding everything together. Tempeh is a great source of texture and protein in vegetarian cooking. Beyond soybeans, many grains, legumes, and some seeds can be included and used to make tempeh. Some store brands sell soy-based tempeh and multigrain tempeh.

UNFERMENTED SOY PRODUCTS

Soy milk: Soaked and ground soybeans that are then cooked, strained of the non-milk material (known as lees/okara which is great in its own way), and then cooked once more. The flavor of homemade soymilk is leagues above store-bought and a great first step to get a handle on if you plan to make tofu.

Soy milk can be used to make a plethora of nondairy items, such as cheese, yogurt, and mayonnaise, like the recipe on page 179.

Yuba: The skin that forms on heating soymilk, often done accidentally if you're me and making soy milk. These skins can be used fresh or dried as a meat replacement or noodles.

Soybean oil: The extracted fat from soybeans. It can be used like any other cooking oil. You're most likely to encounter soybean oil as part of a vegetable oil or processed butter replacement.

Textured vegetable protein (TVP): Often used for meat replacements and is considered a byproduct of soybean oil production. Soybeans go through a defatting process, similar to nuts and seeds, where the oil/fat is extracted. What's left is the defatted material, in this case, TVP. The extraction can be shaped into many different forms including strips, flakes, and chunks. Then it is dehydrated. One of the most popular uses of TVP is soyrizo, a plant-based alternative to chorizo. It's a fun product to play around with, but I typically stick with tofu and tempeh.

FERMENTED SOY PRODUCTS

This is nowhere near an exhaustive list because the fermentation of soybeans has been happening in Asian cultures for generations. And so, this is a list of ones that I often enjoy and use in my cooking.

Miso: A ferment made from cooked soybeans, *koji* (mold-inoculated grains), and salt that results in an umami paste. I often use miso to round out dishes and add just a bit of salty goodness. Although miso can be made from most legumes, soybean-based misos are the most readily available.

Miso comes in different varieties, mostly based on how long it was fermented. **White (*shiro*) miso** is the lightest in color as it's fermented for the least amount of time. This miso is a great all-around addition to broth-based soups, paired with butter, and whipped into salad dressings. **Red (*aka*) miso** is further along in terms of color and time fermented. The flavor is a bit more pronounced. I really enjoy this miso paired with tomato-based and chile-based sauces and stews. *Awase* **miso** is a blend of white and red creating a slightly more assertive white miso.

Doenjang: A fermented soybean paste used in Korean cooking. Cooked soybeans are processed into a brick that is then taken through a drying and fermenting process. Once that is complete, the bricks are aged in a brine until the desired level of fermentation is reached. Then the doenjang is separated from the remaining liquid which is ganjang (a type of Korean soy sauce). Doenjang brings a completely different funk to food. I use it in when looking to bring really deep flavor like in the black bean smash burgers on page 129.

Gochujang: A fermented chile paste using powdered fermented soybeans.

Soy sauce: Traditionally made with soybeans and wheat that goes through a fermentation process. Most of the time soy sauces are categorized by **light** (or thin in the case of Thai soy sauces) or **dark** where the light soy sauces tend to be saltier and the dark soy sauces tend to be slightly sweeter. The average soy sauce you'll find in grocery stores is a Japanese dark soy sauce that balances the salty with just a bit of sweetness.

Beyond the varying levels of salt, soy sauce can also be sweetened or flavored, such as **mushroom soy sauce** which gives an earthy layer to the umami flavor. And soy sauce can be **double-fermented** which means instead of the soybean-wheat mix using a brine to ferment, it uses soy sauce instead. This soy sauce is a bit sweeter and less salty than even the darker soy sauces.

The Korean **ganjang** produced when making doenjang and Japanese **tamari** are both gluten-free as they are created without wheat.

SOYBEAN RECIPES

Bitter Greens Salad with Miso-Citrus Vinaigrette

Serves 4

I've become a bit obsessed with miso, and really all the things *koji* can do (read: miso, soy sauce, tamari, and more). It might be the ultimate magic we as humans wield to make food taste a little better.

This salad is delicious and one of my favorite, slightly punchy companions to meals that have an underlying richness such as pizza, pasta, and risottos. It shows just what a little miso can do to a few simple ingredients, taking a citrus vinaigrette from good to fantastic.

SESAME-ALMOND TOPPING

¼ cup (35 g) raw almonds

½ teaspoon white sesame seeds

½ teaspoon avocado oil

½ teaspoon maple syrup

Hefty pinch of crushed smoked salt

DRESSING

½ large grapefruit

½ orange

¼ cup (60 ml) avocado or other neutral oil

1 tablespoon white miso

1 tablespoon maple syrup

Pinch of salt, as needed

SALAD

1 head radicchio

4 to 5 handfuls of baby arugula

Preheat the oven to 325°F (160°C).

PREPARE THE TOPPING: Coarsely chop the almonds into small pieces. Place on a baking sheet and add the sesame seeds, avocado oil, maple syrup, and smoked salt. Toss to coat the almonds, then spread out in a single layer. Roast until the almonds are fragrant and have deepened in color, 14 to 15 minutes. Let cool.

MAKE THE DRESSING: Heat a cast-iron grill pan or skillet over medium heat. Place the citrus cut side down, in the hot skillet. Sear until charred. Remove from the heat and let cool. Once cooled, squeeze the juice into a measuring cup.

Take ¼ cup (60 ml) of that juice and place it in a jar with a lid. Add the oil, miso, and maple syrup. Shake vigorously until well combined and the miso has broken down. If your miso is a thick paste, use a blender instead. Taste and add salt if needed.

MAKE THE SALAD: Remove the core of the radicchio and remove the leaves. Tear any larger leaves in half, but leave the smaller leaves intact. Place in a bowl along with the arugula. Drizzle with the dressing and sprinkle the almonds on top. Serve immediately.

Notes

The citrus can change based on whatever you might have on hand or your preferred citrus flavors. I like the balance of the slightly tangy grapefruit with the sweet orange. Choose one variety or any combination of lemon (common or Meyer), lime (common or key), grapefruit (red, white, or oro blanco), orange (common or blood orange), or pomelo.

Barbecue Tempeh Bowls with Snap Pea Salad

Serves 4

On one of the main roads in my hometown, a big neon pig highlighted quite possibly the best food smothered in barbecue sauce. And while my love of barbecue sauce started there, it has since become a staple in my vegetarian cooking. Here I've paired my love of barbecue with the vegetarian ingredient I think is most meat-like: tempeh. The fermentation that tempeh undergoes helps create a texture that provides a toothsome bite, different from what tofu provides.

BARBECUE SAUCE

½ small yellow onion

2 garlic cloves

1½ teaspoons kosher salt

1 tablespoon olive oil

3 tablespoons (45 g) tomato paste

½ cup (125 g) canned tomato sauce

3 tablespoons (36 g) dark brown sugar

2 tablespoons molasses

2 tablespoons rice vinegar

1 tablespoon vegan Worcestershire sauce

2 teaspoons yellow mustard

¼ teaspoon ground chile

BOWLS

12 ounces (340 g) tempeh

8 ounces (120 g) snap peas, strings removed and pods thinly sliced on the bias

¼ cup (30 g) crushed roasted peanuts (see page 185), plus more for serving

2 tablespoons minced fresh chives, plus more for serving

3 tablespoons (45 ml) olive oil

1 tablespoon rice vinegar

2 heaping teaspoons stone-ground mustard

Hefty pinch of crushed smoked salt

Cooked farro, bulgur, quinoa, or rice

MAKE THE BARBECUE SAUCE: Combine the onion, garlic, and salt in a food processor and pulse until the onion is in fine pieces, nearly in a paste. Heat the olive oil in a medium saucepan over medium heat. Add the onion mixture and the tomato paste. Cook until the mixture is fragrant, 2 to 3 minutes. Add the tomato sauce, brown sugar, molasses, rice vinegar, Worcestershire sauce, mustard, and ground chile. Bring to a boil, decrease the heat to a simmer, and cook until the sauce has thickened and the flavors have developed a bit, 5 to 10 minutes. Set aside.

PREPARE THE BOWLS: Put the tempeh in a steamer basket and bring water in a saucepan to a boil. Steam the tempeh for 10 minutes. Remove from the steamer, let cool enough to handle, then slice into ⅜-inch (1 cm) slices.

Combine the tempeh with enough barbecue sauce to coat. Let it rest for 30 minutes.

Preheat the oven to 400°F (200°C). Cover a sheet pan with parchment paper.

Put the tempeh on the prepared pan, brush with a bit more barbecue sauce, and bake for 10 minutes. Flip, brush again, and bake for another 10 to 15 minutes, until the tempeh and sauce have significantly deepened in color; keep an eye on it so the sauce does not burn. Remove the tempeh from the oven and brush with more sauce. Set aside.

In a medium bowl, combine the snap peas, peanuts, and chives. Whisk the oil, vinegar, mustard, and salt together in a small bowl until well blended. Add to the snap peas and toss.

TO SERVE: Divide your chosen grain between four bowls and top each with the tempeh and the snap pea salad.

Notes

Don't skip the steaming of the tempeh. Precooking helps to mellow the bitterness occasionally found in store-bought tempeh.

Instead of the snap peas, you could use the Spring Slaw from the Lentil Sloppy Joes (page 163) or a lightly dressed salad.

Caramelized Sweet Potatoes with Soy-Butter Sauce

Serves 4

In the rounds of testing for this recipe, I kept trying to give it more complexity, but the layers never lined up. And so, I did the opposite and let minimalism take hold. The key here is to let the sweet potato get quite soft in the steamer, then caramelize on the grill or in a cast-iron skillet. And let the soy sauce really shine.

The sweet potatoes make a delightful side dish but can also be a good start to a meal. Pair this with grilled tofu, a bowl of rice or other grain, or use the butter to dress noodles, such as udon or ramen, to eat with the sweet potato.

2 large sweet potatoes, quartered
2 tablespoons olive oil
¼ cup (56 g) unsalted butter
4 teaspoons double-fermented soy sauce
2 teaspoons rice vinegar
Smoked sea salt, for finishing

Bring a couple of inches (5 cm) of water to a boil in a saucepan fitted with a steamer basket. Add the sweet potatoes to the basket and steam until the pieces are quite tender, 15 to 20 minutes, depending on the size of the pieces.

If you're grilling, heat the grill to medium-high heat. Brush the sweet potato pieces with the olive oil and place cut sides down on the grill. Grill until charred. Alternatively, heat the olive oil in a large skillet (cast iron is excellent here) over medium-high heat. Add the sweet potatoes, cut sides down, and sear until the edges caramelize.

Heat a small skillet over medium heat. Add the butter, swirling and stirring the pan frequently as the butter melts. Let the butter foam and sizzle, continuing to stir, until it turns a light golden brown—almost a brown butter. Remove from the heat and whisk in the soy sauce and rice vinegar.

Place the sweet potato pieces in a small bowl and drizzle with the soy-butter sauce. Let rest for at least 5 minutes so the sauce can soak in. Sprinkle with smoked sea salt before serving.

Notes

When grilling heartier vegetables, I don't play chance with the texture. Steaming ahead of time ensures a well-cooked vegetable that is intact. From there, charring adds flavor more than anything. This method also works for regular potatoes, winter squash, and cauliflower.

Seasonal Variations: It's hard to go wrong with soy sauce and butter on vegetables (it tastes like a sophisticated step up from the classic butter-and-salt combination). Try this sauce on grilled sweet corn in the summer, broiled asparagus in the spring, and roasted cauliflower or broccoli during fall.

Egg Salad Tartines

Serves 4 and makes 1½ cups (350 g) mayo

When I'm not testing recipes, my go-to lunches are usually some variation of toast or leftover grains. I batch cook soft-boiled eggs for easy meal prep so I often have a few on hand. This tartine embodies my love of egg salad and showcases how great a soy mayo can be.

The fats in soy milk provide such a nice layer of creaminess, and I've found that of all the nondairy milks, it works the best as a 1:1 substitute for dairy milk and in some applications for eggs, like in this mayo. The recipe here makes more than you need for the egg salad because I usually make big batches of the mayo to use throughout the week.

VEGAN MAYO

½ cup (120 ml) unsweetened soy milk, at room temperature

2 teaspoons rice vinegar, at room temperature

¾ teaspoon kosher salt

1 cup (240 ml) avocado or sunflower oil, at room temperature

EGG SALAD

4 large eggs

2 tablespoons dill pickle juice

2 teaspoons stone-ground mustard

1½ teaspoons kosher salt

TARTINES

2 to 3 tablespoons olive oil

4 thick slices of bread

½ cup loosely packed (12 g) chopped fresh dill

Crispy shallots

Ground chile or black pepper, for serving

MAKE THE MAYO: Combine the soy milk, rice vinegar, and salt in a jar large enough to accommodate an immersion blender. Stir to combine, then pour the avocado oil on top. Place the immersion blender in the jar, pressed to the bottom. Start the blender, leaving it pressed to the bottom of the jar until the mayo begins to thicken. Then slowly start moving the immersion blender up and down until the mayo is smooth and thick.

MAKE THE EGG SALAD: Bring a saucepan of water to a boil and have a small bowl filled with ice water ready. Slowly lower the eggs into the hot water and boil for 8 minutes. Transfer to the ice bath.

In a small bowl, whisk together ½ cup (112 g) of the mayo with the pickle juice, mustard, and salt. Once the eggs are cool enough to handle, peel and cut into wedges. Add to the bowl with the mayo and fold together.

ASSEMBLE THE TARTINES: Heat the oil in a small skillet over medium heat. Trim the crust from the bread slices and place in the skillet. Fry until one side is golden and crisp.

Transfer the toast to plates. Top with the egg mixture and garnish with the dill, crispy shallots, and a bit of ground chile, if desired.

Notes

I realize it's a bit funny to make a vegan mayo only to use it on eggs, but I like the flavor of this mayo and the flexibility. The mayo can be stored in an airtight container in the refrigerator for up to 2 weeks. Use in any place where mayo may be called for, such as in dressings, spreads, or sauces.

Whenever I make toast like this with thick slices of whole-grain bread, I turn into a four-year-old and lose the crusts. I find the crispness takes away from the delicate nature of the eggs. Plus, the crust can easily turn into breadcrumbs for topping soups or tossing with roasted vegetables.

You can thinly slice and fry your shallots in a neutral oil until golden, or just buy them fried. I can usually find these at Asian markets.

Tamarind Tofu Skewers

Serves 4

I became enamored with this sauce after cooking a version of it from *The Pepper Thai Cookbook* that I checked out from the library on a whim. The sauce, originally intended for ribs, is a little sweet, a little tart, and the ideal companion for tofu. The original recipe calls for grated tomato and cilantro stems, but I chose to pull out those ingredients and give them a different treatment here.

The toasted rice powder provides a lovely depth of flavor and helps thicken the sauce. Toasted rice powder can be found in any market that carries Thai ingredients. I keep a jar of tamarind concentrate in my pantry for this meal and to make tamarind chutney, among other recipes. Tamarind provides a unique sour flavor that is quite good when made into sauces such as this one. Look for tamarind concentrate at your local Indian grocery store or order online.

TOFU SKEWERS

12 ounces (340 g) firm or super-firm tofu

24 to 32 plump cherry tomatoes

TAMARIND GLAZE

¼ cup (60 ml) soy sauce

¼ cup (48 g) dark brown sugar

2 tablespoons chile-garlic sauce

2 tablespoons fresh lime juice

2 tablespoons tamarind concentrate

¾ cup (180 ml) water

1 tablespoon cornstarch

1 tablespoon toasted rice powder

TO ASSEMBLE

Avocado or other high-heat neutral oil, for grilling

Cooked rice, barley, emmer, or quinoa, for serving

½ cup (10 g) coarsely chopped fresh cilantro

½ cup (70 g) minced red onions

PREPARE THE SKEWERS: Gently press any liquid from the tofu. Cut into 1-inch (2.5 cm) pieces. Combine the soy sauce, sugar, chile sauce, lime juice, and tamarind for the glaze in a medium bowl. Add the tofu and let marinate for 20 minutes.

Thread the tofu, alternating with the cherry tomatoes, onto eight metal skewers. Set aside.

MAKE THE GLAZE: Transfer the marinade to a small saucepan. Whisk together the water and cornstarch in a small bowl, then add to two thirds of the mixture the marinade. Heat over medium heat and cook, whisking frequently, until it has thickened enough to coat the back of a spoon, about 60 seconds. If the mixture is too thin, add 1 tablespoon of the remaining cornstarch mixture at a time to the glaze and cook, whisking, until thick. If the glaze is too thick, add a splash of water.

TO ASSEMBLE: Preheat the grill to medium heat. If using a grill pan or frying pan, preheat with a bit of avocado oil. Brush the skewers with some of the glaze, transfer the skewers to the hot grill, and cook on one side until lightly charred, 2 to 3 minutes. Rotate and repeat until lightly charred all over.

Spoon your chosen grain onto a serving platter. Transfer the grilled skewers to a serving platter or plate. Stir the toasted rice powder into the glaze and brush or spoon the remaining glaze over the skewers. Garnish with the cilantro and minced red onions before serving.

NUTS AND SEEDS

Head into the northern California countryside from Sacramento and it's all but guaranteed that you'll run into a grove of almonds, walnuts, or pistachios. In spring, the almond trees become a spectacle of pink blooms; in late summer, fields of beautiful sunflowers dot the valley landscape; and in fall, I know to check my son's backpack for stowaway acorns he's picked up on his walks.

Nuts and seeds are a great way to alter the texture, flavor, and depth of a dish. A firm bite of a nutty almond! The buttery taste of a soft pecan! The earthy boldness of a crunchy hazelnut! All pair delightfully well with vegetables, grains, and beans.

FATS (THE GOOD KIND)

As nuts and seeds became a larger part of my diet, the last vestiges of the anti-fat 1990s diet culture of my youth chipped away. It is wild to me that we label all fats as bad given our bodies' daily energy requirements. Nuts and seeds are high in naturally occurring fats. When paired with other nutrients, they make great additions to our everyday meals.

BUYING AND STORING

Quite a few years ago on a press tour for California walnuts, someone asked a walnut producer what they wished consumers knew about the nut. I expected an answer around their great taste or good fats for heart health! Their actual answer made me rethink everything I'd thought about nuts. They wanted consumers to treat walnuts more akin to produce than a shelf-stable product.

Out went viewing nuts and seeds as a long-term cupboard item. Instead I started treating them like the produce they are, cared for in the months after harvest and refreshed yearly. I keep all my nuts and seeds in the refrigerator and use them within a year. Nuts and seeds are high in unsaturated fats, which correlates to a higher risk of rancidity thanks to time, light, heat, and oxygen. This risk increases if the nuts are higher in polyunsaturated fats—a reason walnuts and pine nuts are often the first to turn.

Look for nuts and seeds that have a harvest date and store them in an airtight container in the refrigerator for up to six months. For yearlong storage, transfer to the freezer. Often, I'll keep a larger stock in the freezer and refill my jars in the refrigerator as I run out. I also recommend tasting the nuts every once in a while to get an understanding of how they change over time, even into rancidity if it goes that long.

Whole, raw nuts are best for longer storage because roasting or chopping releases oils. Nuts still in their shells will keep longer than shelled nuts, but I often weigh the amount of time it takes to shell the nuts and keep shelled nuts in cold storage.

TYPES OF NUTS

Not every nut is scientifically considered a nut, but for ease of cooking and consumption, I treat everything in this category mostly the same.

Pistachios: The snacking nut of choice in my house, leading me to keep raw pistachios in the shell to flavor as I like. For all other pistachio needs, I always have a jar of raw, shelled pistachios. If raw, shelled pistachios are hard to find, their roasted and salted counterparts can be used but accounted for in the overall salt level of the dish. This is a great option for sprinkles, sauces, and dressings but best avoided if making pistachio milk or flour.

Almonds: Whole, raw almonds are great as snacks, in salads and sauces, and for making almond butter. In slivered form, they can be used for making nut cheeses (page 191) that might be better without the slightly bitter skin.

Pecans and walnuts: I use pecans and **English walnuts** interchangeably, while **black walnuts** have a more concentrated and bold essence—making them delightful for baked goods.

Hazelnuts: Have a wide variety of uses, including nut butters, milks, garnishes, sauces, and dressings. Depending on the usage, it can be helpful to remove the skin from the nut before using (see page 191).

Beyond these nuts, I use chestnuts, Brazil nuts, and macadamia nuts only occasionally because of cost and availability. I don't use cashews very often anymore as harvesting and processing them is extremely tough and often done through manual labor. They are not local for me and can be hard to ethically source.

What About Green Nuts?

Occasionally you might see green almonds or walnuts for sale. These are the unripe fruits, which can be used whole before the pericarp splits. Green almonds can be served raw, used in pastas, salads. Green walnuts are harvested to use in liquors and pickled to use in condiments.

BLANCHING, ROASTING, AND TOASTING

A majority of the recipes in this book call for roasting the nuts and seeds before using. With a little heat, something slightly plain becomes something noteworthy. In my kitchen, toasting is a high-heat, quick cook on the outside while roasting is low and slow, heated all the way through, and usually refers to whole nuts and seeds. To truly get the best flavor, low and slow, with occasional blanching ahead of time, is key.

Blanched Nuts

Occasionally it is helpful to remove the thin skin from around nuts by blanching. While any nut can go through this process, it's most common for hazelnuts, peanuts, and almonds. The thin, papery skin can be a source of bitterness depending on the variety. If nut butter is the goal, the nuts will need to be dried after blanching.

HOW TO BLANCH NUTS

Almonds require just 1 minute of blanching in boiling hot water. Then transfer to an ice bath until cool, strain, and pinch at one end until their skins slip off.

Peanuts require up to 3 minutes of blanching in boiling water, a quick ice bath, and then the skins should easily rub off.

Hazelnuts can be a bit more difficult. Luckily, we have a technique from Julia Child. She recommends 3 minutes of blanching 1 cup (120 g) of hazelnuts in 2 cups (480 ml) of water with 3 tablespoons (32 g) of baking soda followed by an ice bath and rubbing.

Once blanched, nuts can be roasted. Pat dry and follow the instructions for dry roasting (to follow), increasing the time as needed to account for any moisture left after blanching.

Roasting Nuts and Seeds

When it comes to larger nuts and seeds, my preference is usually to roast in the oven. The heat is uneven from top to bottom and side to side when you toast in a skillet, and you're more likely to brown the outside before any of that good flavor penetrates.

Roasting nuts and seeds happens in two stages. Upon heating, nuts and seeds lose moisture from evaporation, which is needed for the next step—the Maillard reaction. In nuts and seeds, heat impacts the amino acids and sugar content, creating the darker color and nutty flavor we all know and love. Sometimes I roast nuts in a drizzle of oil if I plan to add flavor, such as a spice blend, during or right after the roasting process. I use this technique when I want a quick snack or addition to salads.

Dry-roasted nuts are roasted with no added oil. I dry-roast if I'm using nuts in a sauce, as a topping of some kind, or making a nut product such as a cream, milk, or oil.

HOW TO ROAST NUTS AND SEEDS

Preheat the oven to 300°F (150°C). Spread the raw nuts or seeds in a single layer on a sheet pan. If using oil, drizzle with a bit of avocado oil and toss to coat. Roast until golden brown and fragrant, anywhere from 10 to 20 minutes, depending on the density and size of the nut. Stir every 5 minutes or so to ensure even roasting. Once done, remove from the oven, transfer into a bowl, and let cool.

Toasting Nuts and Seeds

Smaller seeds and crushed nuts can be toasted in a skillet on top of the stove to save time. Sometimes I toast nuts and seeds in a bit of oil, which can help even out the browning.

Heat a skillet that is large enough to accommodate all the nuts or seeds in a single layer over medium heat. Add the nuts or seeds and swirl the pan every 30 to 45 seconds, continuing to cook until they are golden.

WHOLE, PIECES, AND MORE

When I use whole or pieced nuts and seeds, I'm often thinking about the experience of the bite from start to finish. Have you ever had a salad where you had to maneuver getting a pecan halve onto the fork? Or had a bite of brownie only to discover the bite was mostly walnut? Different uses require different preparation. As such, here's how I break nuts down (literally and figuratively).

Starting from the top, some nuts and seeds have the option to be purchased in-shell or shelled. The in-shell option is great for longer storage, or if you like the act of cracking shells.

After shelling, nuts are either left in their whole form (or halved form if dealing with pecans and walnuts). This is my preferred way to purchase most nuts and seeds as it gives me the most

options to control the size needed per use and a decent shelf life.

Pieces, usually in regards to pecans and walnuts, are also found in stores. I actually prefer pieces for these two nuts and only buy halves as needed. As a pecan farmer once informed me, keeping the halves during the processing can be tricky which means they are something to be cherished (and pieces are often cheaper).

Almonds can be found in **sliced and slivered** forms. Sliced almonds are just that, thin slices made from whole almonds. Slivered almonds are made by blanching and slicing raw almonds. These are great if you are in need of blanched almonds.

Beyond what you find in stores, I have three different ways I prepare nuts and seeds to use in the recipes found throughout this book. **Chopped nuts or seeds** are similar to the size of pieces you'd find at the store—a few large pieces. I often use this size if I'm looking for even roasting or if I want nuts to be a bit more present in the meal. **Finely chopped nuts or seeds** are in smaller pieces with some meal-like consistency as well. I like to use this size for dressings, sprinkles, and garnishes. Both the chopped sizes are best achieved on a cutting board with a chef's knife. Finally, **crushed nuts** are an even texture of small pieces—about as fine as you can get them. This can be done on a cutting board but is easier using a mortar/pestle or a few pulses in a food processor. I prefer this texture when I'm using nuts and seeds as a coating, in a fine sauce, or in a garnish.

NUT AND SEED PRODUCTS

As plant-based diets have continued to gain popularity, so have the products made from nuts, which is great when looking for a dairy alternative. Best of all, many of the products found in the market can be made at home if you possess a few tools.

Butters and Pastes

The category of nut and seed butters is by far the most used in my kitchen from peanut butter to tahini. Nut and seed butters are also one of the easiest ways to see the benefit of having high-fat ingredients because without the fat, there is no nut butter.

While they are all unique in flavor, the process for achieving luscious butters doesn't require a detailed recipe, just a sturdy food processor, time, and patience.

HOW TO MAKE A NUT BUTTER OR PASTE

The process is straightforward: In a sturdy food processor, puree 4 cups (500 g) of dry-roasted nuts/seeds until you've lost all hope that it will work, then continue going until the fats release from the nuts to help smooth out the paste. After this stage you can add a bit of salt, a little sweetener, or a myriad of other flavors (cocoa powder, turmeric, cinnamon just to name a few). This will yield about 2 cups of nut butter that can be stored in the refrigerator for a few weeks.

Once you have a luscious nut butter, you can lather it on a sandwich, use it as a dip for fruit, use in a dressing or sauce (such as Chile-Walnut Butter Sauce on page 195), stir into a soup for a boost (see Butternut Squash Soup on page 229), or simply eat by the spoonful. One note, store-bought nut butters, especially peanut butter, often contain palm oil to keep it from separating. This is a convenience and not a necessity; I find if I store my jars of nut butters upside down, they separate a bit less.

Common Types of Nut Butters

Peanut butter

Almond/walnut/hazelnut/pecan

Sunflower/pumpkin seed butter (using the kernel/pepita)

Tahini (uses toasted/hulled seeds)/sesame paste (uses toasted/unhulled seeds)

Mix and match: choose two or more nuts/seeds and blend together

MILKS, CREAMS, AND SPREADS

I use nut milks as an easy way to make meals vegan, as with the porridge on page 97. Nut-based creams can be found gracing the bottom of grain bowls or stirred into risottos (see page 202).

Even though most grocery stores provide access to a wide variety of nut milks, I like knowing I can make homemade nut milks if I need them in a pinch or want to add particular flavors. As with peanut butter, homemade nut milks don't require a deep, technical recipe. It's as simple as blending soaked, raw nuts with water then straining.

Which Nuts and Seeds Work Best

For starters, all the nuts, culinary seeds, and peanuts can make great nut milk either individually or as a blend. It's best to use raw nuts as the roasting process draws out the fats that form the base of the creaminess when the nuts are blended. However, a few roasted nuts or seeds can be added to the mix to provide a bit more flavor if desired. For example, if you are using ½ cup (70 g) whole raw almonds, include 2 tablespoons of roasted almonds to the mix.

Soaking: Nuts are made up primarily of storage proteins, which are water and salt-water soluble. Soaking the nuts helps facilitate the breakdown when pureeing. I typically soak the nuts in a ratio of 4 cups (960 ml) room temperature water to 1 teaspoon kosher salt for 4 to 8 hours at room temperature. The larger and harder nuts, like almonds, benefit from the slightly longer soak times, while with the smaller nuts and seeds, like sunflower and peanuts, will be fine with a shorter soak time. Beyond 8 hours, the soaking mixture should be refrigerated to inhibit bacterial growth.

After soaking, drain and rinse the seeds before pureeing.

Pureeing: Most nut milks turn out well with a ratio of 1 part nuts to 4 parts water. This provides a texture akin to 2% milk—just a little creamy and great for using as an all-around milk. Occasionally I like to have a slightly creamier milk and will increase the ratio of nuts to more of a 1.25 parts nuts to 4 parts water ratio. This is all personal preference and can vary from nut to nut. Once you decide on the ratio, the nuts and water need about a minute in a high-speed blender.

Add a pinch of salt and a bit of sweetener—maple syrup, honey, or pitted dates—during blending.

Straining and storing: Once you have the milk mixture, strain through a nut-milk bag or a sieve lined with cheesecloth. Save the pulp to make a meal that can stand in for nut meal (see below) and store the nut milk in a lidded jar in the refrigerator for up to 4 days.

For Creams and Spreads

When making nut and seed creams, I follow the same procedure for soaking the nuts and seeds. After that, it's straight to the high-speed blender with a ratio of 2 parts nuts to 1 part water. I keep the proportion of liquid low so that I can add other ingredients as needed, including a bit of oil to add a boost of richness, alliums or chiles for flavor, vinegar or citrus for punch, and miso or nutritional yeast for a bit of umami.

NUT FLOURS AND NUT MEALS

In my cooking, I use nut and seed meals as complements to other flours and starches, especially if I'm baking muffins or cakes. Nut meals are nice for coatings, like for the tofu on page 225 and the green tomatoes on page 200. In a pinch, the meal can be toasted and used as a sprinkle for finishing salads.

How to Make Nut Meal from Whole Nuts

I recommend roasting the nuts first (see page 186), or for a finer flour, blanching then roasting the nuts. This draws out some of the oil and intensifies the flavor. Once the nuts are cool, pulse in a food processor for a few seconds until finely ground but not a second longer, or else you risk the oils turning your meal into nut butter.

If you're looking for a finer meal, pass the ground nuts through a sieve and return the larger pieces back to the food processor and repeat the process until satisfied.

The **leftover pulp from nut milk** can stand in for nut and seed meal. To use the pulp, spread the pulp on a sheet pan and dehydrate at 200°F (90°C) for upwards of 2 hours. Then, once cool, pulse the dried pulp in a food processor until it resembles flour. I find this version of nut meal isn't as flavorful, but it is a great way to use up the byproduct of nut milk.

Rendering oil from nuts and seeds creates a similar, though defatted, product. While not feasible to do at home unless you own an expeller, defatted nut and seed flours can be found for purchase.

OILS

Nuts and seeds are well suited for the oil-making process thanks to an abundance of fat. This oil extraction can be done from raw nuts, for a more mild oil, or from roasted nuts, for an oil that has a robust quality.

The extraction is done mechanically through an expeller press which, with pressure and force, extracts the oil. Heat is created through this process, but if the oil stays below 120°F (49°C), it can be considered extra virgin. This type of oil is often touted for health benefits and nutrients. Alternatively, oil can be extracted through a chemical solvent. This process is often used to create more shelf-stable, high-heat oils.

Once the oil is extracted it may be used right away or go through a refinement process which is meant to improve shelf life, create a neutral flavor, reduce contaminants, and create an oil that can be used at higher heat. Oils are labeled either unrefined or refined.

Cooking with Nut and Seed Oils

The question becomes which oils do we use and when? While on the surface this feels like an easy question, the more one digs, the more confusion abounds.

For starters, there's the talk of smoke point. All oils have different smoke points (when the oil goes beyond shimmering and sends up smoke). Once an oil starts smoking, the potential for creating harsh flavors and carcinogens that can have an impact on your health increases.

Unfortunately, as much as I wish I could give you a handy chart to tell you exactly when an oil will smoke, there are just too many factors and the charts that are out there have wide temperature ranges. Plus, recent research around olive oil is finding that oils may break down well before or well after smoking begins—it's heavily based on the type of fats found in the oil.

With that said, here are the things to keep in mind when working with nut and seed oils.

The fatty acid makeup matters: Polyunsaturated fats break down faster when exposed to air and light. They also have weaker thermal stability, meaning the oil degrades as the temperature rises, often before the smoke point is reached. Unrefined walnut, sunflower, flax, and safflower oils fall into this category.

Monounsaturated fats tend to have a slower reaction to air and light while having a stronger thermal stability. This means these oils can potentially be okay past their smoke point. Peanut, sesame, avocado, and olive oil are the popular choices in this category.

Almond, hazelnut, pecan, and pumpkin oils have a moderate amount of both polyunsaturated and monounsaturated fats, so while they could be used for cooking, their unrefined versions are better used as a finishing oil.

The production process matters: Refined oil has a much higher smoke point than unrefined and you can often find oils originally high in polyunsaturated fats refined into high-heat oils, such as sunflower and safflower oils. Also, if the oil has a large amount of sediment, that can cause the oil to break down at a faster rate.

All of this is to say that you should use what you find to be the best solution for you. I keep olive oil, avocado oil, and peanut oil on hand for my mid-range heat needs. I sparingly use refined sunflower and safflower oil in dishes that require deep frying.

The real excitement I find, however, is in the unrefined nut and seed oils for flavor. They are great for finishing dips, in salad dressings (see Hot Honey Hazelnut Vinaigrette on page 196), giving a boost to grain bowls, and rounding out flavors in sauces (see Chile-Walnut Butter Sauce on page 195). I also use nut oils in low-heat roasting and baking (see the peanut granola on page 226).

NUT-BASED CHEESE AND YOGURT

Over the last decade, an explosion of cultured dairy-alternative products and recipes made from nuts and seeds has happened. The yogurt aisle of my local co-op is half-filled with nut-based products. Miyokos is one brand that sells nearly every type of product one could desire, and there are cheese companies devoted to the craft of aged nut-based cheeses.

Due to the high levels of fats and proteins in nuts and seeds, fermentation can really only happen through the addition of probiotic cultures. Different types of vegan cultures can be found online and used for making nut-based yogurts, cheeses, and sour cream.

However, if fermented cheese making is not in your future, there are simple ways to play around with the idea of nut cheese, such as the almond ricotta recipe on page 201.

NUT RECIPES

Whipped Goat Cheese Dip with Black Pepper Hazelnuts

Serves 4 to 6
as a snack

While I mostly talk about my love of California produce, I could easily segue to talking about all the delightful cheese made here. One of my top choices: creamy, fresh goat cheese. I love the tangy, earthy flavor of the goat cheese, and it is an easy partner to the rich hazelnuts. Best of all, this dip comes together quickly, making it a good choice for a last-minute party addition.

BLACK PEPPER HAZELNUTS

¼ cup (30 g) raw hazelnuts, chopped

1 teaspoon toasted hazelnut oil

1 teaspoon maple syrup

½ teaspoon ground black pepper

¼ teaspoon kosher salt

WHIPPED GOAT CHEESE

6 ounces chèvre (fresh goat cheese), at room temperature

3 to 4 tablespoons heavy cream

½ teaspoon lemon zest

¼ teaspoon kosher salt

FOR SERVING

Toasted hazelnut oil

Bread and/or crackers

Preheat the oven to 325°F (160°C).

PREPARE THE HAZELNUTS: Put the hazelnuts on a baking sheet. Add the oil, maple syrup, black pepper, and salt. Stir to coat the hazelnut pieces, then spread out in a single layer. Roast until the hazelnuts are fragrant and have deepened in color, 12 to 14 minutes. Let cool.

MAKE THE WHIPPED GOAT CHEESE: Combine the goat cheese, 3 tablespoons (45 ml) of the heavy cream, the lemon zest, and salt in a food processor. Puree until smooth, adding the remaining cream if needed to smooth out the cheese.

TO SERVE: Spoon the whipped goat cheese into a wide, shallow bowl. Top with the roasted hazelnuts and a drizzle of hazelnut oil. Serve with bread and crackers.

Notes

Using hazelnut oil with the whole hazelnuts is just a nice nutty bonus but not a must. A good finishing olive oil would also work to bring the dish together.

Make Ahead: The hazelnuts will be okay for a day or so at room temperature, but after that, they start to soften. The whipped goat cheese will last for 5 to 6 days in the refrigerator. Bring it to room temperature before serving.

Charred Carrots with Dill-Almond Oil

Serves 4

In my opinion, the easiest, most showstopping side dishes consist of two things: a punchy dressing and a charred vegetable. The vegetable could be roasted, grilled, or seared, and the dressing can take a ton of different paths. Here, I use an herb-forward dressing that has the added benefit of built-in crunch from the almonds. By including almonds in the dressing, the nuts cling to the carrots, creating a perfect bite every time.

ALMOND-HERB DRESSING

1 garlic clove

2 tablespoons rice vinegar

¼ teaspoon kosher salt

¼ cup (30 g) whole roasted almonds (see page 185), chopped

2 tablespoons minced fresh flat-leaf parsley

2 tablespoons minced fresh dill, plus extra for finishing

6 tablespoons (90 ml) olive or almond oil

CARROTS

2 tablespoons olive oil

12 ounces (340 g) short, plump carrots, trimmed and halved lengthwise

½ teaspoon kosher salt

MAKE THE DRESSING: Mince the garlic and combine it in a large bowl with the rice vinegar and salt. Let rest for 5 minutes.

Add the almonds to the bowl with the garlic and add the parsley and dill. Whisk in the olive oil until well combined. Set aside.

PREPARE THE CARROTS: Heat the olive oil in a medium cast-iron skillet in a pizza oven or under a broiler. Add the carrots with a sprinkle of salt, return the skillet to the pizza oven or broiler, and cook until lightly charred, 4 to 5 minutes.

Transfer the carrots to a medium serving platter and drizzle with the dressing. Finish with a sprinkle of dill.

Notes

You can easily use large carrots, cut into smaller pieces. Beets, asparagus, and hakurei turnips are also nice in this recipe. For heartier vegetables like beets, steam until just tender before charring—as in the Fennel-Herb Beet recipe on page 219.

Udon Noodles with Chile-Walnut Butter Sauce

Serves 4

I am a creature of exploration, which means recipes I made ten years ago are rarely made again. There are, however, a handful of exceptions, including a peanut noodle bowl. Here I showcase the versatility of other nut butters in a savory sauce. The trio of walnut butter, red miso, and sambal oelek will leave you wanting to eat this sauce by the spoonful.

CHILE-WALNUT BUTTER SAUCE

¼ cup (64 g) walnut butter (see page 188)

3 tablespoons (16 g) red miso

3 tablespoons (45 ml) walnut oil

2 small shallots, minced

1 heaping tablespoon sambal oelek

2 teaspoons cane sugar

¼ cup (30 g) crushed roasted walnuts (see page 185), plus extra for serving

BOWL

1 pound (450 g) green beans, trimmed and cut into 1-inch (2.5 cm) pieces

1 pound (450 g) uncooked udon or similar-style noodle

4 eggs, soft boiled until jammy (7 minutes)

MAKE THE SAUCE: Combine the walnut butter, miso, walnut oil, shallot, sambal oelek, and sugar in a food processor and puree until well combined. Add the crushed walnuts and pulse until combined. Let rest for 5 minutes, then taste and adjust the flavors as desired.

PREPARE THE BOWLS: Bring a medium saucepan of salted water to a boil and have an ice bath ready. Add the green beans and cook until brightened in color and just tender, 2 to 3 minutes. Using a slotted spoon or strainer, transfer to the ice bath and set aside.

In the same saucepan you used to cook the green beans, cook the noodles according to the package directions. Remove ½ cup (120 ml) of water, drain the noodles, and return to the saucepan. Drain the green beans and add to the saucepan along the sauce. Toss until well combined, adding a splash of reserved noodle water as needed to thin the sauce.

TO SERVE: Divide the noodles between four bowls. Peel and cut the eggs in half and top each bowl with two halves. Finish with a sprinkle of crushed walnuts before serving.

Notes

Seasonal Variations: Given this is a year-round meal for me, I've made it with many different vegetables and greens. Think about using wilted spinach in the summer, or kale, roasted Brussels sprouts, or steamed broccoli in the fall and winter.

Vegan Riff: Crumble baked or pan-fried tofu into the mix in place of the eggs.

Grilled Peaches with Hot-Honey Hazelnut Vinaigrette

Serves 4

Honey and nuts are a popular combination for good reason. The sweet, often floral flavors of honey complement the earthy undertone of the nuts—especially in hazelnuts. Here I take the honey-and-nut combination a step further and turn it into a complex vinaigrette that works with greens, vegetables, and my favorite, fresh summer fruit.

These grilled peaches are delightful when paired with cheese. Try them served with grilled halloumi, spooned over ricotta toast, or coarsely chopped, then used as a topping for whipped goat cheese (page 193).

HOT HONEY

¼ cup (85 g) raw honey

1 tablespoon dried red pepper flakes

½ teaspoon rice vinegar

HAZELNUT VINAIGRETTE

¼ cup (55 g) unsalted butter

¼ cup (30 g) crushed raw hazelnuts

2 tablespoons lemon juice

2 teaspoons rice vinegar

½ teaspoon kosher salt

GRILLED PEACHES

1 pound (450 g) just-ripe peaches, pitted and cut into 1-inch (2.5 cm) wedges

1 tablespoon avocado oil

MAKE THE HOT HONEY: In a small skillet over medium heat, combine the honey and pepper flakes. Bring to a simmer, turn off the heat, and let infuse for at least 20 minutes. Strain through a sieve if desiring a smooth honey and stir in the vinegar. Set aside. Wipe out the skillet and return it to the stovetop.

MAKE THE DRESSING: Melt the butter in the skillet over medium-low heat. Stir in the crushed hazelnuts and toast until fragrant and golden. Remove the skillet from the heat and stir in the lemon juice, rice vinegar, and salt and 2 tablespoons of the hot honey.

GRILL THE PEACHES: Preheat the grill to medium heat. Toss the peaches with the oil until well coated in a medium bowl. Grill until lightly charred, 1 to 2 minutes per side.

Return the peaches to the bowl, add a couple tablespoons of the dressing, and toss to combine. Transfer to a medium serving bowl and drizzle with more dressing before serving.

Notes

The best part about making hot honey at home is that you control the flavor and heat. You can easily use the crushed red pepper from stores, which is typically made with cayenne peppers and focuses more on heat than flavor. However, there's a wide world of chile pepper flakes on the market now. I recommend sticking with flakes that have a bit more heat, but play around with different varieties to find flavors you like. My personal favorite: chile de árbol flakes.

Vegan Riff: Maple syrup can stand in for the honey and pairs quite well with the peaches, and from there you can use your favorite nondairy butter or a neutral oil.

Make Ahead: Hot honey will keep, sealed, at room temperature for a few weeks, while the dressing will last up to a few days stored in the refrigerator. As the dressing cools, the butter will solidify the dressing. Simply reheat over low heat until the dressing becomes liquid again.

Paneer Bowls with Pistachio Dukkah and Asparagus

Serves 4

Dukkah is, in my mind, the perfect showcase of blending nuts and spices together to achieve texture and flavor. This Egyptian condiment is often made with hazelnuts and almonds as the base, but my house blend favors the slight piney flavor of the pistachios with the floral coriander and earthy cumin and fennel seeds.

PISTACHIO DUKKAH

¼ cup (35 g) raw pistachios

1 tablespoon white sesame seeds

1 teaspoon coriander seeds

½ teaspoon cumin seeds

¼ teaspoon fennel seeds

½ to 1 teaspoon kosher salt

ASPARAGUS

2 tablespoons olive oil

1 pound (450 g) asparagus, woody ends trimmed

1 tablespoon lemon juice

1 teaspoon lemon zest

½ teaspoon kosher salt

BOWLS

2 tablespoons olive oil

12 ounces (340 g) paneer, cut into ¼-inch (6 mm) thick slices

½ cup (130 g) hummus (see page 157) or similar spread

Cooked emmer, millet, quinoa, or barley

Preheat the oven to 300°F (150°C).

MAKE THE DUKKAH: Spread out the pistachios on a small baking sheet. Roast for 10 minutes, until just golden. Transfer the pistachios to a small bowl and let cool. Spread out the sesame seeds, coriander, cumin, and fennel on the baking sheet and roast for 5 to 6 minutes, until fragrant.

Combine the roasted pistachios and seeds in a mortar and crush, or pulse in a food processor to crush and combine. Add salt and stir to combine.

PREPARE THE ASPARAGUS: Heat the oil in a large skillet over medium-high heat. Add the asparagus and sear, flipping once or twice, until browned but still crisp, 2 to 3 minutes. Remove from the skillet, place on a sheet pan and toss with the lemon juice, zest, and salt.

TO PREPARE THE BOWLS: Wipe out the skillet used for the asparagus, add the oil, and turn the heat to medium. Add the paneer and fry until golden on both sides, 1 to 2 minutes per side. Transfer to a medium bowl. Sprinkle with three-quarters of the dukkah until coated.

Divide and spread the hummus between four shallow bowls. Add the grains followed by the paneer and asparagus. Sprinkle with the remaining dukkah before serving.

Notes

Dukkah can be sprinkled on everything: salads, grain bowls, roasted vegetables, and savory yogurt bowls, to name a few.

Seasonal Variations: I recommend keeping the vegetables light to not overpower the flavor of the dukkah. For the summer months, go with grilled eggplant or tomato wedges tossed in a bit of olive oil. For the cooler months, I like snap peas and roasted cabbage.

Vegan Riff: Swap the paneer for extra-firm tofu.

Pecan Fried Green Tomatoes with Roasted Garlic Mayo

Serves 4 as a snack

Even though I can easily wax poetic about ripe summer tomatoes, part of my heart belongs to their firm, unripe version. The tart green tomato does all the things a ripe tomato cannot do and has become a deep-fried staple in my summer rotation. Using pecan meal in the batter adds an extra layer of buttery flavor and light crunch.

These fried green tomatoes are fantastic in a sandwich with the mayo and a bit of lettuce. Add these tomatoes to salads, such as the Kale Caesar Salad on page 159.

TOMATOES

Avocado oil or other refined high-heat oil, for frying

⅔ cup (160 ml) buttermilk

½ cup (70 g) soft white wheat or all-purpose flour

½ cup (60 g) pecan meal

1 teaspoon kosher salt

1 teaspoon garlic powder

1 teaspoon ground black pepper, plus more for serving

2 large green tomatoes, cored and sliced into ½-inch (1.3 cm) thick wedges

ROASTED GARLIC MAYO

½ cup (120 ml) unsweetened soy milk, at room temperature

4 to 5 peeled roasted garlic cloves (see page 109), minced

2 teaspoons rice vinegar, at room temperature

¾ teaspoon kosher salt

1 cup (240 ml) avocado oil, at room temperature

PREPARE THE TOMATOES: Heat about 2 inches (5 cm) of oil over medium heat in a dutch oven until the oil reaches 350°F (175°C).

Put the buttermilk in one bowl and mix together the flour, pecan meal, salt, garlic powder, and black pepper in a separate bowl. Dredge about half of the tomato wedges in the buttermilk, then the flour mixture. Repeat, dipping in the buttermilk, then the flour mixture. Slip the tomatoes into the hot oil, being careful not to overcrowd them, and fry until the wedges are a deep golden color. Transfer to a wire rack to cool. Then repeat the process with remaining tomato wedges.

MAKE THE MAYO: Combine the soy milk, rice vinegar, and salt in a jar large enough to accommodate an immersion blender. Stir to combine, then pour the avocado oil on top. Place the immersion blender in the jar, pressed to the bottom. Start the blender, leaving it pressed to the bottom of the jar until the mayo begins to thicken. Then slowly start moving the immersion blender up and down until the mayo is smooth and thick. Transfer ¼ cup (60 ml) of the mayo to a small bowl and stir in the garlic. Extra mayo can be stored in an airtight container in the refrigerator for up to 2 weeks.

TO SERVE: Spread a few tablespoons of the mayo in the bottom of a shallow serving bowl. Top with the fried tomatoes and a sprinkle of ground black pepper.

Notes

There are two mistakes I see often when people deep-fry at home. First, the oil isn't properly heated, which means instead of cooking, the green tomatoes absorb the oil and become soggy. If you haven't already, pick up an instant-read thermometer—I use mine daily! Second, make sure you fry long enough. Even though the tomatoes will continue to cook when removed from the oil, you want them to be golden and crisp.

Pulling too early will also result in sogginess!

Vegan Riff: The buttermilk lends a thickness that helps cling to the tomatoes; using a luscious soy milk is a nice replacement.

Potato and Chile Crisp Pizza with Almond Ricotta

Makes one 12-inch (30 cm) pizza

Over the past three years, my love of pizza developed into a serious hobby, infused by a desire to make vegetable-heavy pizzas. This vegan version was inspired by the almond ricotta from *The Little Pine Cookbook* by Moby. Here, the ricotta is balanced with the heat of a good chile crisp and forms a nice layer of topping with the small, diced potatoes.

I like this almond ricotta recipe because it takes the route of using lactic acid to lend a tangy cheese-like flavor. Most recipes call for using lemon or vinegar, which I find all impart their own particular flavors. You can purchase lactic acid at a local home-brew store or online, by searching for food-grade lactic acid.

ALMOND RICOTTA

2 cups (240 g) slivered almonds, soaked overnight

1¼ cups (300 ml) water

1½ teaspoons powdered lactic acid

1½ teaspoons kosher salt

PIZZA

Pizza Dough (see page 38)

4 ounces (115 g) small yellow potatoes, such as Yukon gold, finely diced

¼ cup (60 ml) chile crisp

Flour, for dusting

Small basil leaves, for serving

MAKE THE ALMOND RICOTTA: Drain and rinse the almonds and place in a high-speed blender with the water, lactic acid, and salt. Puree until as smooth as possible. Transfer to a nut-milk bag or cheesecloth and squeeze out about three-quarters of the liquid. Discard the liquid and chill the ricotta.

MAKE THE PIZZA: Let the pizza dough rest at room temperature, covered, while prepping the potatoes and preheating the oven.

Bring a small saucepan of salted water to a boil. Add the potatoes and cook until just tender, 4 to 5 minutes. Drain, transfer to a small bowl, and stir in the chile crisp.

Preheat the oven to 500°F (260°C) with a baking stone and cast-iron pan in place.

Stretch the dough into a 12-inch (30 cm) circle. Place on a floured pizza peel and spread the potato mixture over the dough. Transfer the pizza to the pizza stone and bake, rotating the pizza occasionally, until the crust is golden brown and cooked through.

Once the pizza finishes baking, top liberally with the almond ricotta and basil.

Notes

A nut milk bag is a fairly cheap investment that I use to make nut milks (see page 188), this ricotta, and rinse smaller grains that would normally fall through strainers. They come in all sizes and materials; I prefer the unbleached cotton.

Ricotta will keep for up to 1 week in the refrigerator and can be spread on toast, used as a ravioli filling, or drizzled with a bit of chile oil and served with crackers.

Seasonal Variations: During the summer, I make a similar version of this pizza using fresh sweet corn kernels, which require no cooking preparation. During the cooler months, cooked sweet potatoes or even shaved Brussels sprouts are good.

Barley-Pea Risotto with Pistachio-Herb Cream

Serves 4

Over the years I've made my fair share of grain-based risottos and have a handful of ways I achieve a texture reminiscent of risotto made from arborio rice. One of my most-used ways is to include a nut-based cream. Not only does the cream provide a creamy texture, it also is an easy way to make a rich, satisfying plant-based meal.

I like pairing pistachios with spring produce because of the color (the green!) and the slightly floral flavor pistachios bring to the dish. Just be sure if you're ordering pistachios that you're buying shelled—having to shell the pistachios before use just takes a little more effort.

PISTACHIO CREAM

½ cup (70 g) raw shelled pistachios

¼ teaspoon kosher salt

½ cup (120 ml) hot water

¼ cup loosely packed (6 g) fresh dill fronds, plus extra for serving

¼ cup loosely packed (7 g) fresh flat-leaf parsley leaves

2 tablespoons minced fresh chives

2 tablespoons fresh lemon juice

2 tablespoons olive oil

1 tablespoon white miso

RISOTTO

4 cups (960 ml) vegetable broth

3 tablespoons (45 ml) olive oil

1 small yellow onion, minced

½ teaspoon kosher salt

4 garlic cloves, minced

1 cup (190 g) uncooked pearled barley

¼ cup (60 ml) dry white wine

2 cups (340 g) fresh or frozen peas

MAKE THE PISTACHIO CREAM: Put the pistachios and salt in a bowl of hot water to cover and let soak for 30 minutes. Drain, then place in a food processor or high-speed blender along with the water, dill, parsley, chives, lemon juice, olive oil, and miso. Puree until smooth.

MAKE THE RISOTTO: Heat the vegetable broth in a small saucepan until hot; keep warm while making the risotto.

Heat the olive oil in a medium saucepan or braiser over medium heat. Add the onion and salt. Cook until the onion has softened substantially, about 15 minutes. If the onion begins to brown, reduce the heat to medium-low. Add the garlic and cook for another minute. Stir in the barley and cook for 1 minute. Add the wine and continue to cook for about 2 minutes until most of the wine has cooked away.

Add ½ cup (120 ml) of the broth and stir. Let the risotto cook until nearly all the broth has been absorbed. Add another ½ cup (120 ml) and let absorb again, stirring often. Repeat these steps, adding broth and letting it absorb, stirring frequently, until the barley is just about tender and the risotto has thickened, 30 to 35 minutes. All the vegetable broth might not be used, but it's helpful to have it heated.

Once the barley is tender and most of the liquid has been absorbed, stir in the peas and half of the pistachio cream. Let cook for 3 to 4 minutes, until the risotto and cream are warm.

TO SERVE: Divide the risotto among four bowls, adding a spoonful of extra pistachio cream as desired, and finish with dill before serving.

Notes

To make this a whole-grain version, choose a grain, such as rye or barley, and medium-crack the grains in a mill (see page 25). This helps cut down on cook time and provides a small bit of dust from the grains to help to thicken the risotto.

Seasonal Variations: During summer, I switch out the cool-weather herbs for a basil-heavy pistachio cream and finish the risotto with roasted cherry tomatoes. During the fall and winter months, rosemary makes a lovely addition to the puree, and roasted squash is my vegetable of choice.

CULINARY SEEDS

While nearly every grain, legume, and nut highlighted in this book is a seed, our use of the term "seed" in the culinary sense is quite a bit more limited. Culinary seeds span vegetables (pumpkin seeds or pepitas), flowers (sunflower), herbs (sesame, hemp, flax, and chia), and trees (pine nuts). There are also a handful of flower and herb seeds we use as spices, covered in the section on page 212, and as grains as highlighted on page 24.

Culinary seeds are used in much the same way as nuts. Sunflower and sesame seeds are pureed into excellent butters (sunflower seed butter and tahini, see page 188); pepitas are great for adding a bit of crunch to dishes; and seed oils, such as toasted sesame oil, lend an aromatic, nutty flavor to sauces and dressings.

Seeds play just as important a role in my cooking as their larger nut counterparts, and I often use them interchangeably, especially when cooking for someone who might have a nut allergy.

Sesame seeds: I often have to pull myself back from adding sesame seeds to everything because I love the subtle savory flavor and visual contrast. I keep **white hulled seeds** on hand for making tahini and black seeds for their bolder flavor and their color contrast. **Unhulled brown sesame** seeds are also readily available and can be used in place of their hulled version. Only when used in a large quantity, such as making tahini, is there a noticeable difference—the brown will lend a darker and slightly more bitter flavor.

Sunflower seeds: Along with safflower, hemp, and chia, sunflower seeds are types of fruits that do not open upon ripening—think about the black, sometimes streaked hull of the sunflower seeds

versus the creamy, soft kernel found instead. My love of sunflower seeds started with **unhulled snack seeds** but now I exclusively keep **hulled raw kernels** for making creams and adding bits of crunch to meals.

Pumpkin seeds: As much as I love roasting seeds from the pumpkins we carve at Halloween, I prefer the green **pepitas**, which are the kernels found inside only certain pumpkin varieties.

Pine nuts: A specialty item in my kitchen because of their higher cost due to the few varieties of pine trees that produce this seed and the labor involved in harvesting—a fact I learned firsthand when foraging from the piñon pine. I typically look for pine nuts from Mediterranean regions, which tend to be more expensive, however the quality and flavor is often superior.

Hemp, chia, and flax seeds: These seeds are prized by the health community, but I tend to use them sparingly because I prefer the flavor and texture of sesame and sunflower seeds. I like to puree hemp seeds into sauces and dressings to lend a bit of creaminess. Chia and flax are great as a binder or substitute egg as they both have the consistency of a gel when combined with liquid.

CULINARY SEED RECIPES

Charred Broccoli with Mustard Sunflower Cream

Serves 4

In the world of nut-based creams and spreads, cashew reigns supreme thanks to its neutral flavor and creamy texture. However, as I've moved away from using cashews, I've found an array of other nuts and seeds to fill the void. Here, sunflower seeds provide the silky cream, and the tangy, bold mustard allows the sunflower flavor to take a more neutral tone.

MUSTARD SUNFLOWER CREAM

½ cup (75 g) raw sunflower kernels

1 teaspoon nutritional yeast

⅓ to ½ cup (80 to 120 ml) hot water

2 tablespoons olive oil

1 tablespoon stone-ground mustard

½ teaspoon apple cider vinegar

¼ teaspoon kosher salt

SUNFLOWER SPRINKLE

2 tablespoons raw sunflower kernels

¼ teaspoon fennel seeds

3 tablespoons fried onions

¼ teaspoon finishing salt, such as Maldon

CHARRED BROCCOLI

2 broccoli crowns with stems, stems peeled and trimmed and crowns quartered

2 tablespoons avocado oil

Preheat the oven to 300°F (150°C).

MAKE THE SUNFLOWER CREAM: Arrange the sunflower kernels in a single layer on a small baking sheet. Roast until they just start to deepen in color, 8 minutes. Remove from the oven, sprinkle the nutritional yeast on top, then continue roasting for another 4 to 5 minutes, until the sunflower seeds and nutritional yeast are deeply golden.

Transfer to a high-speed blender or food processor along with ⅓ cup (80 ml) hot water, the olive oil, mustard, vinegar, and salt. Puree until smooth, adding more water as needed to form a thick cream. Set aside and let cool.

MAKE THE SUNFLOWER SPRINKLE: Arrange the sunflower seeds and fennel seeds on the small baking sheet in a single layer. Roast until the sunflower seeds are golden and the fennel seeds are fragrant, about 10 minutes. Let cool. Use a mortar and pestle to crush the seeds along with the fried onions and finishing salt.

PREPARE THE BROCCOLI: Heat a couple of inches of water in a pot and put the broccoli in a steaming basket. Steam the broccoli until just fork-tender, 4 to 6 minutes. Remove the broccoli from the steaming basket, shaking off any excess moisture, and put on a plate.

Heat the oil in a large pan over medium-high heat. Transfer the steamed broccoli to the pan. Cook, turning once, until the cut sides of the broccoli are charred.

TO SERVE: Spread the sunflower cream in the bottom of a medium serving bowl. Place the charred broccoli on top. Finish liberally with the sunflower sprinkle before serving.

Notes

If you find yourself roasting nuts and seeds often, I recommend investing in a few eighth sheet pans. The size is perfect for roasting small amounts of seeds, and you can fit multiple pans into your oven at once.

Roasted Tomatoes with Buttered Pine Nuts

Serves 4

Since I don't keep pine nuts on hand very often because of cost, when I do have them, I like to make them the hero more than a secondary ingredient. For this recipe, the pine nuts are part of one of my go-to finishings: vinegar butter. The tart, rich, and earthy flavors mingle to form a silky drizzle for these tomatoes and more.

1 pound (450 g) Roma or similar tomatoes, halved lengthwise

2 tablespoons olive oil

½ teaspoon kosher salt

¼ cup (55 g) unsalted butter

2 tablespoons pine nuts

1 teaspoon sherry vinegar

Smoked finishing salt

Preheat the oven to 425°F (220°C).

Put the tomatoes cut side up on a sheet pan. Drizzle with olive oil and sprinkle with salt. Bake for 30 to 40 minutes, until the tomatoes are quite soft. Turn on the broiler and continue to cook the tomatoes until the tops are browned, checking every minute or so.

Melt the butter in a small skillet over medium-low heat. Add the pine nuts and cook until the pine nuts are browning and the butter is beginning to foam. Remove the pan from the heat and stir in the sherry vinegar.

Transfer the tomatoes to a medium serving plate and drizzle with the buttered pine nuts. Finish with a sprinkle of finishing salt before serving.

Notes

I'm throwing my roasting and toasting rules of nuts and seeds out the window for this recipe because I feel it's worth it to toast the pine nuts in butter. The butter takes on a little pine-nut flavor while gaining a golden hue. Just watch them closely. These softer seeds have a penchant for turning from golden to burnt before your eyes.

Seasonal Variations: During the cooler months, this pine-nut mixture is stellar tossed with roasted Brussels sprouts, charred cabbage wedges, or roasted parsnips.

Greens with Green Goddess Tahini Dressing

Serves 4

Using nut and seed creams in dressings is a great way to add lusciousness without dairy and provide a slightly sweet, nutty layer of flavor. Tahini is a great option for this because the sesame flavor is not as pronounced as other nut butters, such as peanut butter, allowing the dressing to really be herb-forward.

The real magic of this salad is the dressing, beyond that you can go a bit wild. Some suggestions: add a cup of cooked white beans, leftover grains, roasted sweet potatoes, and/or other types of greens, such as arugula or kale.

GREEN GODDESS TAHINI DRESSING

3 tablespoons (48 g) tahini

3 tablespoons (45 ml) olive oil

1 small clove garlic

¼ cup lightly packed (12 g) basil leaves

2 tablespoons minced fresh flat-leaf parsley leaves

1 tablespoon lemon juice

2 tablespoons minced fresh chives

1 teaspoon white miso

½ teaspoon stone-ground mustard

½ teaspoon kosher salt

SALAD

6 to 7 handfuls baby leaf lettuce

2 small watermelon radishes, thinly sliced

2 cups (200 g) thinly sliced snap peas

1 tablespoon white sesame seeds, toasted (see page 186), for serving

MAKE THE DRESSING: Combine the tahini, olive oil, garlic, basil leaves, parsley, chives, lemon juice, miso, mustard, and salt in a food processor and blend until smooth. Alternatively, mince the garlic, then whisk together with the remaining ingredients in a small bowl.

MAKE THE SALAD: Put the lettuce in a large bowl. Add most of the sliced radishes, snap peas, and 1 teaspoon of the sesame seeds. Drizzle with the dressing and toss until combined.

Finish the salad with the remaining radishes, snap peas, and toasted sesame seeds.

Notes

Make Ahead: The dressing can be made ahead of time and stored for a couple days in the refrigerator.

Pipián Rojo–Braised Winter Squash

Serves 4

Pipián is a classic chile-based sauce found throughout Mexico as either *rojo* (red) or *verde* (green). Pipián rojo has a bit of the complexity of mole but does not require as many ingredients or as much time to make. It can be made ahead of time and stored in the refrigerator for up to a week or frozen for three months.

This squash makes a stunning side dish, but can also work as a main. Use the squash to top a grain bowl with beans and fried cheese, swap the squash for the chipotle sweet potatoes in the quesadilla on page 222, or simply fry an egg, toss it on top, and call it a day.

PIPIÁN ROJO

2 dried mild chiles, such as New Mexico

1 dried medium chile, such as guajillo

1 dried mild smoky chile, such as ancho

¼ cup (30 g) raw pepitas

1 tablespoon white sesame seeds

½ cinnamon stick, or ½ teaspoon ground cinnamon

2 allspice berries, or ¼ teaspoon ground

½ teaspoon cumin seeds, or ½ teaspoon ground

½ large yellow onion

1 tablespoon avocado oil

3 garlic cloves, smashed

2 tablespoons tomato paste, divided

1 cup (240 ml) vegetable broth, plus more as needed

3 tablespoons (30 g) raisins

½ teaspoon kosher salt, plus more to taste

SQUASH

½ medium kabocha squash, seeds removed and cut into wedges

3 tablespoons (45 ml) avocado oil

FOR SERVING

1 lime, quartered

¼ cup loosely packed (14 g) chopped fresh cilantro

Preheat the oven to 300°F (150°C).

MAKE THE SAUCE: Bring a medium saucepan of water to a boil and heat a large dry skillet over medium heat. Add the chiles to the skillet and toast until the chiles are soft and starting to brown, 1 to 2 minutes per side. Let the chiles cool slightly, then remove the stems and seeds. Transfer the chiles to the boiling water, cover, turn off the heat, and allow to soak for 20 minutes.

While the chiles soak, arrange the pepitas, sesame seeds, cinnamon, allspice, and cumin on a small sheet pan in a single layer. Toast in the oven for 15 minutes, until the seeds have darkened in color and the spices are fragrant.

Cut the onion half into four wedges. Return the skillet used for toasting the chiles to medium-high heat with the 1 tablespoon avocado oil. Add the onion wedges and sear until charred, 1 to 2 minutes per side. Add the garlic and half of the tomato paste and cook until the garlic is a deep golden color. Add the vegetable broth and remaining tomato paste. Add the raisins and salt, cover, and let simmer for 5 minutes.

Drain the chiles and place in a high-speed blender along with the seed mixture and the onion mixture. Puree until smooth, adding more vegetable broth as needed to create a sauce. Taste and add salt as needed.

PREPARE THE SQUASH: Wipe out the skillet, add the oil, and heat over medium-high heat, Add the squash wedges. Cook until well seared, flip, and repeat on the other side, 1 to 2 minutes per side.

Reduce the heat to low, pour in the sauce, and shake the pan back and forth until the squash wedges are covered. Cover and let cook until the squash is quite tender, 10 to 15 minutes.

TO SERVE: Transfer the squash and cooked sauce to a serving bowl. Squeeze the lime over the squash and garnish with the cilantro.

Sesame-Gochujang Cauliflower Lettuce Wraps

Serves 4

I could easily eat sandwiches and toasts everyday but, alas, I've had to adapt to enjoy some not-so-bready meals. These wraps feature crispy cauliflower drenched in a gochujang sauce, chewy barley, and sharp pickled onions, so it's not all so bad.

I'm a bit obsessed with sesame seeds. They seem so unimposing but even in small amounts can add a hint of flavor and texture. Not to mention they make tahini and sesame oil, so that's cool too.

PICKLED RED ONIONS

½ small red onion, peeled and thinly sliced

2 tablespoons rice vinegar

½ teaspoon kosher salt

CRISPY OVEN CAULIFLOWER

1 pound (450 g) cauliflower florets

2 tablespoons avocado oil

2 tablespoons cornstarch

2 tablespoons potato starch

1 teaspoon kosher salt

GOCHUJANG-BUTTER SAUCE

¼ cup (56 g) unsalted butter

¼ cup (68 g) gochujang

2 tablespoons honey or maple syrup

2 teaspoons rice vinegar

½ teaspoon kosher salt

1 heaping tablespoon white sesame seeds, toasted

WRAPS

10 to 12 large butter lettuce leaves

2 cups (320 g) cooked pearled barley (see page 55), slightly cooled

½ cup (8 g) fresh cilantro leaves, coarsely chopped

Preheat the oven to 425°F (220°C).

MAKE THE PICKLED ONIONS: Combine the red onion, vinegar, and kosher salt in a bowl; set aside.

PREPARE THE CAULIFLOWER: Put the cauliflower florets on a sheet pan, toss with the avocado oil, corn starch, potato starch, and salt. Arrange in a single layer. Bake, stirring every 10 minutes or so, until the cauliflower is golden and crisp, 25 to 30 minutes.

MAKE THE SAUCE: Melt the butter in a medium skillet over medium-low heat. Whisk in the gochujang, honey, vinegar, and salt. Increase the heat to medium and whisk until the mixture bubbles and thickens slightly. Turn off the heat and stir in the sesame seeds. Add the crispy cauliflower and stir to coat.

ASSEMBLE THE WRAPS: Lay the lettuce leaves on a large serving platter. Divide the barley among the leaves, followed by the cauliflower. Finish each wrap with cilantro and pickled onions.

Notes

Lettuce is really key to making a good wrap. I suggest butter lettuce because the heads tend to be the perfect size so that leaves are little cups. Plus, the lettuce has enough crispness to it that the leaves can hold up to a small pile of ingredients. In lieu of butter lettuce, go for cabbage leaves or a similar variety of head lettuce, such as bibb.

SPICE SEEDS

The seeds we eat are varied and encompass a wide swath of categories, one of which is a category we typically label as "spices." These seeds do contain fats; however, they are less likely to go rancid and more likely to just lose potency over time. You should refresh your spice drawer each year.

IN MY KITCHEN

Spices have a large impact on flavor, but can really only make a difference when they are fresh—not something pushed to the back of your pantry.

Whole cumin seeds, coriander seeds, fennel seeds, and black peppercorns: Used for foundational flavor, as in a stew (page 49), a sauce (page 216), or a finish (page 199).

Vanilla beans, nutmeg, allspice, star anise, cloves, fenugreek, and white pepper: Kept for a variety of sweet and savory spice needs—often used as foundational flavors to soups, curries, and sauces.

White, yellow, black mustard seeds: Great for homemade mustards (see page 218), adding to spice blends, or using in a *tadka* (see page 215). The variety of mustard seeds range in heat levels.

I also keep **black** and **green cardamom** in the spice drawer. These two varieties are from different plants and have distinct characteristics. Black cardamom is harvested when just ripe and dried over fire, creating a pungent, smoky flavor while the green cardamom is harvested while unripe and dried for a more warm, smooth finish.

WHOLE, GROUND, AND HOW TO SWAP

If I could convince you of one thing, it would be to buy whole spices and grind them as needed—either with a spice grinder or mortar/pestle. I know it takes a couple extra steps but if you're looking for the best flavor possible, fresh ground spices are key.

However, I also understand ground spices are a much-needed convenience. Most recipes in this book call for whole spices but swapping is possible.

Smaller seeds, like cumin, can be swapped near 1:1 with the ground version, while larger seeds, like coriander, will be closer to a 1:2 ratio of ground to whole seeds. Also, depending on how old your ground spices are, you may need to increase the amount of ground to achieve a similar flavor. For the most part, a little extra spice is never a bad thing, unless it's cloves. Never add too many cloves.

PREPARING SPICES

In the introduction on page 15, I mention my preference for oven-roasting nuts and seeds with a few caveats. Those caveats were mostly included for the seeds in this section. Due to their size, spices toast quickly, and I'm always relying on sight and smell to know when they are done. That's not easy in the oven.

There are two methods for toasting spices: dry toasting and blooming in fat. Whole, cracked, and ground spices can be dry toasted or bloomed in fats such as ghee, olive oil, and butter. Spices contain fat-soluble flavor compounds, which means the flavors of the spices are extracted and then absorbed into the fats. This creates a more robust, even distribution of the spice flavor and is the basis for tadka (see page 215).

Dry toasting seeds: Put the spices in a thin layer in a dry skillet over medium heat, shaking the pan occasionally to even the toasting. This method pulls out the oil to enhance the flavor and is great if you plan to grind or use whole in a dry mix, such as the dukkah on page 199. Just note, spices toast very fast and it's best to err on the side of extreme caution. Once spices burn, there's no saving them.

Blooming in fat: The Indian technique of blooming the spices in oil goes by many regional names including tadka and *chhonk*. The goal is to infuse as much flavor into the oil as possible without burning any ingredients. Heat oil or ghee over medium heat until it begins to shimmer, 1 to 2 minutes. Add the spices and cook for 45 to 60 seconds, until fragrant and browning. Watch closely as they can burn quickly.

SPICE SEED RECIPES

Avocado Toast with Cumin-Chile Tadka

Makes 4 toasts

As a millennial Californian, I'm obligated to include an avocado toast recipe. Avocado toasts can be served for breakfast, lunch, and occasionally dinner. Using a *tadka* is a quick way to add bold flavor to the toast, while the microgreens are my way of making this just a bit extra (they are completely optional). Finally, I like serving with a few pickled items on the side to act as a bit of an interlude between bites of the buttery avocado.

Beyond this recipe, avocado toast is the perfect base for a few different larder recipes highlighted in this book. Good toppings for this toast include salsa negra (see page 88), charred scallion sauce (see page 40), peanut dressing (see page 80), and chimichurri (see page 134).

AVOCADO TOAST

4 thick slices whole-grain bread

2 tablespoons avocado oil or butter

2 large ripe avocados

CUMIN-CHILE TADKA

½ cup (120 ml) avocado oil

4 teaspoons cumin seeds

2 teaspoons coriander seeds

2 garlic cloves, minced

1 heaping tablespoon lemon zest

1 teaspoon medium-heat ground chile

1 teaspoon kosher salt

FOR SERVING

Microgreens

Pickles of your choice (cauliflower, beets, carrots, and radishes make great choices)

MAKE THE TOAST: Heat the oil in a medium skillet over medium heat. Add the bread and toast until each side is golden and crisp, 1 to 2 minutes. Transfer to a plate. Thinly slice the avocado. Use a spoon to scoop the flesh from the skin. Fan half on each slice of toast.

MAKE THE CUMIN-CHILE TADKA: Heat the avocado oil over medium heat in the same medium skillet from before until it begins to shimmer, 1 to 2 minutes. Add the cumin and coriander seeds and cook for 45 to 60 seconds, until fragrant and browning. Watch closely as they can burn quickly. Remove the pan from the heat and add the minced garlic, lemon zest, ground chile, and salt. Swirl to combine and immediately spoon over the avocado toast.

Finish the toast with microgreens and serve with your choice of pickles on the side.

Notes

A Bit of Avocado Wisdom: Want to make a single serving with only half an avocado? Store the avocado half with the pit in the refrigerator with nothing covering it. Then, when you are ready to use it, simply slice off the thin layer of browned flesh. You don't need any fancy tips or tricks. Also, store your avocados in the refrigerator just as they turn ripe. I buy avocados on the firm side and check them each morning. The second I feel any give when I gently, and I do mean gently, squeeze, they go in the refrigerator. I swear by this method and unless the avocados are lost in the refrigerator, I rarely have one go bad.

Paneer and Snap Pea Skewers with Red Chermoula

Makes 8 skewers

I hold the firm belief that nearly any vegetable can be grilled and paired with a sauce for a meal that will impress even the biggest skeptic. Here paneer and spring snap peas are drizzled with a red chermoula, a savory spice and oil-based condiment with roots in North Africa.

When grilled, the snap peas keep their crispness while mellowing a bit of the raw flavor and the paneer gets just a bit crispy. Then the skewers are finished with the chermoula, soaking in all the delicious flavors.

RED CHERMOULA

1 teaspoon toasted cumin seeds (see page 212)

1 teaspoon toasted coriander seeds (see page 212)

1 tablespoon minced preserved lemon

¼ cup loosely packed (7 g) fresh cilantro, minced, plus extra for serving

¼ cup loosely packed (7 g) fresh flat-leaf parsley, minced, plus extra for serving

3 garlic cloves, minced

1 teaspoon ground Aleppo pepper

1 teaspoon ground sweet paprika

½ teaspoon kosher salt

6 tablespoons (90 ml) olive oil

SKEWERS

8 ounces (230 g) paneer, diced into 1-inch (2.5 cm) cubes

1 pound (450 g) snap peas, threads removed

2 tablespoons avocado oil

Cooked bulgur, spelt, or quinoa, to serve

MAKE THE CHERMOULA: Combine the cumin and coriander in a spice grinder or mortar and pestle and grind to a coarse consistency. Transfer to a small bowl and add the preserved lemon, cilantro, parsley, garlic, Aleppo pepper, paprika, salt, and oil. Stir to combine and set aside.

MAKE THE SKEWERS: Thread the paneer and snap peas onto eight metal skewers. Place on a large plate and brush with the avocado oil.

Preheat a grill or grill pan to medium heat. Once hot, transfer the skewers to the grill and cook on one side until lightly charred, 2 to 3 minutes. Rotate and repeat until all sides of the skewers are lightly charred. Remove the skewers from the heat and immediately spoon the chermoula over the skewers.

TO SERVE: Divide the grain between four plates and top each with two skewers. Sprinkle with extra cilantro and parsley before serving.

Notes

When grilling paneer, or really any cheese or tofu, ensure your grill is hot and scrubbed free of debris. This will help ensure the paneer chars well and does not stick to the grill.

Seasonal Variations: During summer, zucchini and summer squash are my go-to skewer vegetables; in the fall, it's all about sweet potatoes—just be sure to steam them until tender before using (see page 178).

Vegan Riff: Use tofu or tempeh in place of the paneer.

Grilled Asparagus with Caraway Butter

Serves 4

When it comes to my spice drawer, I try hard to make sure that I use whatever is in there for more than one purpose. I keep caraway on hand for batches of sauerkraut and the occasional caraway-tinted rye bread. However, I've found I also like pairing the earthy anise flavor with a myriad of vegetables, like asparagus. If caraway isn't in your pantry, this butter is also delicious with toasted fennel seeds, coriander, or cumin.

CARAWAY BUTTER

1 teaspoon crushed caraway seeds

¼ cup (55 g) unsalted butter

1 teaspoon minced preserved lemon, or ½ teaspoon lemon zest

¼ teaspoon kosher salt

ASPARAGUS

1 pound (450 g) asparagus, woody ends trimmed

1 teaspoon avocado oil

Black pepper, for serving

MAKE THE CARAWAY BUTTER: Heat a small pan over medium heat and add the crushed caraway seeds. Toast until the seeds are fragrant and starting to brown, shaking the pan occasionally. Add the butter, reduce the heat to low, and let the butter melt and meld with the caraway. Transfer to a small metal bowl and stir in the preserved lemon and salt. In a larger bowl that will fit the smaller bowl, fill the bottom with ice. Place the small bowl with the melted butter on top and whip until the butter has firmed to room temperature.

Preheat your grill, grill pan, or broiler to medium–high heat.

TO PREPARE THE ASPARAGUS: Toss the asparagus with the oil. Grill, turning a couple times, until the asparagus is charred but still has a bit of firmness to it, 3 to 5 minutes.

Transfer the asparagus to a medium serving platter and place dollops of butter on top. Finish with freshly cracked black pepper.

Notes

You could choose to skip the step of bringing the butter back to a solid once it's been infused with the caraway. However, I believe the process of whipping the butter together with the preserved lemon provides better distribution and as such, better flavor.

Cheese Toast with Fermented Mustard

Makes 4 thick pieces of toast, plus ¾ cup / 180 ml leftover mustard

I owe thanks to my mom and Cowgirl Creamery for this recipe. My mom for sharing her enjoyment of cheese, pickles, and mustard in a sandwich and Cowgirl Creamery for their cheese toastie that added caramelized onions to the mix. And now, with the help of fermented mustard, it's toast that has nearly all the flavors I love in one bite.

I know not everyone is ready to tackle fermentation, and sometimes the craving hits and there's no time to wait. Whole-grain mustard is the next best thing, but really any mustard will work—I won't judge.

FERMENTED MUSTARD

½ cup (100 g) yellow mustard seeds

2 tablespoons brown mustard seeds

½ cup (120 ml) water

¼ cup (60 ml) plain kombucha

1 tablespoon kosher salt

¼ cup (60 ml) apple cider vinegar

1 tablespoon maple syrup

CARAMELIZED ONIONS

3 tablespoons (45 ml) olive oil

2 large yellow onions, sliced ⅛-inch (3 mm) thick

1 teaspoon kosher salt

CHEESE TOAST

4 semi-thick slices of wheat bread

¼ cup (56 g) unsalted butter, at room temperature

4 ounces (115 g) shredded sharp cheddar

Sweet pickles, for serving

MAKE THE FERMENTED MUSTARD: Using a mortar and pestle, crush the yellow and brown mustard seeds until most are no longer whole. Transfer to a pint jar along with the water, kombucha, and salt. Seal the jar airtight and let sit at room temperature for 3 days. Taste and continue to ferment until a balanced salt level is reached.

Stir in the vinegar and maple syrup. Taste and adjust flavors as desired. Store in a sealed container in the refrigerator. This mustard will keep for up to 6 months.

MAKE THE CARAMELIZED ONIONS: Heat a large skillet over medium heat with the olive oil. Add the onions and salt, cooking until the onions begin to soften, 12 to 14 minutes. Reduce the heat to medium low and continue to cook, stirring occasionally, until the onions are deeply golden, around 1 hour.

Preheat the broiler.

MAKE THE CHEESE TOAST: Butter one side of each slice of bread and place butter-side up on a sheet pan. Broil 4 inches (10 cm) from the heat source, flipping once, until the bread just starts to crisp, 30 to 60 seconds per side. Keep an eye on the toast—this will happen quickly.

Remove the bread from the oven and smear on 2 to 3 teaspoons of the fermented mustard. Divide the caramelized onions between the toasts and top with the cheese. Return to the broiler and broil until the cheese is melting and bubbly, 60 to 90 seconds. Serve the toasts with sweet pickles.

Notes

Use the mustard as you would any good stone-ground mustard. It is perfect for sandwiches and adding to nut creams or making a salad dressing mustardy.

Vegan Riff: You could easily swap in a vegan cheese, but for a non-cheese alternative, I suggest turning this into a summer sandwich with mustard, the caramelized onions, pickles, and a thick slice of salted tomato.

Storage: Mustard will last for a while in the refrigerator—it's fermented!

Fennel-Herb Beets

Serves 4

In the realm of vegetable side dishes, beets may not be at the top of your list. However, give me enough time, and I'll try to convince you they should be. The earthy flavor makes a sturdy canvas to paint with brighter flavors like the fennel and herbs in this recipe. Serve these beets on a nut cream or hummus, toss with black lentils, and/or add seared wedges of halloumi.

4 medium-sized beets (about 1 pound / 450 g), trimmed

2 teaspoons fennel seeds, cracked

1 teaspoon nutritional yeast

2 scallions, whites and greens trimmed and thinly sliced

½ cup loosely packed (14 g) fresh flat-leaf parsley leaves, minced

¼ cup loosely packed (6 g) fresh dill fronds, minced

2 teaspoons olive oil

2 teaspoons rice vinegar

½ teaspoon kosher salt

Bring a few inches of water to a boil in a saucepan fitted with a steamer basket. Put the beets in a steamer basket and steam until the beets are tender but can still hold their shape, 40 to 60 minutes (start checking around 40 minutes and adjust time accordingly).

While the beets cook, heat a small dry skillet over medium heat. Add the fennel seeds and nutritional yeast. Toast, swirling the pan occasionally, until fragrant and deepening in color, about 2 minutes. Remove from the heat and transfer to a bowl. Add the scallions, parsley, and dill and toss to combine.

Once the beets are cooked, let them cool enough to handle. Using a knife or paper towel, scrape or rub the skin from the beets, then cut them into ¼-inch (6 mm) wedges. Transfer to a medium bowl and add the olive oil, vinegar, and salt, then toss until the beets are well coated. Add the fennel-herb mixture and toss to combine. Taste and add more salt as desired.

Notes

I typically use red beets for this type of dish because I think the color is stunning. However, they can cause a lot of mess. Yellow or chioggia beets work as well.

Make Ahead: The beets can be prepped up to 3 days ahead of time, peeled, and stored in the refrigerator until assembly.

PEANUTS

Peanuts hold a dear spot for me. The peanut butter sandwiches I endlessly ate as a kid, the bag of peanuts in my lap as I watched the Cubs play baseball at Wrigley Field in Chicago, and the afternoon bourbon (soda for me) and beer nuts with my grandfather in the summer afternoons (inspiring the recipe on page 223).

Technically a legume and not a nut at all, the peanut plays the role of a nut amazingly well thanks to its high monounsaturated fat content. Anything a nut can do, the peanut can do as well with the added benefit of being an annual crop. Around the world, peanuts and other types of groundnuts are used for flavor and texture, including in a few of my favorites like Ghanaian groundnut stew, Indonesian *gado-gado*, Mexican *salsa de cacahuate*, and Indian groundnut chutney.

TYPES OF PEANUTS

There are four main categories of peanuts that contain most peanut varieties, and the types play a role in how I use peanuts in my food.

Runner peanuts: The most popular type of peanut, known for high yields. These peanuts are used for peanut products, most notably peanut butter. This variety is what's sold in stores as "peanuts" and is my all-around peanut.

Spanish peanuts: Known for their red skin and slightly higher oil content. Spanish peanuts were originally used for peanut butter until runner peanuts became popular. I reach for Spanish peanuts if I'm making a shelled peanut snack, like the Sweet Chile Peanuts on page 223.

Virginia peanuts: Reigning supreme in the snack realm, these large peanuts are considered more gourmet and therefore used mainly for peanut snacks and ballpark peanuts.

Valencia peanuts: The sweetest type and often sold in-shell for snacking and occasionally used to make natural peanut butter. I use in-shell Valencia peanuts as a cocktail-hour companion.

Occasionally you might see **green peanuts**. Peanuts sold in stores have been dried to retain only 10% of their moisture, ensuring their long-term storage, whereas green peanuts are freshly harvested and contain upwards of 50% of their moisture content. These peanuts are used for boiled peanuts and green peanut oil.

PEANUT RECIPES

Chipotle-Peanut Sweet Potato Quesadillas

Serves 4

Quesadillas are great as a basic tortilla with just melted cheese but also can be filled with ingredients to make just about anyone happy. My vegetarian quesadillas are often filled to the brim with vegetables and served with more vegetables as a topping.

Here roasted sweet potatoes in an easy chipotle sauce are smashed into a filling with the melty cheese. Then I serve it with a pile of pickled onions. Occasionally I'll also add salted and massaged cabbage.

SWEET POTATO

1 large sweet potato, cut into ½-inch (1.3 cm) cubes

1 tablespoon avocado or olive oil

½ teaspoon kosher salt

CHIPOTLE SAUCE

1 tablespoon avocado oil

2 garlic cloves, smashed

2 tablespoons roasted peanuts (see page 186)

1 chipotle in adobo

2 tablespoons adobo sauce

½ teaspoon kosher salt

½ teaspoon rice vinegar

QUESADILLAS

4 large flour tortillas

Avocado or olive oil, for brushing

6 ounces (170 g) Oaxaca or Monterey Jack cheese, shredded

FOR SERVING

Crema

Fresh cilantro leaves

Quick pickled onions (see page 210)

Preheat the oven to 425°F (220°C).

PREPARE THE SWEET POTATO: Arrange the sweet potato cubes on a sheet pan. Drizzle with the oil and salt and toss to coat. Spread out into a single layer. Roast for 20 to 25 minutes, until the sweet potatoes are tender and browning.

MAKE THE CHIPOTLE SAUCE: While the sweet potato roasts, heat the avocado oil in a small skillet over medium heat. Add the smashed garlic cloves and cook until golden on both sides, 2 to 3 minutes. Transfer the garlic to a mortar or small food processor. Add the peanuts, chipotle, adobo sauce, salt, and vinegar. Pound or puree the sauce until the peanuts are crushed and the sauce is well combined.

Add the chipotle sauce to the sweet potato. Toss to coat, then return the pan to the oven. Bake for another 5 to 10 minutes until the sauce begins to brown.

MAKE THE QUESADILLAS: Heat a large skillet over medium-low heat. Warm two tortillas in the dry skillet and remove. Brush the skillet with avocado oil. Add one tortilla followed by one-quarter of the cheese, half the sweet potatoes, another one-quarter of the cheese, and the second tortilla. Press down until the quesadilla is even and the filling is evenly distributed. Cook until the cheese begins to melt, 2 to 3 minutes. Turn up the heat to medium and continue to cook until the tortilla is golden and crisp, 1 to 2 minutes. Flip, cook the second side until crisp, then remove from heat. Repeat the assembly and cooking process for the second quesadilla.

TO SERVE: Cut each quesadilla into wedges and drizzle with the crema. Finish with a heavy sprinkle of cilantro and pickled onions.

Notes

If you make your own corn tortillas (see page 88), you can use those in place of the flour tortillas to make smaller quesadillas. The pipián sauce from page 209 makes a fantastic swap for the chipotle sauce, and the salsa negra on page 88 is great to drizzle on each bite you take.

Sweet Chile Peanuts

Makes 1½ cups (360 ml)

While a can of beer nuts was a staple in my childhood, the snack has made its way into my adult life by becoming a quintessential road-trip snack. The slightly sweet, slightly salty mix can satisfy many a craving while also giving me a boost of protein. This recipe is my riff on the American classic beer nut, perfect for a happy hour or road trip.

If you can find Spanish peanuts, use them here. The blend of peanuts, skins, and finishing sugar makes a gratifying mix of textures.

FINISHING SUGAR

2 teaspoons cane sugar
1 teaspoon kosher salt
½ teaspoon medium-heat ground chile
¼ teaspoon MSG

PEANUTS

¼ cup (60 ml) water
¼ cup (50 g) cane sugar
2 tablespoons maple syrup
1 tablespoon unsalted butter
¼ teaspoon kosher salt
1½ cups (180 g) raw shelled peanuts

MAKE THE FINISHING SUGAR: Combine the sugar, salt, ground chile, and MSG in a small bowl and set aside.

Preheat the oven to 350°F (180°C). Line a sheet pan with parchment paper.

PREPARE THE PEANUTS: Combine the water with the sugar and maple syrup in a small pan. Heat over medium-high heat until the mixture is vigorously bubbling. Continue to cook, stirring once or twice with a spatula, until the mixture has a honey-like viscosity, 2 to 3 minutes. Remove from the heat and stir in the butter and salt, followed by the peanuts once the butter has melted.

Transfer the peanut mix to the prepared sheet pan. Bake for 10 minutes, stir, then bake for another 8 to 10 minutes, until the nuts have darkened in color and the sugar mixture is quite bubbly.

Remove from the oven and let cool for 2 minutes. Stir in half the finishing sugar and let the peanuts cool for another 2 minutes. At this time, the peanuts should be starting to crisp. Finishing with the remaining sugar mixture, toss well to combine, and let cool completely before eating.

Notes

This recipe also is good to use with other types of nuts—especially walnuts and pecans. Also, try swapping the maple syrup for honey for a slight floral undertone.

The peanuts can be chopped and added to salads, tossed with roasted vegetables, or used as a finishing flair for soup.

Storage: Peanuts will last, stored at room temperature, for a few days.

Peanut-Fried Tofu Bowls

Serves 4

There are few things in this life that make me as happy as crispy tofu. This recipe takes fried tofu and adds crushed peanuts, which provide just a hint of nutty savoriness. I recommend crushing the peanuts in a spice grinder or mortar—the resulting fine texture will better mix with the flour.

QUICK PICKLES

1 cup (100 g) sliced cucumber

¼ cup (60 ml) vinegar

2 tablespoons water

1 teaspoon cane sugar

½ teaspoon kosher salt

TOFU

12 ounces (345 g) firm tofu

6 tablespoons (45 g) crushed raw peanuts

3 tablespoons (25 g) cornstarch

3 tablespoons (30 g) potato starch

½ teaspoon kosher salt

6 tablespoons (90 ml) whole milk

3 to 4 tablespoons avocado oil or other neutral high-heat oil

MAPLE-HOISIN SAUCE

1 tablespoon avocado oil

2 garlic cloves, minced

3 tablespoons (50 g) hoisin sauce

3 tablespoons (45 ml) water

4 teaspoons maple syrup

4 teaspoons soy sauce

½ teaspoon five-spice powder

BOWLS

Cooked rice

Roasted crushed peanuts

MAKE THE PICKLES: Place sliced cucumbers in a pint jar. In a small pot, combine the vinegar, water, sugar, and salt. Bring to a boil and cook until the sugar is dissolved, then immediately pour over the cucumbers. Set aside.

PREPARE THE TOFU: If the tofu feels overly moist, use a tofu press or two plates and a heavy book to press the tofu for about 30 minutes. Pat the tofu dry, then cut into slices ½ inch (1.3 cm) thick. In a medium shallow bowl, combine the crushed peanuts, cornstarch, potato starch, and salt. Place the milk in a separate medium shallow bowl.

Heat a large skillet over medium heat with 3 tablespoons (45 ml) of the oil and place a drying rack over a plate. Dredge the tofu in the peanut mix, then in the milk, then back to the peanut mix. Shake off any excess and transfer to the heated skillet. Repeat with the remaining tofu slices, adding more oil as needed. Cook until the tofu is crisp and golden brown, 4 to 5 minutes per side. Transfer to the drying rack and continue until all the tofu is cooked.

MAKE THE SAUCE: Wipe out the skillet used for cooking the tofu and return to the stovetop over medium-low heat. Add the oil, then the garlic and cook until fragrant, about 1 minute. Stir in the hoisin, water, maple syrup, soy sauce, and five-spice powder. Bring to a boil and cook until slightly thickened, 1 to 2 minutes.

Turn off the heat and add the tofu. Toss until the tofu is coated.

PREPARE THE BOWLS: Divide the rice between four bowls and top each with tofu, crushed peanuts, and the pickled cucumbers.

Notes

The key to the tofu is to use well crushed peanuts (see page 186) and to make sure the heat is hot enough to crisp the tofu but not hot enough to burn the peanuts. Your oil should be shimmering in the pan but not smoking.

Peanut Granola Yogurt Bowls

Serves 4

This granola bowl is my ode to the classic peanut butter and jelly sandwich. The peanut granola has an extra boost of peanut flavor thanks to using crushed peanuts, peanut butter, and peanut oil. As for jelly, the strawberry compote is how I typically make jam, just cooked for a bit less time to leave it in a softer, swirl-able form.

PEANUT GRANOLA

½ cup (58 g) rolled oats

½ cup (60 g) roasted peanuts (see page see page 186)

2 tablespoons maple syrup

2 tablespoons smooth peanut butter

1 tablespoon peanut oil or neutral oil

½ teaspoon kosher salt

½ teaspoon vanilla extract

STRAWBERRY COMPOTE

8 ounces (225 g) strawberries

2 tablespoons cane sugar

1 tablespoon maple syrup

1 tablespoon lemon juice

FOR SERVING

3 cups (680 g) whole-milk or nondairy yogurt

Preheat the oven to 325°F (160°C).

MAKE THE GRANOLA: Pulse the rolled oats and peanuts together in a food processor or blender until only a few noticeable pieces of peanut remain. In a medium bowl, combine the maple syrup, peanut butter, oil, salt, and vanilla extract. Whisk to combine. Add the oat mixture and mix using a spoon or your hands (my preferred method) until everything is well mixed.

Transfer the oats to a baking sheet and evenly spread into a thin layer. Bake for 30 minutes, turning the tray halfway through. Granola should be lightly browned and beginning to crisp. Remove from the oven, let cool slightly, then break apart. Return to the oven and continue to bake until the granola is evenly golden, 10 to 15 minutes. Let sit until cool.

MAKE THE STRAWBERRY COMPOTE: Combine the strawberries with the sugar, maple syrup, and lemon juice in a small saucepan. Cook over medium heat, stirring occasionally, until the fruit starts to fall apart but some pieces remain, about 15 minutes. Transfer to a heat-safe jar and let cool slightly.

TO SERVE: Divide the yogurt between four bowls. Swirl in a few tablespoons of the strawberry compote and finish with a rather indulgent sprinkle of granola.

Notes

No fruit on hand? Store-bought jam can be used instead.

Seasonal Variations: Peaches or blueberries are great in summer, while apples or pears make a nice jam in the cooler months.

Make Ahead: Granola will last for up to a week stored in an airtight container at room temperature. The strawberry compote will last for up to 2 weeks in the refrigerator.

Butternut Squash Soup

Serves 4

I like to use nut butters to add an underlying richness to savory sauces, marinades, and stews that is often only found in the form of fat from meat-based items. This soup takes a spin on the classic butternut squash soup with influence from Ghanaian groundnut soup, where peanut butter and tomatoes provide a deep flavor companion to the butternut squash.

This soup makes a nice base for experimenting with garnishes and finishes. Try swapping the peanut oil for the cumin-chile tadka (see page 215), mix the roasted peanuts with fresh herbs you might have around, or crush and use the Sweet Chile Peanuts from page 223.

2 tablespoons olive oil
¼ medium yellow onion, diced
1 teaspoon kosher salt
2 to 3 garlic cloves, minced
1-inch (2.5 cm) piece of fresh ginger, peeled and minced
1 teaspoon ground cumin
1 teaspoon ground coriander
2 tablespoons tomato paste
2 tablespoons smooth peanut butter
4 cups (440 g) peeled and cubed butternut squash (1 small squash)
4 to 5 cups (960 ml to 1.2 L) vegetable or tomato broth, divided
½ teaspoon rice vinegar
Crushed roasted peanuts (see page 186), for serving
Roasted peanut oil, for serving

Heat the olive oil in a medium saucepan over medium heat. Add the onion and salt and cook, occasionally stirring, until the onion is tender and starting to deepen in color, about 8 minutes. Stir in the garlic, ginger, cumin, and coriander. Cook for a minute or two until fragrant. Stir in the tomato paste and cook for 1 minute. Then stir in the peanut butter, butternut squash, and 3 cups (720 ml) of the vegetable stock. Bring to a boil, reduce to a simmer, and cook until the squash starts to fall apart, about 15 minutes.

Use an immersion blender or regular blender to puree the soup, adding ½ cup (120 ml) of the remaining stock at a time to reach a good soup consistency. Bring the soup back to a simmer, add the vinegar, taste, and adjust the salt level as needed.

Divide the soup between four bowls and finish with the crushed peanuts and a drizzle of the peanut oil.

Notes

This soup would be excellent thickened slightly and used as a sauce for tofu or paneer—a great option if you happen to have leftovers the next day.

Butternut squash is great, but this soup is equally tasty with red kuri, kabocha, Hubbard, or buttercup winter squash.

Make Ahead: The soup will keep for a few days in the refrigerator or can be frozen for extended storage.

RESOURCES

This is but a small list of people and companies doing right by grains (both whole and flour), legumes, and seeds. As always, support local when you can.

Anson Mills
ansonmills.com

Barton Spring Mill
bartonspringsmill.com

Blue Bird Grain Farm
bluebirdgrainfarms.com

Boonville Barn Collective
boonvillebarn.com

Burlap & Barrel
burlapandbarrel.com

Capay Valley Mill
capaymills.com

Carolina Ground
carolinaground.com

Community Grains
communitygrains.com

Diaspora Co.
diasporaco.com

Early Bird Farms
earlybirdnc.com

Farm & Sparrow
farmandsparrow.com

Farmer Mai Nguyen
farmermai.com

Grist & Toll
gristandtoll.com

Hayden Flour Mills
haydenflourmills.com

Janie's Mill
janiesmill.com

Jovial Foods
jovialfoods.com

Kandarian Organic Farms
kandarian-organic-farms.
myshopify.com

Koda Farms
kodafarms.com

Laura Soybeans
laurasoybeans.com

Maine Grains
mainegrains.com

Maskal Teff
teffco.com

Meadowlark Farm and Mill
meadowlarkorganics.com

Primary Beans
primarybeans.com

Rancho Gordo
ranchogordo.com

True Origin Foods
trueoriginfoods.com

Yolélé
yolele.com

Zürsun Beans
zursunbeans.com

REFERENCES

This book was written with great help from all the authors and researchers who have come before, and there's so much more information and inspiration beyond the pages of this book.

First and foremost, **Harold McGee**'s *McGee on Food & Cooking* overhauled my relationship the ingredients in this book. So much of how I cook now is directly impacted by reading this book and diving deep into the science of seeds.

GRAINS

My early passion for grains was deeply fueled by *Ancient Grains for Modern Meals* and *Simply Ancient Grains* from **Maria Speck**, *Everyday Whole Grains* by **Ann Taylor Pittman**, and *Nourishing Traditions* by **Sally Fallon**. In recent years *Grist* by **Abra Berens**, *Mother Grains* by **Roxana Jullapat**, *Flour Lab* by **Adam Leonti**, *The Miller's Daughter* by **Emma Zimmerman**, and *Grains for Every Season* by **Joshua McFadden** stoked the fire. All these books are wonderful ways to explore even more uses for grains and whole-grain flours.

A small shelf is devoted to rice books, including *Seductions of Rice* by **Jeffrey Alford** and **Naomi Duguid**, *The Rice Book* by **Sri Owen**, *Rice* by **Michael W. Twitty**, and *Koji Alchemy* by **Jeremy Umansky** and **Rich Shih**. Whether you're looking to expand your rice repertoire or try your hand at homemade koji, these books have it all.

A few single-subject books changed my relationships with individual grains: *The Fonio Cookbook* by **Pierre Thiam**, *Masa* by **Jorge Gaviria**, *The Rancho Gordo Pozole Cookbook* by **Steve Sando**, and *Einkorn* by **Carla Bartolucci**.

Beyond cookbooks, *Small-Scale Grain Raising* by **Gene Logsdon** and *Grain by Grain* by **Bob Quinn** dive into growing grains on vastly different scales, but focus on the importance in today's agriculture (and guide you if you decide to grow grains!). The *Encyclopedia of Grain Science*, the newer *Encyclopedia of Food Grains, Pseudocereals and Less Common Cereals* edited by **Peter S. Belton** and **John R. N. Taylor**, and *Sorghum and Millets: Chemistry, Technology, and Nutritional Attributes* edited by **Kwaku G. Duodu** and **John R. N. Taylor** are invaluable resources for more than you would ever want to know about grains (but a truly delightful way to nerd).

LEGUMES

Most of my bean knowledge has been through learned experience but *Bean by Bean* by **Crescent Dragonwagon** and *Cool Beans* by **Joe Yonan** are great bean resources.

Soy, however, has extensive resources, ready to help make nearly any soy product you would like. *Asian Tofu* by **Andrea Nguyen** and *The Book of Tofu* by **William Shurtleff** and **Akiko Aoyagi** are the perfect guides for making all types of tofu at home while *Miso, Tempeh, Natto, and Other Flavorful Ferments* by **Christopher Shockey and Kirsten Shockey** and *The Book of Miso* by **William Shurtleff** and **Akiko Aoyagi** provide support of the wonderful world of soy-based ferments.

GENERAL COOKBOOKS

Beyond the specific books referenced, quite a few cookbooks have impacted my cooking style and general cooking knowledge around the ingredients used in this book. These books include *Ethiopia* by **Yohanis Gebreyesus**, *Burma Superstar* by **Desmond Tan**, *Made in India* by **Meera Sodha**, *Diasporican* by **Illyanna Maisonet**, *The Nourished Kitchen* by **Jennifer McGruther**, *My Korea* by **Hooni Kim**, *Nopalito* by **Gonzalo Guzmán**, and really any book ever written by **Heidi Swanson**, **Deborah Madison**, **Bryant Terry**, and **Yotam Ottolenghi**.

RESEARCH CITED

Adamcová, Anežka, et al. "Lectin activity in commonly consumed plant-based foods: Calling for method harmonization and risk assessment." *Foods* 10, no. 11 (2021): 2796

"Arsenic in Your Food." *Consumer Reports*, November 2012, www.consumerreports.org/cro/magazine/2012/11/arsenic-in-your-food

Balakireva, Anastasia, and Andrey Zamyatnin. "Properties of gluten intolerance: Gluten structure, evolution, pathogenicity and detoxification capabilities." *Nutrients* 8, no. 10 (2016): 644

Brouns, Fred. "Phytic acid and whole grains for health controversy." *Nutrients* 14, no. 1 (2021): 25

Feng, Yaohua, et al. "Growth and survival of foodborne pathogens during soaking and drying of almond (*Prunus dulcis*) kernels." *Journal of Food Protection* 83, no. 12 (2020): 2122–2133

Graf, E, et al. "Phytic acid. A natural antioxidant." *Journal of Biological Chemistry* 262, no. 24 (1987): 11647–11650

Gupta, Raj Kishor, et al. "Reduction of Phytic Acid and Enhancement of Bioavailable Micronutrients in Food Grains." *Journal of Food Science and Technology*, U.S. National Library of Medicine, Feb. 2015

Ikehashi, Hiroshi. "Why are there indica type and japonica type in rice? — history of the studies and a view for origin of two types." *Rice Science* 16, no. 1 (2009): 1–13

Kumari, Shivani, et al. "Does 'activating' nuts affect nutrient bioavailability?" *Food Chemistry* 319 (2020): 126529

Li, Hongyan, et al. "The molecular structural features controlling stickiness in cooked rice, a major palatability determinant." *Scientific Reports* 7, no. 1 (2017)

Masud, Tariq et al. "Influence of processing and cooking methodologies for reduction of phytic acid content in wheat (*Triticum aestivum*) varieties." *Journal of Food Processing and Preservation* 31, no. 5 (2007): 583–594

Menon, Manoj, et al. "Improved rice cooking approach to maximise arsenic removal while preserving nutrient elements." *Science of the Total Environment* 755 (2021): 143341

Rasheed, Faiza, et al. "Modeling to understand plant protein structure-function relationships—implications for seed storage proteins." *Molecules* 25, no. 4 (2020): 873

Singh, K. B. "Chickpea (*Cicer arietinum L.*)." *Field Crops Research* 53, no. 1–3 (1997): 161–170

ACKNOWLEDGMENTS

Thank you to my parents and grandparents, who have always given me the space to explore, learn, and make my own path forward. Mike, for being my foundation and always supporting my wild whims and creations. Mack for keeping me humble and providing endless laughs. Christina, for being the best dinner date; Emma, my best food nerding-out partner; Erin, for supplying me with endless amounts of olive oil; and Melanie, for giving me sourdough starter every time I've been neglectful.

The team at Hardie Grant, specifically Carolyn, for making this process enjoyable and for helping me create the best book possible. Erin, for taking these beautiful images and reassuring me I did indeed not have to do it all, and Lillian, for making everything look beautiful. To Lizzie, for bringing everything to life in these pages with your design.

And finally, the people who have been a constant support through Naturally Ella and Casual. Without your support and excitement, I would have never made my way here.

INDEX

Hardie Grant North America
2912 Telegraph Ave
Berkeley, CA 94705
hardiegrantusa.com

Published in the United States by Hardie Grant North America,
an imprint of Hardie Grant Publishing Pty Ltd.

Library of Congress Cataloging-in-Publication Data is available
upon request.

ISBN: 9781958417430
ISBN: 9781958417447 (eBook)

Printed in CHINA
Design by Lizzie Allen
Food styling by Lillian Kang
First Edition

FSC
www.fsc.org

MIX
Paper | Supporting
responsible forestry
FSC® C020056